THE FALL OF THE RED WALL

'THE LABOUR PARTY NO LONGER
REPRESENTS PEOPLE LIKE US'

STEVE RAYSON

For my father.

ACKNOWLEDGMENTS

∼

I am grateful to my former LSE tutors Nick Anstead, Charlie Beckett and Damian Tambini for giving me the confidence to write this book. I also want to thank Damian for talking through the concept of public narratives with me as I was developing the analysis and manuscript. Thanks also to Paula Surridge, for her values analysis and allowing me to reproduce her charts in this book.

I particularly want to thank my family Christine, Rebecca and Matthew, who listened to me talk endlessly about the book with good humour. I am particularly grateful for their love, understanding and support.

Thanks go to my editor, Lyndsey Jenkins, and to Kate Chesterton, for her design of the cover.

Thanks also go to all those that took the time to read all or parts of the manuscript and give me their comments: Stephen Walsh, Charlie Beckett, John O'Brien, John Helmer, Phillipe Shoosmith, Damian Tambini, Rob Ashton, Peter Kilmister, Peter Fairfax, Jan Morgan, and Donald Clark.

Finally, my inspiration in writing this book was my father, who never lived to see the book, but whose thoughts were with me throughout its development.

CONTENTS

Introduction   ix

PART I
THE RED WALL: LONG TERM TRENDS AND STRUCTURAL WEAKNESSES

1. Defining the Red Wall   3
2. The 2019 Earthquake   16
3. Increasing Political Volatility in UK General Elections   35
4. Deindustrialisation and Economic Decline in Towns   45
5. Labour's New Electoral Coalition and Declining Working Class Vote   53
6. Labour's Values Disconnect and Cross-Pressured Voters   70

PART II
WAR OF WORDS: NARRATIVES, CHANGE AND ELECTIONS

7. The Importance of Narrative   89
8. Political and Public Narratives   102
9. Understanding Social and Political Change   115
10. Developing an Effective Election Campaign Narrative   131

PART III
THE RED WALL COLLAPSE

11. The 2019 Election: An Overview of the Major Party Campaigns   149
12. Red Wall Public Narratives and the Labour Party In 2019   179
13. A New Challenger Narrative in Red Wall Seats   201
14. Summary: The Perfect Storm Which Brought Down the Red Wall   214

PART IV
THE FUTURE

15. Labour's Challenge 223
16. Crafting an Effective Political Narrative 236

Afterword 241
Notes 243
About the Author 281

INTRODUCTION

On December 12th, 2019 polling stations had been open for nearly an hour when the sun rose at 7.57am. It was a damp day. More rain fell than on the days of the ten previous general elections combined. Sunset was at 3.51pm. As the sun went down it was setting not just on Labour's hopes, but on an entire political era. In traditional Labour constituencies across the Midlands and the North, a 'never Tory' generation put aside historic narratives of being Labour towns and Labour people and voted for the Conservatives. This is the story of one of the most dramatic political turnarounds in UK political history.

Drawing on analysis of long-standing trends, extensive academic research, and interrogating the detail of election results, focus groups and interviews in forty-one Red Wall constituencies, this book demonstrates the importance of public narratives in determining political contests. While all political parties are preoccupied with their own narratives - the messages they want to present to voters - this book demonstrates that the public narrative - the stories that the public themselves are sharing - is far more significant.

In many long-held Labour constituencies a powerful 'Labour towns and Labour people' narrative kept the party's vote disproportionately high in the face of unfavourable economic and demographic changes. This narrative with its strong antipathy to the Tories, disguised the growing disconnect between Labour and its traditional working-class voters. Social pressures led many people to conceal their changing preferences which, when revealed, led to the rapid breakdown of previous norms and the collapse of the Labour vote.

In 2019, the Labour Party failed to understand that in traditional working-class communities the public narrative had shifted, it had become 'the Labour Party no longer represents people like us'. The fall of the Red Wall provides a cautionary tale to political parties of failing to understand the public narrative. It also provides important lessons about effective political storytelling. This book sets out key principles to guide the development of a new Labour narrative and the development of effective political narratives more generally.

Prior to June 2017 there were 41 parliamentary seats which formed part of a Red Wall that stretched from the Vale of Clwyd in the West to Great Grimsby in the East. These were long-standing Labour seats which had elected Labour MPs for decades. Ironically, however, changes in the cultural and demographic characteristics of these seats meant that they increasingly looked similar to many Conservative seats in the South. They were culturally conservative, older, and disproportionately white with strong English identities. Based on the cultural and demographic characteristics of these constituencies the Labour vote was disproportionately high prior to 2019. Rather than looking at why voters left Labour in 2019, one could turn the question on its head and ask 'why did these voters stick with Labour for so long?' And why did they finally give up on the party on 2019?

The answer lies in the public narrative, *the stories that people share about themselves, their communities and their vision for the future.* The power of these stories lies in their reception, interpretation and retelling. Within the public sphere some narratives become familiar and influential. They are the narratives that resonate and that are repeated the most often. These narratives are co-created. They are a social act and they shape people's lives, views and behaviour.

In Red Wall seats, in traditional working class communities, the public narrative was centred around the idea of Labour towns and Labour people. This narrative shaped the collective memory, identity and politics of these communities. It was this narrative that sustained the Labour vote in the face of adverse trends such as deindustrialisation, economic decline and a growing disconnect between the Labour Party and many of its traditional supporters. In these seats the Labour Party was seen as synonymous with local working class communities. Parents and grandparents passed down stories of Labour standing in solidarity with local working people in the mines, textile factories and the potteries. For decades industrial communities in Red Wall towns felt Labour 'had their back'. That Labour was 'on their side'.

Alex Niven, from the University of Newcastle, has observed that "when it came to election time, almost everyone would vote instinctively for the Labour party, because it was visibly an extension of their community's interests."[1] Fundamentally the Labour Party represented 'people like them'.

This narrative was accompanied by an antipathy to the Conservatives, reinforced by the loss of local manufacturing and mining jobs under the Tories in the 1980s. A northern Tory campaigner commented prior to the election that Labour voters in these seats given a choice between voting Conservative and selling their children, would sell their children. While voting Labour was seen as an act of community solidarity, voting Conservative made you a social pariah. People were afraid that family and friends would disown them if they voted Conservative.[2] The taboo on voting Tory led many of Labour's culturally conservative voters to conceal their growing preferences for the Conservative Party. It was these concealed preferences that also created the conditions for rapid political change.

The 2017 election provided a clear foreshock of what was to come. There was the highest ever recorded level of Labour to Conservative vote switching. Six Red Wall seats, collectively held by Labour for over 300 years, were lost to the Conservatives in 2017. However, these seismic rumblings were largely lost in the story of Labour's increased national vote share, its highest since 2001. Despite Labour's increased national vote share in 2017, the party had become increasingly disconnected from its traditional industrial voters in Red Wall towns. The disconnect stemmed from a confluence of trends including deindustrialisation, educational divides, economic decline, new divides between cities and towns, the growing salience of cultural issues, cross-pressured voters, falling party loyalty, new age divides, increasing political volatility and Labour's focus on a new broader electoral base.

An analysis of hundreds of focus groups and interviews, involving thousands of Red Wall voters, reveals that the growing disconnect was increasingly finding expression in a new public narrative. Former Labour voters were increasingly sharing stories about the Labour Party's lack of aspiration for their areas and of taking them for granted. They shared stories about Labour no longer representing their values, stories of betraying them on Brexit, and stories of the party looking down on them. From 2016 a combination of Brexit and Jeremy Corbyn was exacerbating this disconnect between traditional Labour voters and the party. Strand by strand, the stories shared by disillusioned Labour voters plaited together to form a new public narrative: 'Labour no longer represents people like us'. It was this new public narrative which gave people the confidence and 'permission' to vote Conservative, as they were increasingly aware that their friends, neighbours and community felt the same way.

∾

In political terms an earthquake took place on the 12th December 2019. The seismic activity broke records on the political Richter scale, exemplified by the highest ever swing from Labour to the Conservatives, an astonishing 18% swing in Bassetlaw. In seats that had never voted Conservative in a general election, the Labour vote collapsed as voter after voter switched their allegiance to the Tories. A further 35 long-held Labour seats fell to the Conservatives. Forty-one in total including the six that fell in 2017, and which voted Conservative in even greater numbers in 2019.

The dramatic nature of the voting realignment that took place is exemplified by events in Mansfield. The constituency had been held by Labour since 1923. In 2019 the Conservatives didn't just win the seat: they won 64% of the vote and now have a 16,000 majority. Mansfield is not an isolated example. A number of former long-held Labour seats returned Conservative majorities of over 20%, such as Dudley North (31.3%), Bassetlaw (27.6%) and Great Grimsby (22.2%).

In January 2020, a Labour Party internal review of the election laid the blame for their losses on Brexit and Labour's second referendum policy. Four months later, Labour's new leader Keir Starmer, the architect of Labour's Brexit policy, disagreed. He claimed the losses were primarily due to Jeremy Corbyn's leadership.[3]

Both analyses are wrong. At its heart the Red Wall story is a twenty year story of Labour's growing disconnect with traditional voters which was reflected in the emergence of a new public narrative that Labour no longer represented traditional working class communities. This narrative gained momentum and quickly took hold because it aligned with the concealed preferences of many voters. As the narrative grew stronger, former Labour voters became more confident in revealing their frustrations with the party and their preference for the Conservatives. This created a cascade effect as voters felt increasingly confident to give voice to their concealed preferences, and as more voters voiced their views, this in turn gave others the confidence they needed to speak out. Where there is a high level of concealed preferences this process can be like a dam bursting. In such circumstances existing norms and narratives collapse very quickly. The speed and scale of Labour's losses in 2019 was a consequence of such a process, a rapid unravelling of the historic 'Labour towns and Labour people' narrative.

It is important to note that the collapse in the Labour vote did not reflect an overwhelming endorsement of the Conservatives but one of disillusionment with Labour. Many voters actively spoke of lending the Conservatives their support and many supported them with a heavy heart. This can be viewed at one level as good news for Labour. However, the disconnect between the Labour Party and its traditional supporters in these seats is very real. The close ties between many working class families and Labour have been broken.

The key challenge for Labour is to create a new political narrative which recognises, responds to, and reshapes the public narrative. Labour's new narrative has to create a new imagined future that resonates with these communities, which is supported by multiple stories, is familiar to the audience, which reflects their perceptions of reality, and which is capable of being conveyed concisely using everyday language.

A particular challenge for Labour is creating a narrative that can connect with both traditional voters in Red Wall seats and with Labour's growing electoral base of students, young people and progressive professionals in cities. This book identifies potential areas of common ground. It also highlights how the coronavirus pandemic presents an opportunity for the Labour party to create a new overarching political narrative linked to themes emerging from the crisis, such as the focus on community, greater national self-sufficiency and more active government intervention.

An analysis of the changing public narrative in Red Wall seats is at the heart of this book. This is based on a review of the themes and ideas that were frequently repeated across hundreds of focus groups and interviews with thousands of people in these constituencies. The book also includes original analysis of 2019 British Election Survey (BES) data for the relevant seats.

The fall of the Red Wall was one of the most important moments in British political history, and it has important lessons for politicians, campaigners, academics and commentators. It highlights the crucial role of public narratives in electoral contests and the conditions that may lead to rapid political and social change. The collapse of Labour's vote in its heartland seats will continue to reverberate for years to come. Labour's challenge is to rebuild its connections with these voters and to create a new narrative. As many people within and beyond the party have argued, this can only be done if Labour acknowledges the real reasons that voters abandoned them. Hearing and understanding the stories that people themselves tell is therefore absolutely critical if the party is to respond to these people and their communities, winning back their hearts, minds and votes.

Finally, the fall of these long-held Red Wall seats offers crucial lessons in political storytelling, not only for Labour, but for any political organisation or campaign seeking to convey their message to the public. This book provides fresh insights into political communication, and sets out practical guidance and advice for those seeking to craft effective political narratives.

PART I

THE RED WALL: LONG TERM TRENDS AND STRUCTURAL WEAKNESSES

1

DEFINING THE RED WALL

In 1918, Thomas Walter Grundy, a former miner, was elected as Labour MP for Rother Valley. In 1922, Henry Twist, a former checkweighman at Bamfurling coal mine, won the parliamentary seat of Leigh for Labour. In the same year another former miner, Thomas Williams, was elected as the Labour MP for Don Valley. For the next 97 years these three constituencies repeatedly elected Labour MPs as their representatives. These seats—and dozens of others like them—were the bricks that built the Red Wall.

On the 27th July 2019, the Prime Minister, Boris Johnson, made a speech in Manchester. It is worth quoting in full an extract from this speech:

> The centre of Manchester – like the centre of London – is a wonder of the world. But just a few miles away from here the story is very different. Towns with famous names, proud histories, fine civic buildings where unfortunately the

stereotypical story of the last few decades has been one of long term decline. Endemic health problems. Generational unemployment. Down-at-heel high streets. The story has been, for young people growing up there of hopelessness, or the hope that one day they'll get out and never come back.

And in so far as that story is true and sometimes it is, the crucial point is it isn't really the fault of the places and it certainly isn't the fault of the people growing up there - they haven't failed. No, it is we, us the politicians, the politics, that has failed. Time and again they have voted for change, but for too long politicians have failed to deliver on what is needed.[1]

It is clear from this speech that the Conservatives were targeting the post-industrial towns outside of the major cities. Winning these seats was critical if the Conservatives were to secure a sizeable majority at the General election.

In August 2019, a series of tweets by Tory strategist James Kangasooriam revealed the thinking behind this strategy. Kanagasooriam, an advisory board member of Onward, and a strategy consultant at OC&C, first mentioned the concept of the Red Wall in a tweet on 14th August 2019, as part of a 16-part Twitter thread.[2] Kanagassooriam noted there is a huge 'red wall' where the "entire stretch shouldn't all be Labour but is."

According to Kanagasooriam "the Red Wall is dominated by rural, small market-town seats which hug the more diverse safe Labour seats in the cities of the Midlands and the North."[3] In a tweet of 1st November 2019, Kanagasooriam suggested there were 41 seats in the Red Wall that on a demographic basis should have a higher Conservative vote but do not for cultural reasons.[4]

In November 2019, Sebastian Payne wrote an article in the *Financial Times* highlighting how the Conservatives were targeting a line of seats in the North and the Midlands, that ran from the Vale of Clwyd to Great Grimsby. These constituencies were historically Labour heartland seats. Payne also noted that pollsters were referring to these seats as the Red Wall.[5]

In early December 2019, James Johnson, the former adviser to Theresa May, confirmed that the Tories were not only thinking the unthinkable, but acting on it—and believed they could win in dozens of previously unwinnable seats. Johnson commented that the entire election result depended on these Labour seats in the North and the Midlands, adding this was "a segment of the electorate that we tracked closely when I ran private polling at No 10, they remain essential to the Conservative Party's route to victory."[6]

These Red Wall constituencies, targeted by the Conservative election strategists, had three specific characteristics. Firstly, they had voted to Leave the EU in 2016. Secondly, large proportions of each constituency population identified as English rather than British or any other national identity. Finally, these seats were culturally conservative according to polling by Lord Ashcroft. These characteristics gave the Tories encouragement that they could prise voters away from Labour.

It would not be a simple task for the Conservatives to win these seats. As many of these constituencies had voted Labour for generations and there was an historic antipathy towards the Tories. Focus groups in traditional Labour seats revealed significant social pressure within families and communities to vote Labour or to abstain altogether rather than vote Conservative. This social pressure prompted Guy Opperman, Conservative MP for Hexham, to note "it's exceptionally difficult to win Labour seats in the north."[7]

Despite these potential obstacles Conservative strategists were encouraged by the fact that the Tory vote had increased in many Red Wall seats in the 2017 election, and that a number had returned Conservative MPs for the first time such as Middlesbrough South, East Cleveland and Mansfield. A key part of the Conservative election strategy was to focus on these seats and to persuade Labour voters to switch to the Conservatives with their 'get Brexit done' message and with their policies on issues such as crime and immigration.

The Red Wall concept

The Red Wall became a heuristic used by journalists in the media, rather than a specific, defined set of seats. The concept was criticised by political analyst Lewis Baston for being too widely drawn, as in addition to former Labour heartland mining and industrial seats, it was often used to refer bellwether seats such as Warrington South, Bury North, Keighley, and Stockton South.[8] These seats typically swing in line with national trends and are in stark contrast to seats such as Workington, Rother Valley, Don Valley and Bassetlaw which were held by Labour for over 90 years. Commentators also used the Red Wall to refer to the Brexit voting towns of supposedly 'left-behind Britain', namely areas with low house prices, low wages, low ethnic diversity, a large older population and low numbers of graduates.[9] Thus the Red Wall became a shorthand for these types of areas rather than a defined set of seats.

Defining the lost Red Wall

The original Red Wall concept reflected the fact the constituencies held by Labour across the North and the Midlands resembled a wall when looked at on a map. This fairly contiguous grouping of seats comprised a large number of Labour seats including those in cities as well as in towns. In this book we are interested in the long-held seats that Labour lost, most of which had never elected a Conservative MP in their history i.e. the 'lost Red Wall'. For the purposes of this book, the lost Red Wall is defined as the 41 seats won by the Conservatives in 2019 which were historically held by the Labour Party for many tens of years. Collectively these seats were held by Labour for over 2,300 years (well over 50 years on average) before they were lost to the Conservatives. This group of seats excludes bellwether seats that regularly change hands in line with national trends. They are also seats which voted to Leave in the EU referendum.

These 41 seats include six seats which were actually won by the Conservatives in 2017. These were the first Red Wall seats to fall post the 2016 EU referendum. These constituencies are Copeland, Derbyshire NE, Mansfield, Middlesbrough SE and Cleveland, Stoke-on-Trent South, and Walsall North. These six seats were held by Labour continually for decades apart from a three year period when Walsall North was held by the Conservatives following a by-election in 1976. Given their long history of Labour voting, and their economic and demographic similarities to the rest of the Red Wall, they have been included as lost Red Wall seats.

Five of the 41 seats are in the East Midlands, ten are in the West Midlands, seven are in the North East, nine are in the North West, five are in Yorkshire and Humberside and three are in Wales. The seats tend to be more rural, outside or on the edges of major cities and populated by smaller towns. These constituencies are listed below:

41 Red Wall Seats Won By The Conservatives In 2019

West Midlands

- Birmingham Northfield
- Dudley North
- Newcastle-under-Lyme
- Stoke-on-Trent North
- Stoke-on-Trent Central
- Stoke-on-Trent South
- West Bromwich East

- West Bromwich West
- Wolverhampton North East
- Walsall North

East Midlands

- Ashfield
- Bassetlaw
- Bolsover
- North East Derbyshire
- Mansfield

North West

- Barrow and Furness
- Blackpool South
- Bolton North East
- Burnley
- Bury South
- Copeland
- Heywood and Middleton
- Hyndburn
- Leigh
- Workington

North East

- Bishop Auckland
- Blyth Valley
- Darlington
- North West Durham
- Redcar
- Sedgefield
- Middlesbrough South and East Cleveland

Yorkshire and Humberside

- Don Valley
- Great Grimsby
- Penistone and Stocksbridge
- Rother Valley
- Scunthorpe
- Wakefield

Wales

- Clwyd South
- Delyn
- Wrexham

These 41 lost Red Wall seats were all long-held Labour constituencies with a couple of recent exceptions:

- Burnley, which was held by Labour since 1935 with the singular exception of 2010 to 2015 when it was held by the Liberal Democrats.
- Redcar, which was held by Labour since 1974 with the singular exception of 2010 to 2015 when it was held by the Liberal Democrats.

Given the economic and demographic nature of these constituencies, their long history of Labour voting and the fact the Conservatives had never won them, they have been included in the group of 41 lost Red Wall seats, though one could make the case for their exclusion.

It is important to recognise there are also very similar Red Wall seats which the Conservatives failed to win in 2019 such as Hartlepool, where the Brexit Party may have saved Labour by providing an alternative home for Leave voters. The Brexit

Party candidate, Richard Tice, picked up 26.8% of the vote, and the combined Brexit Party and Conservative vote was 54.7% compared to Labour's 37.7%.

It is also important to recognise that while these constituencies can be grouped together as Labour's lost Red Wall they often have vastly different local political contexts. For example, in Ashfield the Conservatives actually won fewer votes in 2019 than they did in 2017 when they failed to win the seat. Labour's loss in Ashfield has a lot to do with Jason Zadrozny, the independent leader of Ashfield District Council, who stood as an independent candidate and won 27.6% of the vote. Labour's vote collapsed from 42.6% in 2017 to 24.4% in 2019. In Bassetlaw, an acrimonious candidate selection process meant local supporters were angry and frustrated before campaigning was even underway, exacerbating existing difficulties. Labour members in Bassetlaw had selected Sally Gimson. However, the national party deselected her and imposed Keir Morrison. The Labour Party refused to comment on the internal selection process but it was reported the deselection came after complaints relating to allegations concerning "protected characteristics"—which can relate to issues surrounding race, disability, and sexuality. Many felt it was ideological and 'a Momentum stitch up'.[10] According to Hugh Casswell, the BBC's Radio Nottingham political journalist, local supporters were "incandescent with rage" at the deselection.[11] Labour lost Bassetlaw with a record 18% swing to the Conservatives.

The changing demographics of the lost Red Wall

Though it has been frequently claimed that these seats are older, whiter, and less educated than the rest of the country, a more precise understanding of these claims is essential. Some caution must be exercised here, since many statistics are based on the 2011 census and there will have been changes since then.

This analysis reveals that though the seats are only slightly older than the national average, they appear to be ageing at a greater rate. More significantly, however, they are less ethically diverse than the national average, and have far fewer people educated to degree level. Demographically, socially and culturally, these seats have a lot in common with places which tend to vote Conservative.

Age

The proportion of the population aged 60 or over in the 41 lost Red Wall seats, according to the 2011 census, was 23.94%. The average for constituencies in England, Scotland and Wales was 22.96%. Thus, the proportion of elderly people in lost Red Wall seats in 2011 was not significantly different from the national average. It was city seats that were the outliers. For example in Islington North, the proportion of the population aged 60 or over was just 13%.

There will have been changes since the 2011 census and it is possible that the average age of the population in towns and smaller communities has increased faster than the national average. There is some evidence to support this assumption as small towns in the North and Midlands had been ageing at a faster rate than the national population in the decades before 2011. This reflected a national trend where the populations in large towns and cities were getting younger while the populations in villages and smaller towns were growing older. A report by the Centre for Towns shows that from 1981 to 2001 there was a significant increase in the numbers of 26 to 44 year olds in core cities and a decline in the number of people aged 65 plus.[12] By contrast villages, communities, small towns and medium towns all saw a marked decline in the numbers of 16-24 year olds and increases in the number of those aged 65 plus. The table below shows the nature of the population changes in selected Red Wall constituencies.

Changes in Population in Selected Constituencies (1981 to 2011)

Town	Change in Population Over 65s	Change in Population 18-24 year olds
Workington	+14.0%	-28.4%
Bury	+27.3%	-7.3%
Southport	+12.4%	-21.8%
Bishop Auckland	+34.8%	-24.9%
Darlington	+21.2%	-16.6%
Hartlepool	+26.9%	-24.5%
Redcar	+8.9%	-24.3%
Grimsby	+39.6%	-19.1%
Scunthorpe	+39.6%	-21.0%
Wakefield	+29.0%	-10.5%
Mansfield	+30.3%	-14.4%
Kirkby-in-Ashby	+41.3%	-15.5%
Bolsover	+35.2%	-16.1%

Source: The Centre for Towns

This growth in the proportion of elderly people in Red Wall towns is exemplified by Bishop Auckland where, according to the Centre for Towns, the number of over-65s has increased by a third since 1981, while the number of 18- to 24-year-olds has fallen by a quarter. In 2019, the Conservatives won Bishop Auckland for the first time with an 8,000 majority, making it a relatively safe Conservative seat.

The age profile of constituencies and the demographic change matters because age has become one of the most significant dividing lines in British politics. Age has become a primary predictor of voting behaviour with the Conservative vote share increasing as people get older. In 2019, the Conservatives won 57% of the vote among over-60s and 67% among over-70s.[13] The relationship between age and voting intention is highlighted by YouGov data which shows that the Labour vote consistently declines as voters get older while the Conservative vote consistently increases. It is not yet clear, however, whether this is because there is an age effect—where people become more conservative as they get older—or a cohort effect where these younger voters will retain their support for Labour as they get older. This is discussed in more depth in Chapter 6.

Older people are also far more likely to vote than younger people. Research by Brunel University shows that in the twenty constituencies with the highest proportion of voters under 35, average turn out was just 63 per cent, and in the twenty constituencies with the lowest proportion of voters under 35, turnout was 72 per cent.[14]

Retired population

The proportion of the population that was retired in the 41 lost Red Wall seats, according to the 2011 census, was 16.06%. This was higher than the average for constituencies in England, Scotland and Wales which was 14.28%. Thus, in 2011, while a higher proportion of the population in Red Wall had retired, it wasn't much higher than the national average. However, again all the indications are that the populations in Red Wall seats have continued to age. This, in turn, would lead to larger numbers of retired people.

Ethnicity

The 2011 census shows that the proportion of the population that was white in the 41 lost Red Wall seats was 92.97%. This was higher than the average for constituencies in England and Wales which was 86%.[15] Red Wall seats were and remain more ethnically white than average.

Education

According to the 2011 census the proportion of the population that had a degree in the 41 lost Red Wall seats was 9.67%. This was significantly lower than the average for constituencies in England, Scotland and Wales which was 15.1%. Thus, Red Wall seats had fewer people with degrees and far less than inner city seats such as Islington North, where 43% of the population held a degree in 2011.

Home ownership

According to the 2011 census the proportion of the population that owned their own home in the 41 lost Red Wall seats was 65.04%. This was slightly above the average for constituencies in England, Scotland and Wales which was 64%. Both are significantly higher than the proportion in cities, for example, in Islington North the percentage was just 30%.

Leave vote

In the 2016 EU referendum, the 41 lost Red Wall seats voted on average 64.32% to Leave and 35.68% to Remain. This compares to the national result of 52% to 48%. These constituency figures are based on Hanretty's constituency estimates of the 2016 vote.[16] Thus, these 41 historic Labour seats were significantly more pro-Leave than the population nationally.

Conservative targeting of Red Wall seats

The economic and demographic characteristics in Red Wall seats aligned with predictors of Conservative support. This may partially explain the growing vote for the Conservative party in many rural and semi-rural post-industrial areas in the North with older populations. However, what was particularly notice-able about Red Wall seats was that despite these economic and demographic features, the Labour vote remained relatively high until very recently. A powerful public narrative sustained the Labour vote in these communities, namely that these were 'Labour towns and Labour people'.

This narrative went back to the 1920s and the emergence of Labour as a political force. A narrative where Labour was seen as synonymous with working people and where there was historic antipathy to the Conservatives. This gained new force in the 1980s, when Margaret Thatcher branded unions 'the enemy within', and communities grappled with the economic, political, social and cultural ramifications of the miners' dispute. It was a narrative that erected cultural and social barriers to voting Conservative.

To Conservative strategists these Red Wall seats with their older, culturally conservative populations; low levels of formal education; and high levels of support for Brexit; became ideal electoral targets. These constituencies were to make up the bulk of Conservative target seats in the 2019 election.

2

THE 2019 EARTHQUAKE

In 1923 Frank Varley won the Mansfield constituency for the Labour Party. For the next 94 years the constituency voted Labour.

In 2005, the Conservatives received just 7,035 votes or 18% of the vote. The Conservative vote did increase in subsequent elections but by 2015 it was still only 28%, significantly below the 39.4% received by the Labour candidate. However, something was changing. Just two years later in 2017, the Conservatives won the seat, albeit with a wafer thin majority of just 57. Then in 2019, the Conservatives won by a staggering margin, gaining 63.9% of votes cast. The candidate, Ben Bradley, won a majority of over 16,000 - more than double the Labour vote. Mansfield is now a Conservative safe seat.

Dan Jarvis, Labour MP for Barnsley, has argued the Labour Party needs to undertake an honest analysis of what happened in 2019, and suggested that without such an analysis "we risk the bond between heartland seats across the Midlands and North of England and Labour being irrevocably broken."[1]

In this chapter we are going to look at three things. Firstly, a detailed analysis of the voting patterns. Secondly, why the most frequently mentioned causes for Labour's collapse such as Brexit and Jeremy Corbyn are overstated and fail to tell the whole story. Thirdly, the importance of long term trends within these constituencies and why these trends accelerated so dramatically in 2019.

The 2019 election results

Labour MPs in Red Wall seats had long felt the rumblings of a political earthquake to come. Labour MP for Wigan, Lisa Nandy, said she could feel the ground quaking.[2] Former Labour MP for Leigh (2015-2017), Jo Platt, says, "from the moment of my election, I could feel the electoral tectonic plates gradually shifting."[3]

In 2019, the earthquake finally hit. In Great Grimsby, the Conservatives won just 26.3% of the vote in 2015, but only four years later in 2019 they won 55%. In Leigh, which Labour had held for 97 years since 1922, the Conservatives gained just 22.6% of the vote in 2015. Four years later in 2019, the Conservatives unexpectedly won the seat with 45.3% of the vote. It was even a surprise for the winning Conservative MP, James Grundy, who commented: "I came here tonight expecting to lose with dignity."[4]

In Bassetlaw, which had been held by the Labour Party since 1929, there was a record swing of 18% from Labour to the Conservatives. This is the highest ever swing in the UK despite the previous election being only two years earlier. Labour lost almost half their votes in Bassetlaw in just two years. To put the scale of change into context, after the election there were

Conservative majorities of over 20% in former Red Wall seats such as Dudley North, Mansfield, Bassetlaw, Middlesbrough and South East Cleveland, Stoke-on-Trent South, Walsall North and Great Grimsby.

The national picture

Nationally Labour lost over two and a half million votes in 2019 across England, Scotland and Wales. The table below shows the shift in votes between the main parties from 2019 to 2019.

Main Party Votes 2017 and 2019 General Elections

	2017	2019	Change	Share (%)
Conservative	13,636,684	13,966,454	329,770	43.6
Labour	12,877,918	10,269,051	-2,608,867	32.1
SNP	977,568	1,242,380	264,812	3.9
LibDems	2,371,861	3,696,419	1,324,558	11.6
Green	525,665	865,715	340,050	2.7
Plaid	164,466	153,265	-11,201	0.5
Brexit (UKIP)	594,068	644,257	50,189	2

Source: House of Commons Library

These national figures hide a large degree of switching between parties. In 2019, many Labour and Conservative voters switched to the Liberal Democrats who gained over 1.3m votes. Many other people who had voted Labour in 2017 switched to the Scottish National Party, or the Greens in 2019. As a consequence Labour actually lost a larger share of its 2017 vote in 'affluent remain' areas in England and Wales than in Red Wall areas.[5] However, these votes were less critical in determining the outcome of seats with a few exceptions, most notably Putney and Canterbury.

The number of 2019 Labour voters switching to the Conservatives has been estimated at between 1 million and just over 1.2 million voters.[6] Thus Labour lost more votes in 2019 to other parties than to the Conservatives but it was the direct switching to the Conservatives and the collapse in the Labour vote in Red Wall seats which was critical.

Regional variations in vote share

The nature of the UK first past the post electoral system means that it is more efficient electorally for a party's voters to be spread across the country, rather than piling up votes and winning large majorities in constituencies. This is clearly demonstrated by the results of the EU referendum. The vote was famously 52% Leave and 48% Remain. However, the Leave vote was more evenly spread across constituencies, there was a majority of Leave voters in over 400 seats. Thus, if the referendum was fought on a first past the post basis, Leave would have won over 60% of the country's 650 parliamentary constituencies.

The 2019 election was always going to create problems for Labour as its vote was less efficiently distributed across constituencies and around two-thirds of Labour-held constituencies had a pro-Brexit majority in 2016. Nationally, the Conservatives only increased their total votes by 2.3%. However, there were large regional variations as shown in the table below. These variations were critical in delivering a Conservative majority.

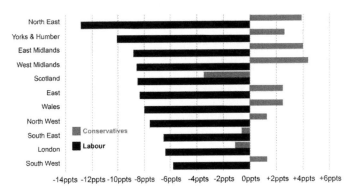

Regional change in major parties' vote share between 2017 and 2019

North East
Yorks & Humber
East Midlands
West Midlands
Scotland
East
Wales
North West
South East █ Conservatives
London █ Labour
South West

-14ppts -12ppts -10ppts -8ppts -6ppts -4ppts -2ppts 0ppts +2ppts +4ppts +6ppts

Source: Resolution Foundation analysis of Britain Elects House of Commons Library
General Election 2017: Full results and analysis January 2019

The North East, Yorkshire and Humberside, East Midlands and West Midlands were the areas where the Conservatives made their largest gains. They were also the areas where Labour's vote fell the most. Data from the Resolution Foundation found that Labour's biggest fall in vote share regionally was in the North East, in Yorkshire and Humberside, and in the East and West Midlands.[7] These were also the four areas where the Conservative vote share increased the most though the fall in Labour's vote share was much larger, between 8 and 12 points compared to Conservative gains of between 2 and 4 points. The aggregate vote swings from Labour to the Conservatives regionally were:

- North East 16.7%.
- West Midlands 13.0%.
- East Midlands 12.8%.
- Yorkshire and Humber 12.7%.

The fall in Labour's vote share was over 20% in some Leave

voting constituencies, for example:

- Bassetlaw, fall of 24.9% (67.8% Leave).
- Wentworth & Dearne, fall of 24.67% (70.28% Leave).
- Barnsley Central, fall of 23.79%, Barnsley East fall of 21.91% (Barnsley 68.3% Leave).
- Doncaster North, fall of 22%, Doncaster Central, fall of 17.9% (Doncaster 69% Leave).
- Normanton, Pontefract & Castleford, fall of 21.58% (69.26% Leave).
- Jarrow, fall of 20.05% (61.78% Leave).

Labour switchers and first time Tory voters

One of the unusual aspects of the 2017 and 2019 elections was the high level of direct switching from Labour to the Conservatives, which was particularly marked in Red Wall seats. Historically, the level of direct vote switching from Labour to Conservative has been lower than other swings, such as from Labour to the SNP or to the Liberal Democrats. It has been assumed this is because there are much greater ideological differences between Labour and the Conservatives. Thus, whilst a Labour voter might switch to the Liberal Democrats, they would rarely switch directly to the Conservatives. Former Conservative MP, Rory Stewart, argued this was even less likely if the Tory party did not tack to the centre.[8]

Datapraxis estimate about one million habitual Labour voters backed the Conservatives in the 2019 election.[9] The majority of these were in traditional Labour seats where an estimated 700,000 to 800,000 voters transferred their vote directly to the Conservatives. Robert Langley writing in *the Spectator* argues the election "was a watershed moment. My grandfather, who picketed alongside the likes of Arthur Scargill went out and voted for Boris Johnson's Conservative party. It is almost incomprehensible to believe that the people my grand-father addressed as they burned an effigy of Thatcher six years ago went out in their hundreds and voted Conservative too."[10]

BES data on vote switchers

The BES panel data for 2019 includes data on 1,077 people who voted Labour in 2017 and Conservative in 2019. This data gives us some insights into the characteristics of people across the country that switched such as age, gender, employment status, ethnicity, and their views on a range of matters including their views on the EU referendum.

Age group

The data suggests that most Labour to Conservative vote switchers were older people. 55% of switchers were 56 or over and 77% of switchers were aged 46 or over. The table below shows the age groups of people who switched directly from Labour to Conservative in 2019.

Age Profile of Voters That Switched from Voting Labour in 2017 to Conservative in 2019

Age Group	Percentage
18-25	4.1
26-35	7.7
36-45	11
46-55	21.7
56-65	37.9
66+	17.4

Source: BES 2019

These figures are not surprising when we consider the national picture. Age has become a major divide within UK politics with older voters much more likely to vote Conservative.

Employment status

The analysis of the employment data reveals that the single biggest category of people switching directly from Labour to the Conservatives were retired people. This supports and reinforces the age profile data.

Labour to Conservative Vote Switchers by Employment Category (2019)

Category	Percentage
Working full time	30.5
Working part time (8-29 hours)	13.6
Working part time (less than 8 hours)	1.8
Full time student	1.1
Retired	38.8
Unemployed	2.4
Not working	9.5
Other	2.3

Source: BES 2019

Nationally, in the 2019 General Election it is estimated that 62% of pensioners voted Conservative, as opposed to just 18% of pensioners who voted Labour. It is significant that 38% of Labour to Conservative switchers were also retired. As we noted in the previous chapter, there is a higher proportion of retired people in Red Wall seats, 16% compared to 14% nationally.

Ethnicity

94% of people who switched from Labour to the Conservatives identified as White British. Again, this will have hurt Labour more in Red Wall seats which have a higher proportion of White British voters than average.

Gender

Nationally, slightly more women (46%) voted Conservative than men (44%). However, the gender gap was both significant and reversed in the 18-24 year old age group with 65% of women supporting Labour and 15% Conservative, compared to 46% of men supporting Labour and 28% Conservative. By contrast the numbers of men and women voting Conservative in the older age groups was very similar with 50% of women and 51% of men aged 50 to 64 voting Conservative and 64% of both women and men aged 65 plus voting Conservative. These older groups were more likely to switch their votes from Labour to the Conservatives. The BES data nationally shows that 11.1% of male 2017 Labour voters switched to the Tories in 2019 compared to 12% of women.

Views on the EU referendum

The BES data shows that 79.5% of Labour to Conservative switchers identified with the Leave side of the EU referendum debate. This is the group to whom the 'get Brexit done' message was targeted in Red Wall seats and which appears to have resonated strongly. There was a particularly strong swing in seats that had voted heavily to Leave in 2016, as shown in the table below.

2016 Brexit Vote and 2019 Labour to Conservative Swing in Selected Constituencies

Constituency	Brexit Leave Vote (%)	2019 Swing (%)
Bassetlaw	68.3	18.4
Redcar	67.7	15.4
Grimsby	71.4	14.7
Scunthorpe	68.7	12.8
Sedgefield	59.4	12.8
West Bromwich East	68.2	12.1
Leigh	63.3	12
West Bromwich West	68.7	11.7
Bolsover	70.4	11.5

Source: House of Commons Library

Party identity

Analysis of the British Election Survey data indicates that the Conservatives more successfully held on to voters who identified as Conservative than Labour held on to their identifiers.[11] The Conservatives doubled their vote share from Labour identifiers from 5% to 10% and increased their share of votes from those who do not identify strongly with a particular party.[12]

It is striking that one in five of new Conservative voters in 2019 still identify with the Labour Party. This supports the notion, discussed later in this book, that many Labour voters lent their votes to the Conservatives in 2019 to 'get Brexit done' but may have seen this as a necessary but temporary switch.[13]

The loss of Red Wall seats swung the 2019 election for the Conservatives

The Tony Blair Institute for Global Change argues that the primary reason for Labour's defeat was the loss of traditional Labour voters in the Midlands and North of England – the fall of the Red Wall.[14] The switching of formerly Labour voters to the Conservatives, often for the first time, contributed to record swings from Labour to the Conservatives and to Labour's worst election defeat since the 1930s. The 41 Red Wall seats won by the Conservatives—35 from Labour—were critical in delivering a majority of 80 seats for Boris Johnson.

Labour lost seats like Darlington, Bishop Auckland, Dewsbury, Wakefield, Bolsover, Warrington South, Sedgefield, Redcar, and Blyth Valley. This was a very different set of seats to those Labour lost in 1983, where the biggest loss of votes was in southern seats such as Buckingham, Horsham, New Forest, Portsmouth North, Winchester, Wokingham, and Yeovil. Most of the seats lost by Labour in 2019 were in Labour heartlands and were lost as a consequence of former Labour voters switching directly to the Conservatives.

In 2017 Theresa May had created major cracks in the Red Wall, increasing the Conservative vote share on average in these seats to 42%. In 2019 Boris Johnson broke through the wall entirely, winning 41 critical Labour heartland seats and, like many others, referring to the result as an earthquake.[15]

Brexit and Corbyn: significant factors not causes

Two of the most commonly cited reasons for Labour's loss in 2019 are Brexit and Jeremy Corbyn. However, while these factors were both significant, their significance was in accelerating trends that were already well underway, rather than the cause of the shift away from Labour.

Commentators, politicians, and analysts were quick to point to the correlations between Leave voters in 2016 and Conservative voters in 2019. 62% of pensioners voted Conservative in the 2019 election, this almost exactly matched the 60% of pensioners who voted for Brexit in the 2016 referendum.[16] Peter Kellner argued the large swings to the Conservatives in Red Wall areas were caused in large part by the fact two-thirds of those Labour voters who voted Leave in 2016, and who defected from Labour in 2019, switched straight to the Tories.[17] According to private YouGov MRP research, licensed to Datapraxis, almost one in four Labour Leave voters "crossed the rubicon" and voted Tory for the first time.[18] This analysis matches similar analysis by Ashcroft polling which found that 25% of 2017 Labour Leave voters switched directly to the Conservatives. The Labour Party's own internal report on the election in early 2020 drew upon much of this data to argue that the primary reason for Labour's loss was Brexit.[19]

This was contradicted in May 2020 by Labour's new leader, Keir Starmer, who argued that the main reason the party lost the 2019 general election was because of "the leadership" of Jeremy Corbyn.[20] It may be no surprise that Keir Starmer, as the chief architect of Labour's Brexit policy, argues the main reason for the party's loss was the Party's former leadership not Brexit. However, there is some support for this argument in the polling data. While the polling found that the top reason people gave for voting Conservative nationally was Brexit, it also found that the most popular reason Labour voters gave for deserting the party in 2019 was not Brexit but Jeremy Corbyn. The Ashcroft poll of more than 10,000 people, which included 18 focus groups in seats Labour lost, found the most popular reason for Labour voters switching to the Conservatives or Lib Dems was not Brexit but rather "I did not want Jeremy Corbyn to be Prime Minister."[21] It is also important to note that 62% of 2017 Labour voters who switched, said they would still have voted Tory even if Brexit hadn't been at stake.[22] It appears that both Brexit and Jeremy Corbyn were important. The Ashcroft survey gave participants a list of reasons for switching to the Conservatives and asked which of the reasons applied to them. 75% of Labour to Tory switchers in 2019 said keeping Jeremy Corbyn out of No 10 applied to them and 73% said that 'getting Brexit done' also applied to them.[23]

Ashcroft's analysis of Labour's defeat also points to issues that influenced vote switching beyond Brexit and Corbyn. His research suggests former Labour voters felt that the party:

> could not be trusted with the public finances, looked down on people who disagreed with it, was too left-wing, failed to understand or even listen to the people it was supposed to represent, was incompetent.. and disapproved of their values and treated them like fools.[24]

Underlying long term trends

Labour's internal report in early 2020 noted that Labour's share of the vote had been declining for the last six elections, with the exception of 2017, in former coalfield areas and recognised "there are long-term issues at work here, reflecting economic, social and demographic change."[25] A Datapraxis analysis for the 2020 Labour Together election review found that Labour had been losing socially conservative, anti-immigration voters for some time. Four in ten of those who voted Labour in 2010 and Leave in 2016 had already been lost by the Party in 2015.[26] Thus forty percent of this group of voters were lost before Brexit or the election of Jeremy Corbyn as Leader.

Lucy Powell, Labour MP for Manchester Central notes that the election loss was not simply about Corbyn's leadership and Brexit, commenting "our disconnect goes further back and is deeper."[27] Alex Niven writing in *The Guardian* in 2020 about Red Wall seats commented: "Labour has been losing support in these parts of the country since the last millennium."[28] Something deeper and more complex had been taking place with Labour losing votes in Red Wall seats that voted heavily to Leave long before the 2016 referendum. For example, between 2005 and 2015 Labour's vote share declined 14% in Bolsover, 12% in Don Valley, and 9% in Bishop Auckland. Peter Kellner noted that the two regions where Labour's support fell the most since 2005 were the North East and East Midlands. MPs Ian Lavery and Jon Trickett argue that Brexit "merely served to speed up a decline in our heartlands that had been decades in the making."[29] Immediately after the election, Aditya Chakrabortty wrote in *The Guardian*: "I can say with certainty that this week's meltdown is the culmination of trends that stretch back decades."[30] Former Labour MP for Leigh Jo Platt agrees, she says, "The decline of Labour support in seats like Leigh has been years in the making. Brexit certainly did not disconnect them from Labour; it just vastly accelerated a process well underway."[31]

Academic research appears to justify these views. Cutts *et al* argue that "while Labour's post-mortem focused on Brexit, the reality is that its collapse was a long-time coming. The 2019 election was not a 'critical election' as such but rather marked a continuation of the long-term trends of dealignment and realignment."[32] Political sociologist, Paula Surridge, points out "while it is accurate to say that Labour has been gaining seats that voted remain and losing seats that voted leave in the EU referendum it was doing so in 2010 and 2015, prior to the formation of 'leave' and 'remain' identities in the electorate. Labour was losing leave areas in 2010 before Brexit was a politically salient issue."[33]

The Tees Metro mayor, Conservative Ben Houchen

commented: "If you look at every general, local or European election since 2005, Labour have gone backwards in this region."[34] He added that continued Labour losses reached a point when "for the first time in forever, you had a region that didn't just have strong Labour councils since the war."[35] Labour's losses in local elections were not about Brexit, particularly prior to 2016. IPSOS-Mori public opinion surveys also show that Europe was not an important issue until 2016 and the EU referendum. Thus, whilst Brexit might have accelerated this process, it could not have been the sole cause of it.

However, it is clear that Labour's losses have accelerated since 2016. Katy Balls, deputy political editor of *The Spectator*, argues the initial Tory breakthrough in the North East of England came in 2017 when Conservative Ben Houchen beat the Labour favourite to become Tees Metro mayor. In May 2019, Labour performed particularly badly in many traditional heartland areas in the North losing control of Bolton, Hartlepool, North East Derbyshire, Bolsover, Burnley, Darlington, Middlesbrough, Stockton and Wirral. In Bolsover Labour lost 14 councillors and lost control for the first time in its 40-year history.[36] In Darlington, Labour lost nine councillors, while the Tories gained five seats to become the largest party on the council. This was described as "a surprising shift to the Tories" in *The Guardian*.[37] However, the reality is that for those who were looking, this shift had been underway for quite some time.

Jeremy Corbyn wasn't elected as Labour leader until after the 2015 general election and hence was not the cause of the losses in Leave voting constituencies in 2010 and 2015. Also, Corbyn was unlikely to be a particularly salient factor in local elections or Mayoral elections. The reality is that the picture is more complex than Brexit or Jeremy Corbyn. Correlation does not equal causation. The fact large numbers of Labour to Conservative switchers also voted Leave does not mean that it was simply their views on Brexit which caused them to switch to the Conservatives. Sienna Rodgers, the editor of Labour List, sums up the reality. "The truth is that neither Labour's Brexit position nor Corbyn's unpopularity can be solely responsible for the losses. It was both, but a whole lot more, including a disconnect that has been growing for decades."[38]

The Red Wall story is a story of long term trends that were accelerated by factors in 2019. Labour MPs and Labour's own analysis recognised the importance of these longer term trends. For example, Ruth Smeeth, former Labour MP for Stoke-on-Trent North, has commented that the loss of 'red wall' seats "had been coming for a long time."[39]

There has been a lot of discussion about the dramatic falls in the Labour vote in 2019 and these were undoubtedly significant. However, if we look back over a longer time period, we can see that equally significant was the fall in Labour's vote and the increase in the Conservative vote share over the previous eighteen years. The chart below shows each party's average vote share across 40 Red Wall seats, Penistone & Stocksbridge was not included in this analysis as the constituency did not exist prior to 2010.

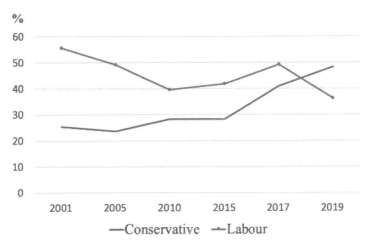

Average Vote Share 40 Red Wall Seats

%

—Conservative —Labour

Source: Analysis of BES 2019 data

The chart shows a steady fall in Labour's vote share since 2001, with the 2017 result appearing to be an outlier. 2019 was the key crossover point.

The Conservative vote in Red Wall seats increased significantly in 2017. Theresa May's strategists had focused on the leave-voting constituencies of the North and the Midlands anticipating they would fall to the Conservative Party. This strategy was successful in that the Conservative vote in the 41 lost Red Wall seats increased significantly from an average of 29.18% in 2015 to 42% in 2017. Former Don Valley MP, Caroline Flint, argues that "Theresa May sowed the seeds in reducing majorities in my seat and elsewhere."[40] The review of Labour's 2019 election performance by Labour Together agrees with this analysis, noting that in 18 of the Red Wall seats lost for the first time since 1945, the Conservatives increased their vote share by an average of 14% in 2017.[41] The review concluded: "the Conservatives had already paved the way to victory in these seats back in 2017."[42]

These Conservative advances in Red Wall seats in 2017 were

overshadowed at the time by the national stories about the dramatic increase in Labour's national vote share. Labour's vote share of 40%, was its highest since 2001, much higher than Tony Blair achieved in his election victory of 2005. In many Labour circles, the 2017 election was almost seen as a victory. This deflected attention away from the Party's growing vulnerability in Red Wall seats. Several commentators were cognisant of the risks, not least the Labour MPs who held on in these constituencies. Caroline Flint commented: "We didn't heed the warning signs in 2017 when we lost places like Mansfield." She also added that Labour not only ignored the warnings in 2017 but also in 2015 and 2010, saying the issues "had been brewing for some time."[43] Labour's vulnerability in these areas was further highlighted in the 2018 and 2019 local elections. Labour lost control of Labour heartland councils such as Bolsover, Bolton, Burnley, Darlington, Hartlepool, Middlesbrough, North East Derbyshire, Stockton, and the Wirral.

Perfect storm: a confluence of changing trends and narratives

Labour's loss in 2019 reminds one of the famous Ernest Hemmingway line from the novel *The Sun Also Rises*. In the novel one character asks another, "How did you go bankrupt?" The reply is: "Two ways. Gradually, then suddenly." This sums up the reality of Labour's long slow decline followed by a catastrophic loss of support in Red Wall seats in 2019.

Labour's seismic losses in 2019 were the consequence of a confluence of long term trends and a rapidly changing public narrative that was accelerated by Brexit and Jeremy Corbyn's leadership. Multiple factors combined in a perfect storm. To understand this confluence in Red Wall seats we must first understand four long term core contextual trends, namely:

- Increasing political volatility and declining party identity.
- Deindustrialisation and economic decline in towns.
- Labour's focus on a new electoral coalition and declining traditional working class support.
- Cultural realignment, cross-pressured voters and Labour's increasing disconnect with traditional working class values.

These four trends helped to undermine the historic 'Labour towns and Labour people' narrative. The narrative that had kept the Labour vote high relative to the demographics of Red Wall constituencies. The stories shared by voters that undermined and changed this public narrative are explored in detail in Chapter 12.

The next four chapters explore the four long term contextual trends.

3

INCREASING POLITICAL VOLATILITY IN UK GENERAL ELECTIONS

"When I was growing up as a child, my grandad was Labour. This is back in Wales in the 80s when I was growing up. My grandad always told me 'always vote Labour, son, always vote Labour'."

Dean, TalkRadio caller, November 2019.[1]

I n the 1970s, the loyalty of voters to political parties was often seen as something that was passed on within families from generation to generation. People came from Labour families and they voted for the party consistently. This party loyalty has declined over many years and we now live in an increasingly volatile political world. In the 2017, election 33% of people changed their vote from 2015.[2] Over the four elections from 2005 to 2017 around 60% of people voted for different parties. While swing voters are often referred to as a small group that can swing election results, they now make up the majority of voters across the UK. In this chapter we look at some of the underlying factors that may be increasing electoral turbulence.

Party dealignment and increased voter volatility

There has been significantly more voter volatility in recent years.[3] Individual-level volatility, measured by the percentage of voters choosing a different party from the previous election, has increased significantly since the 1960s. In 1966 when the BES began, 13% of voters switched parties. In 2015, 43% of voters switched parties.[4] This increased volatility correlates in large part with weaker party loyalties, or what academics refer to as dealignment.[5] Declining party identification has been documented by Dalton.[6] Across many countries. Interestingly, the UK has historically had some of the highest levels of party identification and hence there is the potential for dealignment to have a more significant impact on election results.

Party identification goes to the heart of a person's identity. Classic voting theory proposes that party identification is socialised in the family and community at an early age.[7] Partisans with a strong party identity are less likely to seek out or consider information that contradicts their existing viewpoints. They're more likely to vote Labour because they are a Labour person from a Labour family and community. By contrast, those with less partisan attachments are prepared to listen to political arguments, to respond to new information and events, and to switch parties.

Smaller party success increases volatility

Green *et al* draw on BES data to argue that increased voter volatility is only partly a consequence of party dealignment.[8] They argue it has also been caused by electoral shocks and the success of smaller parties, who are subsequently unable to hang on to their voters. Secondary elections, such as local elections and European parliament elections, give smaller parties the opportunity to increase their visibility, to gain votes and to demonstrate they are a viable alternative to the established larger parties. For example, in the 2019 European Elections the two parties with the largest vote share were the Brexit Party with 30.5% and the Liberal Democrats with 19.6%. By contrast the Conservative Party gained just 8.8% of the vote. For this reason the European Parliament elections have been described as "midwives to the birth of new parties in Europe."[9]

In the UK the creation of elections for devolved institutions such as the Scottish Parliament or the Welsh Assembly; combined with European, city mayors and local elections; have provided more opportunities for voters to cast their votes for new or different parties. When voters are unhappy with mainstream parties, they may cast their vote for challenger parties in secondary elections to show their displeasure.[10] This voting has a psychological impact on voters. Bolstad *et al* found that once a person had voted for a party, even if the vote was a tactical vote, they held a more positive view of that party.[11] This might be explained by seeking to minimise cognitive dissonance, for example it is easier to convince yourself and defend your vote choice if you have a more positive view of the party you chose to vote for.

Once voters have switched party, albeit in a secondary election, they may be more willing to consider voting for a different party in a general election. This can lead to greater success for smaller parties. However, history shows that smaller parties have difficulty holding on to their voters. In the UK, the Liberal Democrats and UKIP are good examples. In the 2010 election, the Liberal Democrats won 23% of the vote. In the following election they gained just 7.9%. In 2015, UKIP came third gaining 12.3% of the vote. Just two years later in 2017, UKIP's vote share fell to 1.8%. The failure of smaller parties to hold on to their voters increases electoral volatility as these voters become open to persuasion by other parties and to vote switching.

Smaller parties may also act as a stepping stone. For example, many Labour voters may have felt more comfortable voting UKIP rather than Conservative in the 2017 general election, or in the 2019 European parliament elections. Once they had taken this step, they may have found it easier to vote Conservative at a subsequent election. It being a much smaller jump from UKIP to the Conservatives than moving directly from Labour.

Frequency of elections and referendums

From 2014 to 2019 we saw three General Elections, two referendums (on Scottish independence and and Brexit) and two European Elections, in addition to local and regional elections. The increased frequency of major democratic votes, particularly three General Elections in five years, gave people the opportunity to reconsider their vote.

Voter volatility: the example of the Scottish referendum

The ideological competition between Labour and the Conservatives has historically been around economic issues such as taxation, redistribution of wealth and social provision of services funded through taxes versus the free market. The Scottish and EU referendums of 2014 and 2016 have highlighted a cultural dimension to party competition and created more cross-pressured voters. A cross-pressured voter is one who may agree with the economic policy of a party but prefers another party's social or cultural policies. The Scottish referendum is a good example.

The data shows that around ninety percent of those that voted 'Yes' for independence in the referendum subsequently voted for the SNP in the 2015 General Election. Their preference for an independence policy trumped their preference for Labour's economic policies. They could not bring themselves to vote for a unionist Labour Party in the general election. As a consequence, Labour's vote collapsed as it lost nearly half of its 2010 voters to the SNP at the 2015 general election. This led to its worst defeat in Scotland for almost 100 years. Not since 1918 had Labour fared so badly. The lesson from the referendum appeared to be that where political parties campaign on one side of a referendum debate, it increases the prospect of voters feeling cross-pressured and reconsidering their party choice depending upon the salience of the issue.

If a person's social identity can be determined by political partisanship and support for a political party, then Fieldhouse *et al* argue it is plausible that "other salient political divisions might also act as a basis for social identities."[12] The SNP created a positive story focused on history and created a vision of an imagined future and what an independent Scotland could achieve. The SNP created an overall narrative rather than simply offering a set of policies. It characterised the conflict as a populist struggle with the old enemy in Westminster. This story shaped the discourse of the debate and increased the salience of the nationalist versus unionist divide. Following the Scottish referendum debate, a person's identity was more likely to be determined by whether they were a nationalist or a unionist than by their party loyalty. People felt more strongly that they were a nationalist than a supporter of a unionist Labour party, which the SNP argued was incapable of functioning "without remote control from their London masters."[13]

In 2014, 84% of the BES cohort of Labour supporters in Scotland who voted 'Yes' in the referendum identified with the Labour Party. A year later this figure had fallen to only 37%. This shift to the SNP may have been made easier by the relative closeness of Labour and SNP policies on economic and cultural issues. The referendum also led to a reduction in British identity amongst Scottish voters.

The impact of the referendum in Scotland on voting in the

2015 general election was significant. There were record breaking swings from Labour to the SNP. In Glasgow North East, the swing from Labour to the SNP was an incredible 39.3%. The SNP vote increased from 4,000 to 22,000. In 2015, Labour won just one seat in Scotland, compared to 40 in 2010. By contrast the SNP won 56 seats compared to just 6 in 2010. The referendum acted "as a catalyst for Labour's collapse in Scotland in 2015, leading to a realignment of voters and parties according to whether they supported Scottish Independence."[14]

In 2017, the SNP support declined. The party lost over a quarter of their vote share and 21 of the 56 seats they had won in 2015. However, Labour only made modest gains, a 2.8% vote share increase, and won back only six seats. By contrast the Conservatives almost doubled their vote share in Scotland from 15% in 2015 to 29% in 2017, winning 12 seats and becoming the second largest party in Scotland. It is of particular interest to note that almost a quarter of 2015 Labour voters switched to the Conservatives in 2017, a high level of switching between the two main parties.

The impact of the 2014 Scottish referendum on the 2015 General Election should have been a major warning to the Labour Party about the potential realignment of voters but like so many others it was ignored. The issue of cross-pressured voters and cultural values is discussed in more detail in Chapter 6.

Non-voters

Referendums also appear to be able to engage people that don't vote in general elections. The turnout for the Scottish Referendum in 2014 was 84.6%. This is the highest recorded for an election or referendum in the United Kingdom since the January 1910 general election, which was held before there was universal suffrage. The turnout in the EU referendum in 2016 was 72%, higher than any general election since 1992. Elections can become more volatile if large groups of people who previously abstained start to vote or vice versa.

New parties gain votes by persuading voters to switch but they can also mobilise voters that didn't previously vote. There is some evidence that new populist parties such as UKIP have mobilised non-voters.[15] The high turnout in the EU referendum was put down to many former non-voters turning out to vote.

A 2019 Hansard Society report states "the strongest feelings of powerlessness and disengagement are intensifying" in the UK which can lead to lower levels of voting.[16] Over thirty percent of people did not vote in the 2017 and 2019 elections. The groups least likely to vote are young people, ethnic minorities, unskilled workers, and the long term unemployed.[17]

Over the last thirty years there has been a relative decline in the proportion of working class people that vote. In the 1980s the difference in turnout between the working class and the middle class was five percent. This increased to almost twenty percent in 2010[18] and to almost thirty percent in 2017.[19] Labour has traditionally gained from increases in turnout. According to political scientists Oliver Heath and Matthew Goodwin, in 2017, "in the twenty constituencies where turnout increased the most, Labour made an average gain of 12.7 percentage points, whereas the Conservatives made an average gain of only 0.8 points."[20] In 2019, it appears it was the Conservatives that gained most by mobilising former non-voters, potentially those that voted in the 2016 referendum but not in previous general elections.[21]

Electoral shocks and volatility

Green *et al* argue that dealignment combined with electoral shocks has led to "substantial and dramatic increases in vote-switching."[22] They argue that shocks which are salient and relevant to party choice cause people to re-examine their historic party loyalties. These shocks also must be substantial to change the status quo in political systems. Green *et al*, give examples of five electoral shocks. These are:

1. **Immigration and the rise of UKIP.** Following the decision of the Blair government in 2004 to allow unrestricted immigration from the EU accession countries, immigration became a growing concern for the electorate which resonated in elections, most notably in the rise of UKIP.
2. **The 2008 financial crisis.** Green *et al* argue the 2008 economic crisis led to a major policy shift focusing on austerity which had long lasting consequences. This shock also allowed the Conservatives to successfully question Labour's economic competence coming as it did at the end of a period of Labour government.
3. **The collapse of the Lib Dems after the coalition government.** The Lib Dems decision to join the Conservatives in government in 2010 angered their left-leaning voters, and they deserted the party in 2015.
4. **The Scottish referendum.** As we discussed above, the 2014 referendum caused a major political realignment in Scotland causing a collapse in the Labour vote. The SNP went from third in 2010 to first in 2015.
5. **Brexit and the 2017 election.** The authors argue the result of the EU referendum was the biggest shock to British politics in decades. While 82% of people voted for the two main parties in 2017, there was an underlying realignment with a record number of

people switching between Labour and the Conservatives. 11% of the electorate switched between the two main parties. The authors comment: "In 2017, for the first time in modern history, non-economic attitudes including immigration and Europe were equally as important as left-right in sorting Conservative from Labour voters."[23]

Volatility during campaigns

Declining party loyalty has led to more people making up their minds during the election campaign. These late deciders mean that campaigns become more important as there are more voters open to persuasion during the period of the campaign. In the 2016 referendum, surveys found up to 30% of people only decided in the last week and up to 15% on the day of the vote.[24] Lord Ashcroft's analysis of the 2019 election revealed that "more than half of voters said they made up their minds within the last month, with a quarter saying they did so within the last few days, including 16% saying they decided on election day or the day they filled in their postal ballot."[25] The presence of more late deciders means there are more people that could be influenced by a particular public narrative taking hold during a campaign.

Summary

Most of the UK voting public are now vote switchers. Across three General Elections between 2010 and 2017, it is estimated that sixty percent of people voted for different political parties at least once. This increased volatility is due to several factors:

- Falling party identification and party dealignment.

- Greater frequency of elections.
- Smaller party success and failure.
- Major shocks that are salient and relevant to vote choice.
- More cross-pressured voters leading to realignment.
- More late deciders during campaigns.

Importantly, between the 2015 and 2017 elections there was also the highest recorded level of Labour to Conservative vote switching.[26]

4

DEINDUSTRIALISATION AND
ECONOMIC DECLINE IN TOWNS

"In the UK, the defining feature of the economy over the last thirty or forty years has been the big shift away from industry as an employer and generator of wealth."[1]

The former industrial towns in the North and Midlands have been subject to long term structural changes which means they are no longer centred around particular industries. For the Labour party this has meant that many of the communities they used to represent simply do not exist any longer.

In many advanced economies, manufacturing has become less important as the economy changes. In the UK business services, retail and financial services grew in importance while factories were gradually replaced by offices, warehouses or stores. Consequently, over fifty years UK manufacturing employment fell from 8.9 million to 2.9 million: a loss of over six million jobs.

In 1952 around 40% of the workforce was employed in manufacturing, by 1981 it had fallen to 22% and today the figure is less than 8%. The decline in manufacturing employment from 1978 is shown below.

UK Manufacturing Employment 1978-2016

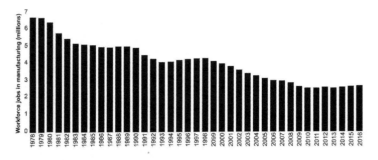

Source: Office for National Statistics

Manufacturing jobs have been lost consistently under both Conservative and Labour governments. Under New Labour, the manufacturing workforce halved from 4.5 million to 2.5 million between 1997 and 2010.[2]

The loss of well-paid secure jobs in manufacturing in Britain between 1995 and 2015 is exemplified by the numbers employed in the following four industry sectors.

Manufacturing Jobs by Sector 1995 to 2015

Industry Sector	Employment 1995	Employment 2015
Clothing	200,000	70,000
Leather goods	200,000	40,000
Machinery	400,000	250,000
Medical equipment	150,000	30,000
Total	950,000	390,000

Source: House of Commons Manufacturing Briefing Paper

This represents a loss of 560,000 industrial jobs in just four sectors across 20 years.

Regional impact of industrial decline

The loss of manufacturing jobs did not equally affect all regions of the country. Beatty and Fothergill note that "Industrial job losses were concentrated in specific parts of the country – mostly but not exclusively in 'older industrial Britain.' Towns and cities in the North of England, and to a lesser extent in the Midlands, were especially badly hit."[3] The peripheral towns around Manchester, Sheffield and Leeds lost their industries but did not have good transport links to enable their workers to easily commute to new jobs elsewhere.

In the last ten years, the ongoing loss of manufacturing has continued to hit the North and Midlands hard. A GMB study found the UK manufacturing sector had lost 600,000 jobs between 2008 and 2018, with the North and Midlands being the hardest hit.[4]

Manufacturing Jobs by Region 2008 and 2018 (Jan to Dec)

Region	2008	2018	Change Number Jobs	Change Percentage
North East	153,900	129,500	-24,400	-15.9%
North West	438,300	344,900	-93,400	-21.3%
Yorkshire & Humberside	330,800	286,800	-44,000	-13.3%
E Midlands	336,300	290,800	-45,500	-13.5%
W Midlands	374,300	342,000	-32,300	-8.6%

Source: GMB Report 2018

These changes have reinforced regional inequalities. The average wealth of households in the South East is already 2.6 times higher than in the North East. According to figures from the Office for National Statistics over 20% of workers in the North West, North East and Yorkshire are on low pay, compared with 9% in London.[5]

A 2020 report from accountancy firm EY predicts that the economic imbalances between the north and south of England will continue to widen in the future.[6] They anticipate that small towns in Red Wall constituencies across the North East, Yorkshire and the West Midlands will be the worst hit. EY forecast that the gross value added (GVA), that measures the increase in the value of the economy that results from the production of goods and services, will grow annually at 2.2% on average in the largest cities, compared with just 1.6% for towns. If these forecasts are correct, the growing number of job opportunities in cities may cause people from towns to either relocate or commute elsewhere, further weakening their local economies.

The 2010 Marmot Review into health inequalities in England, highlighted the impact of economic decline on health inequalities.[7] The report noted that life expectancy was on the decline in the most deprived communities in the North and that the highest rates of male suicide are in the North East and Yorkshire. In 2020, a follow up report by Health Equity in England found that regional differences in life expectancy have continued to increase.[8]

Impact of deindustrialisation on workers

The loss of secure, relatively well-paid manufacturing jobs has been part of a process of deindustrialisation. The proportion of workers in industrial employment in the UK has fallen steadily for over fifty years. In 1957 the proportion of workers in industrial employment in the UK was 48%. By 2016 this had fallen to 15%.[9]

Industrial jobs provided those with low educational qualifications—but often with very high levels of industry-specific skills—secure and relatively well-paid jobs. By contrast, employment in the services sector offers less secure and well-paid jobs to those who lack formal educational qualifications. Recent decades have seen a rapid growth in the numbers of insecure and poorly paid jobs within areas such as the care services and retailing. Dave Etherington, of Staffordshire University, refers to what he terms a 'Sports Direct' economy, saying of the giant distribution centre in Bolsover that it offers "crap pay, minimal rights, and barely enough for workers to live on."[10]

Globalisation shifted manufacturing jobs to lower cost locations which improved company profit margins and offered consumers lower cost products. In contrast, for former employees, secure, well-paid jobs have been replaced by insecure, low paid employment. David Goodhart argues that "The one major group that has lost out from the most recent wave of globalisation are poorer people in rich countries."[11]

The cultural and political impact

The towns of the Midlands and the North have often been referred to as 'left behind'. The industrial decline and regional inequalities have had an impact on perceptions and politics. The Centre for Towns, in partnership with Professor Gerry Stoker, the University of Canberra, and Sky Data, conducted a national survey asking people how central they and their area are to British society. The findings highlighted "the sense of relative social, political, and economic deprivation felt by many in towns across the country."[12] The loss of industrial jobs accelerated regional inequalities and resulted in people in towns having lower health prospects and feeling less important than people in major cities. In short many people in towns felt less central to British society, not cared about by politicians, and less financially well off than other people.

Aditya Chakrabortty, writing in *The Guardian* in 2019 about life in towns after deindustrialisation comments:

> In North East Derbyshire last month, I saw up close what was left: warehouses and care work. Bullying bosses, zero-hours contracts, poverty pay and social security top-ups. Smartphones to tell you whether you have a shift that morning, and Facebook to give you the news, or some dishonest fragment of it. Across the UK, mines were turned into museums, factories swapped for call centres, meaningful local government replaced by development quangos.[13]

Ian Lavery and Jon Trickett, who represent former mining communities in Parliament, talk of a 'silent desperation' in their communities. These communities were suffering from decades of economic stagnation; the loss of stable, secure employment which was replaced by increasingly precarious work; the impact of austerity including cuts to local government; the decline of the high street; and the loss of young people who moved to work and study and work elsewhere.

The impact of deindustrialisation on these working class communities was also political. Former Labour MP for Redcar, Anna Turley, noted that voters frequently laid the blame for the decline of their town centres at the door of Labour councils. British sociologist, Lisa Mckenzie, argues that in the former mining towns of North Nottinghamshire the sense of collectivism, pride and stability was "hollowed out along with the manufacturing industries themselves, and it was precisely this absence of solidarity that had made this area change from a

Labour and union stronghold to an area with much less clear political leanings."[14]

Professor Jim Tomlinson argues that deindustrialisation rather than globalisation is a key part of the Brexit story. He contends that deindustrialisation "has left a legacy of a much more polarised service sector labour market, with large numbers of people condemned to poorly paid and insecure jobs."[15] In these towns the industrial past is often remembered nostalgically, not only by older generations of working class people, but also by society in general which has contributed to 'community nostalgia' narratives.[16] These are groups where the message 'take back control' resonated in the 2016 EU referendum.

Immigration and employment

Immigration was seen as a big factor in the 2016 referendum. As with other factors the impact of immigration is not consistent across all areas. Immigration tends to be higher in areas where there are lower skilled jobs. Since 2010 there has been a significant increase in immigration from the EU in lower skilled occupations according to data from the Labour Force Survey.

Whilst overall immigration has been found to have a positive impact on economies, the impact is less clear cut for lower skilled workers. The Bank of England found marginal but significant negative effects of immigration on the wages of lower skilled workers. The Bank's 2015 report comments:

> The static results suggest that the statistically significant negative effects of immigration on wages are concentrated among skilled production workers, and semi/unskilled service workers. In the latter cases, the coefficients indicates that a 10 percentage point rise in the proportion of

immigrants working in semi/unskilled services — that is, in
care homes, bars, shops, restaurants, cleaning, for example —
leads to a 1.88% reduction in pay.[17]

Immigration is a much discussed and contested area. Whatever the actual facts of the matter, there remains widely held
perceptions among voters in these constituencies that immigration has further reduced the position of traditional industrial
and low-skilled workers. It is these perceptions that have been
leveraged by certain political narratives.

Summary

Deindustrialisation has resulted in a steady loss of secure, well-
paid jobs for lower skilled workers. The industrial communities
that the Labour party was created to represent are no longer
industrial nor are they particularly coherent as communities.
Writing in the *New York Times,* Alex Niven notes that "at the
root of Labour's waning support in England's post-industrial
regions is a basic historical fact: The industrial communities
that gave rise to the birth of the labour movement no longer
exist."[18]

The union organisations, clubs and community associa-
tions that sustained Labour support became much weaker or
closed completely. Aditya Chakrabortty argues that "practically
any institution that might incubate a working class provincial
political identity was bulldozed."[19]

The economic changes that have taken place over the last
fifty years have undermined Labour's support by undermining
the industrial communities which were at the very heart of the
'Labour Towns and Labour people' narrative. Former Labour
MP Jo Platt adds that even under a Labour government "we
never saw the place-based investment needed to rebuild towns
left reeling from deindustrialisation."[20]

5

LABOUR'S NEW ELECTORAL COALITION AND DECLINING WORKING CLASS VOTE

"In the mines of County Durham, the pottery workshops of Staffordshire and the textile factories of Lancashire, workers felt their identity to be synonymous with the Labour cause."
Alex Niven [1]

The Labour Party's roots are in communitarian organisations and institutions, and in its deep connection in industrial towns to the working class. For decades industrial communities in Red Wall towns felt Labour 'had their back'. This notion of being 'on your side' had strong historical resonance in Labour communities. The protest song 'which side are you on?' written during a mining dispute by Florence Reece in 1931, has been used and adapted by Labour unions as a rallying cry over the last 90 years. In the 1980s it was adapted by Billy Bragg in the bitter dispute between Margaret Thatcher and the miners in the 1980s. Director Ken Loach also used the title for his documentary about the miners' strike in Britain.

Historically, Labour held a significant lead over the Conservatives amongst traditional working class voters (based on occupational classifications) which can be seen from British Electoral Survey data. Evans and Tilley argue that this class-based voting was largely static from the 1940s to the 1990s.[2] However, from the 1990s onwards, they argue the relationship between class and party began to disappear as New Labour sought to broaden its appeal as a centrist party. Working class perceptions of Labour began to change and the Party's lead amongst these voters gradually declined.

By 2010, Labour no longer held an electoral lead amongst D2 voters. In 2015, Labour became, for the first time, less popular amongst working class voters than among the population as a whole. In reviewing the 2015 general election Paul Hunter of the Smith Institute observed that "Labour didn't lose because middle class voters deserted them. It was mostly working class voters who lost faith over the last decade in the Labour project."[3]

In 2017 the Conservatives secured 44% of votes from C2DE voters. In 2019 this increased further to 48% and Peter Kellner highlighted the significant gap that the Conservatives opened over Labour amongst working class voters. He noted that though this was not the first election in which working class voters had backed the Tories rather than Labour, they had in 1983 (when Thatcher won a landslide) and also in 2017. However, in 2017 the gap was only two points. In 2019, it was fifteen.[4]

The results of the 2019 General Election highlight the remarkable turnaround in class-based voting in the UK over the last twenty years. In 2019 the Conservatives did better amongst C2DE voters (48%) than they did amongst ABC1 voters (43%). This chapter explores Labour's growing detachment from its traditional working class vote and the implications in Red Wall seats.

Defining working class

According to the British Social Attitudes survey the number of people defining themselves as working class has remained consistent over the last three decades, with sixty percent of people saying they are working-class. However, the term 'working class' has been fiercely debated. Commentators such as Dalton have argued that class is a less useful concept these days as there are more overlaps between classes and class is no longer the same predictor of voting behaviour that it once was. It is therefore worth spending a little time exploring the concept.

Traditionally occupational classifications were used to define 'working-class' and distinctions were made between manual and non-manual occupations. Other classifications have drawn on further factors such as education, income, security, and lifestyle. Evans and Tilley grouped together the following set of socio-economic classifications to define working class jobs: skilled manual, semi-skilled manual, unskilled manual and farm worker, together with traditional jobs such as machine operators and labourers and newer jobs such as HGV driver, gardener, order picker and packer.

Another group of academics have argued for a new categorisation that distinguishes between three types of working class, namely:

- Emergent service workers, employed in low-paid jobs in areas like hospitality or customer service.
- The precariat, who work as cleaners, care workers or van drivers.
- The traditional industrial working class.[5]

In constituencies with a higher proportion of precariat workers there has not been any decline in Labour's support over the last ten years.[6] Also if we take the most deprived constituencies in England, the top 16 are all Labour seats, though these are largely in cities. Thus the disconnect with Labour appears to be concentrated amongst the traditional industrial working class. Unlike the precariat, which is spread across the country, this group is geographically concentrated in the areas of industrial heritage such as mining, pottery or textile towns.

This analysis suggests that Labour is not becoming detached from all the working class but primarily from the traditional industrial working class which is concentrated in seats such as the Red Wall constituencies. This thesis is supported by Cooper and Cooper who point out that "areas with high levels of deprivation and ethnic diversity remain solidly Labour in most of Britain. For example, of the 20 constituencies with the highest levels of child poverty in Britain, 19 of them have a Labour MP in the new Parliament."[7]

Jennings and Stoker also point out that between 2005 and 2017 Labour actually increased its vote in constituencies "with a higher share of 'precariat' and emerging service workers."[8] These studies indicate that Labour is still strongly supported by poorer voters in new insecure service industries but losing support in traditional working class Red Wall seats that are characterised by manual workers with older, less educated populations. In these seats Labour had been slowly but significantly losing the support of voters directly to the Conservatives since the turn of the millennium.

New Labour and a new electoral coalition

As highlighted in the previous chapter, deindustrialisation was reshaping the UK economy and reducing the number of people that worked in traditional industrial working class occupations. The New Labour project in the 1990s focused on developing a new strategic electoral coalition to widen their base of support. Its strategy for electoral success was based on attracting the median voter and winning from the centre. As a consequence New Labour, under Tony Blair, made a less direct appeal to the industrial working class. Prior to the 1990s it was common for the Labour Party to position itself as 'the political wing' of a 'Labour movement' of which the trade unions were "the industrial wing." This positioning was dropped by New Labour as it increasingly sought to gain the support of the progressively minded middle-class voters of London and Britain's major cities. This focus on building a wider coalition of electoral support successfully broadened Labour's appeal and resulted in the party's victory in the 1997 General Election with 13.5 million votes, 43% of the votes cast. According to Cambridge academic Chris Bickerton, this victory "was built upon a shift in the composition of the Labour vote: more middle class, more concentrated in the home counties."[9]

Labour's success in appealing to a new electoral coalition began to reshape the political geography of the UK. Jennings and Stoker note that between 2005 and 2017 "Labour's vote share has tended to rise in urban areas (i.e. major cities), with younger and more diverse and more educated populations often working in 'cosmopolitan' industries, whereas the Conservative vote has tended to increase in less densely populated towns and rural areas, with older and less diverse populations."[10] This Labour tilt to the cosmopolitan axis reflected trends across Western democracies where parties on the left have been losing votes in areas with a high concentration of working class occupations, but gaining in areas with a high proportion of highly educated voters. The decline in manufacturing employment has been cited as a key factor in the decline of social democratic parties across the continent.[11]

Given that broader social and economic changes have reduced the numbers of traditional working class voters and diversified the nature of the working class, many commentators have strongly supported Labour's shift in focus from the traditional industrial working class to a wider progressive coalition. Many have argued that Labour's most important electoral base is no longer the traditional working class but rather middle class and younger voters in cosmopolitan areas. For example, London-based writer Alexander Mercouris has claimed that "not only is Labour's new middle-class base now much bigger than its old working class base, it is also the part of Labour's fastest-growing base, and which is more articulate and more dynamic. To say it straightforwardly, it is the part of Labour's electoral coalition which it most needs in the future."[12] As a consequence, Labour's new heartlands are now larger cosmopolitan cities whether they are in the North or the South.

The Labour party's change in electoral focus was also reflected in the nature of the Party's membership. The latest Labour Party membership figures show that the party is now dominated by middle class members. According to the latest figures, 77% of party members are middle-class, defined as ABC1 social groups, compared to a national average of 62%.[13] These changes have also been reflected in the backgrounds of Labour MPs. For example, the proportion of Labour MPs who have had experience of manual work declined from 16% in 1979 to 3% in 2018. In the 1990s and 2000s many London based Labour grandees were parachuted in by New Labour to represent traditional industrial working class areas. For example, Peter Mandelson (Hartlepool), David Miliband (South Shields), and Ed Miliband (Doncaster). This was nothing new in itself. Working class seats had often been represented by leading party figures rather than local representatives. For example, the rather aristocratic figure of Hugh Dalton in Bishop Auckland or Stafford Cripps in Bristol in the 1930s and 1940s, or Tony Crosland in Grimsby in the 1960s and 1970s. Nevertheless, the imposition of these figures was met with increasing resentment. So why did things feel different in the early 2000s?

The reasons include a complex mix of deindustrialisation, declining respect for politicians, Labour's policies being driven increasing from a city perspective and the sharp decline in the overall number of Labour MPs from working class backgrounds. Professional, middle class graduates, often from outside the area, increasingly won the nominations for traditional Labour seats rather than a community representative. Gone were the days of a miner representing a mining community. MPs Ian Lavery and Jon Trickett wrote in 2020 that "a new political class came to be dominant in our party to the extent that in 2017 only four Labour MPs came from a background of manual labour while 137 came from a professional political background."[14] Working class Labour voters were increasingly being asked to vote for a party that was no longer 'theirs'.

This change in electoral focus and membership also changed the focus of Labour's priorities and policies. Analysis by Diane Kirkwood from the University of York, shows that between 2010 and 2017 Labour's policies became much more socially liberal.[15] Caroline Flint, commented that Labour started "listening too much to the metropolitan cities and university towns" and not enough to core Red Wall towns.[16] Former MP for Stoke-on-Trent Central, Gareth Snell argued that policies were being developed by people that lived in cities, hence the focus was not on the concerns of those that lived in towns.[17] In policy terms, this was exemplified by focusing on trains not buses and on universities not colleges. This gave rise to a widespread perception - vocally expressed by Northern Labour MPs - that Labour was too London-centric.

Taking traditional voters for granted

Critics of New Labour approach have argued that the Labour Party took it for granted that the traditional working classes in the north would always vote in Labour MPs as a matter of tribal allegiance and would not countenance voting for the Conservatives. Former MP Ruth Smeeth and current representatives Ian Lavery and Jon Tricket have all argued that the Party assumed these voters would never leave.[18] This meant substantially less money was invested in campaigning in these areas. In Bolsover, one Labour Party member said, "they barely bothered to campaign."[19]

The decline in Labour's working class vote

These changes have been reflected in voting behaviour for a long time. For example, between 1997 and 2015 Labour's share of the vote fell by 25% in Hartlepool, 23% in Bolsover, 24% in Sedgefield, and 22% in Workington. Political sociologist Paula Surridge found that the seats Labour lost from 2010 to 2019 had a higher proportion of working class occupations than the seats they gained. She comments: "The picture is one of Labour becoming weaker in working class areas but doing so gradually over the last four elections rather than sharply in 2017 or 2019."[20]

Peter Kellner has found that most of the fall in Labour support in the North East and East Midlands took place before 2015, not after.[21] He has also highlighted the successive falls in the Labour vote share during the years when they were in government. Overall, New Labour lost five million votes, around a third of its entire vote. A pressure group—Five Million Votes—was formed to address the issue, and a report was published by the Smith Institute, highlighting that Labour's heaviest losses were in the Midlands, the North East, and Yorkshire and Humberside.[22] However, lessons were not learned.

Kellner's analysis of the voters that Labour had lost suggested "a marked decline in Labour's working class" support.[23] Kellner argued that this was due to a change in the economic structure and there simply being less working class voters rather than such voters being alienated by New Labour. However, his analysis also revealed that the core defectors from Labour were culturally conservative. David Skelton writing in 2013 commented that as the Labour Party became 'lattefied' its views "gradually moved out of sympathy with voters in working class areas, on issues ranging from the EU to housing and crime and justice."[24] This is reflected in Kellner's 2012 findings that Labour defectors had very strong feelings about immigration and the EU, long before the 2016 referendum. Many commentators at the time observed a distancing of Labour from the traditional working class.

The Conservatives had been steadily gaining votes from the DE demographic and their votes from this group increased quite sharply in 2017 and increased again in 2019. The Conservative vote amongst DE voters increased from 29% in 2015 to 47% in 2019. Over the same time period the Labour vote share amongst these DE voters fell from 37% to 34%.

The decline in Labour's lead amongst working-class voters is highlighted by a group of academics who developed the concept of the 'falling ladder', a series of charts over time showing falling support for Labour in constituencies with a higher proportion of blue-collar jobs.[25] They highlighted that the previously healthy lead that Labour enjoyed in working class constituencies in 2010 "gradually dissolved" in each successive election.[26]

The decline in Labour's vote share in Red Wall seats has been accompanied by growing support for the Conservatives. In 2019, the vote swing to the Conservatives was positively correlated with the proportion of the share of workers in low skilled jobs.[27] In simple terms the greater the proportion of low-paid workers in a constituency the greater the swing to the Conservatives.

The importance of low-income voters, and their decreasing tribal loyalty, was highlighted by the Joseph Rowntree Foundation both before and after the 2019 general election.[28] The 2019 report notes that most of the Conservative Party's new low-income votes in 2019 came direct from former Labour voters and argues low-income voters have played a central role in putting the Conservatives into power and Labour into opposition.[29] The report makes the following observation:

Remarkably, the Conservatives are now more popular among people on low incomes than they are among people on high incomes. .... The Labour Party that Sir Keir Starmer recently became leader of is today just as popular among the wealthy as it is among those on low incomes.[30]

In the 2019 election, in constituencies with a high percentage of people in low-skilled jobs, the Conservative vote share increased by an average of six percentage points while the Labour share fell by 14 points. In terms of low pay the Tories led Labour by 11% (45% to 34%) among people with a household income of less than £20,000.[31]

It is remarkable that in the 2019 election, the best predictor of Labour's fall in vote share was how 'working class' the constituency was (measured as the proportion of the electorate in routine or semi-routine occupations). According to Paula Surridge "this appears to predict more strongly Labour's fortunes in a constituency in 2019 than age, education levels, ethnicity or the Leave share of the vote."[32]

Labour's growing disconnect with the traditional working class

In many ways 2020 feels like 1960. Then the Labour Party had lost three elections in a row and the Conservatives had increased their majority each time. This prompted much reflection and the publication of 'Must Labour Lose?'[33] The book argued Labour's liabilities were its leadership, its nationalisation policies and most importantly, the fact it was strongly identified with only one segment of the population - the industrial working class. Ironically, in 2019 it was Labour's lack of identity and disconnect with this group of voters that became an issue in Red Wall seats.

Ruth Smeeth, Jon Trickett and Ian Lavery have all suggested their constituents were variously stereotyped as "backward looking, racist or reactionary'.[34] This sense of disconnect was exemplified by the infamous encounter between Gordon Brown and Gillian Duffy in 2010 when he described her as 'sort of a bigoted woman'.[35] These incidents made former Labour voters suspicious of the party. In 2018, a Fabian Society report highlighted a 'growing hostility' between Labour's old traditional voters and its new core voters.[36]

These tensions were further highlighted by the Brexit debate. Caroline Flint, claimed in a Sky interview with Sophie Ridge that Emily Thornberry said to an MP of a leave voting seat "I am glad my constituents aren't as stupid as yours."[37] This was denied by Thornberry but there is no denying the growing cultural tension between Labour's metropolitan supporters and the older, white, traditional Labour voters in Red Wall seats.

Many Labour voters began to openly question the party. Some were angry with their local Labour councils for their lack of aspiration for their areas. Some felt Labour didn't share their values on issues such as crime and immigration. Some felt they had taken them for granted. Others felt more strongly and argued Labour looked down on them and had betrayed them over Brexit. From this confluence of stories, a new narrative began to emerge from focus groups, namely that Labour no longer represented people like them. Deborah Mattinson has commented:

> Some focus groups I did in Crewe a couple of years ago were saying the Labour Party is not the party that represents people like me anymore. It doesn't sound like me or look like me. It is all about people who live in north London."[38] In these focus groups, Mattinson asked voters what Labour's 'Come Dine with Me' dish would be, and was told that it used to be a pie and a pint, but was now quinoa.[39]

The Labour Together review of the 2019 election comments: "Labour's electoral coalition had been fracturing for a long time and was broken in 2019. We were rejected by many of the communities we were founded to represent."[40]

Decline in voting Conservative taboo

Based on a demographic analysis alone the Labour vote in Red Wall seats was artificially high.[41] A Conservative election strategist speaking to the *Financial Times* before the 2019 election argued that in the Red Wall were "dozens of seats that would have 20,000 Tory majorities if they were in the south of England."[42] However, there was a strong antipathy to the Conservatives amongst working-class communities in Red Wall seats. This comes across clearly from focus groups with voters saying their grandfather would turn in their grave if they knew they were considering voting Conservative. James Kanagasooriam argues the reason these voters stayed with Labour was "a cultural barrier to voting Tory."[43]

In traditional working class communities in Red Wall seats it was seen as socially unacceptable to vote Conservative. These were 'Labour towns and Labour people'. These feelings are summed up in a focus group quote from Michelle, a school-teacher in Bury South and single mother. When asked how she would vote, she wrote down Conservative. However, she then talked about how she struggled to even write down the word 'Conservative' and commented:

> The family, my mum, I feel like if I uttered those words in front of my mum, she'd disown me. I'm a teacher and Conservatives generally have always been for the elite. I teach special needs, I teach re-sits at GCSEs, kids who have been deemed failures their whole lives. So, for me to even think about a party that has gone against everything that I've ever believed in, it is massive, a heavy heart.[44]

Traditional working class people thinking of switching to Conservatives were acutely aware of the social pressures. In 2017, a HuffPost UK-Edelman focus group found Northern Labour voters switching to Theresa May had strong fears that they would be "disowned" by their friends and family for backing the Tories.[45]

However, the taboo against voting Conservative was slowly but steadily eroding in Red Wall seats. The Conservative vote share had been growing since the millennium. Of those that voted Labour in 2005 in Red Wall seats, 12% switched to the Conservatives in 2010, 15% in 2015, 24% in 2017 and 34% in 2019.[46]

In some seats the level of switching was much higher. This can be seen in the Conservative vote share for the following constituencies over the last five elections.

Conservative Vote Share in Selected Constituencies

Year	2005	2010	2015	2017	2019
Leigh	16%	21%	23%	36%	45%
Mansfield	18%	26%	28%	47%	64%
Walsall North	28%	34%	34%	50%	64%

Source: House of Commons Library

At each election, as more people voted Conservative in a Red Wall seat, the taboo was weakened. You started to become less of an outlier if you voted Conservative. As Labour's vote fell in traditional working class constituencies, the Conservative vote increased and highlighted "the growing appeal of the Conservatives to the working class."[47] This appeal was primarily based on cultural factors which we discuss in the next chapter and was brought into sharp relief following the Brexit vote in 2016.

The Copeland by-election in February 2017 was won by the Conservatives on a 6.5 % swing in the first by-election gain for a governing party since 1982. Even more significantly, the constituency and its predecessors had returned Labour MPs to the House since 1935. Former Labour candidate, Rachel Burgin, argues this should have "sounded the alarm bell that Labour was getting things very, very wrong."[48] Yet this warning was not heeded.

Following the success in Copeland, Theresa May specifically targeted Labour Red Wall seats that had voted heavily to Leave the EU in the general election later that year. The Conservatives made significant advances in these constituencies. While they increased their vote share nationally by 5.5 percentage points in 2017, in the 41 Red Wall seats they increased their vote share, on average, by over 12 percentage points. This should have been a major warning shot to Labour. It revealed how the taboo against voting Conservative was weakening. Despite Labour's success nationally the Conservatives were making significant gains in Red Wall seats and six Red Wall seats fell to the Conservatives in the 2017 election.

According to Datapraxis Labour's seismic losses to the Conservatives across its traditional heartlands in 2019 had been "a long time coming."[49] The taboo on voting Conservative meant it had been a long slow journey impeded by great social pressure. Even as Labour voters turned to the Conservatives many did so with a heavy heart. Journalists reporting from Bassetlaw, where there was the largest ever swing from Labour to the Conservatives, said that the ghosts of generations of miners would be turning in their graves. John Ray commented on ITV: "We're in Robin Hood country. And it's as if they'd voted for King John."[50]

Labour's towns problem

While Labour has significantly grown its support in metropolitan cities it has been losing support to the Conservatives in smaller towns and in the areas on the periphery of larger cities.

These problems were already apparent in a review of the 2015 election, which found that Labour's 'biggest failings were in suburbia, small towns and new towns'.[51] A Policy Network report in 2017 found that despite the positive national election performance, Labour had gone backwards in 126 constituencies, mainly towns in the Midlands and North including Mansfield, Rotherham, and Burnley.[52] The report suggested that the swing to the Conservatives in these areas could break up the Labour coalition, just as the New Deal coalition in the USA had been broken in the late 1960s. Ben Houchen has claimed that the town-city divide rather than the north-south divide helps explain the growth in support for the Tories and is likely to form a lasting battleground.[53]

Disproportionate abstentionism amongst the traditional working class

Labour's challenge in holding on to traditional working class seats, such as Red Wall seats, was made harder by disproportionate abstentionism in these seats. While class declined as a significant indicator of vote choice, it became a strong indicator of abstentionism. As noted in Chapter 3 the 2019 Hansard Society report into voting patterns was concerned about communities that had low levels of electoral participation. Over thirty percent of people did not vote in the 2017 General Election.

Hostility to politicians as a collective group has also discouraged some voters from participating in elections. For example, Demos found that there was hostility to professional political pathways which was seen to have disconnected politicians from ordinary people.[54] Demos found this to particularly be the case within the North East of England where participants in focus groups derided politicians.[55]

Voter turnout in the Red Wall seats that the Conservatives won in 2019 has been consistently low relative to the national average as shown in the table below.

Turnout in 41 Red Wall seats

Year	National Turnout %	'Red Wall' Average Turnout %	Difference
2005	61.4	57.36	-4.04
2010	65.1	61.67	-3.43
2015	66.4	61.14	-5.28
2017	68.8	64.97	-3.83
2019	67.3	63.05	-4.25

Source: House of Commons Library

68

This lower turnout is likely to disproportionately affect Labour's vote share as young people, ethnic minorities, unskilled workers and the long term unemployed are all more likely to abstain.

In 2019, Labour failed to persuade supporters in Red Wall seats to turn out and vote for them, and voter turn out actually fell in these places. Those who stayed at home were more likely to support Labour.[56] Brexit may have caused some traditional Labour voters to stay at home. In the Vale of Clwyd, Lee Williams – a postal worker in his 30s and union member commented: "I don't think I'm voting this time. The votes weren't listened to before. Everyone has lost interest at work."[57]

Summary

Labour's vote share amongst traditional industrial working class voters fell slowly and steadily in Red Wall seats. Over a period of twenty years Labour lost support in smaller towns amongst traditional industrial workers as it built a new coalition of professional, university educated and younger voters in the major cities. The seats Labour gained from 2010 to 2019 had a lower proportion of working class occupations than the seats they'd lost. There is evidence that in building the new coalition Labour took its former heartlands for granted and assumed that they would not vote Conservative given the historic antipathy to the Tories. As Labour steadily lost support in Red Wall seats from 2001, there was growing support for the Conservatives. By 2019 these seats were at a tipping point.

6

LABOUR'S VALUES DISCONNECT AND CROSS-PRESSURED VOTERS

There has been a deep "disconnect with our working class voters." The party has lost its connection with traditional working class voters including "their values and what they believe in."

Caroline Flint[1]

The simple story of British politics since the 1930s is that the main political cleavage is between those on the left and those on the right. Historically this left-right division has been seen as a class division.[2] With parties such as the Labour Party established to represent the working class. Over time the concept of left and right ideologies developed, where the left has become associated with greater government intervention; particularly in areas such as redistributive economic policies and social justice; while the right has become associated with views that government restricts the economic benefits and growth that free markets create. Broadly a distinction between those that support collectivism and those that support individualism. As with all stories the reality is more nuanced and complex.

An analysis of Labour to Conservative vote switchers in 2019,[3] reveals that this group of voters is what academics call cross-pressured, this means they are to the left of the average member of the public on economic issues but to the right on social values. On economic issues this group of voters is closely aligned to the Labour Party. However, on cultural issues and values they are to the right, not only of the general public, but to the right of Conservative Party members and even further to the right of Conservative MPs.[4]

This chapter explores the growing disconnect between Labour's value and those of its traditional working class supporters in Red Wall communities. It also examines the new methods that academics are developing to understand cross-pressured voters and move beyond the simple story of a left-right axis.

Labour's 'values disconnect'

The disconnect between Labour and voters in Red Wall seats is something that has been highlighted and discussed repeatedly in recent years. Ian Lavery and Jon Trickett argue this disconnect is not a recent development and comment "over the last 30 years we have seen a disconnect between the values of our Northern heartlands and the Labour party."[5] Writing for CAPX, Glen O'Hara has similarly argued that Labour has "been drifting away from modes of speaking, feeling and believing in many working class communities. No-one with family in those communities ... can fail to see that."[6]

Rachel Burgin, the Vice-Chair of Labour's National Committee Business group, has noted that "communities like Copeland and Workington – and I believe similar communities such as Northwest Durham, Bishop Auckland, Blythe Valley,

Rother Valley and Don Valley – have their own very distinct set of values. Those values are hardwired into the communities and their people."[7] Jon Trickett and Ian Lavery argue these communities have deeply rooted values of hard work, fairness, solidarity, and caring for one another. Many voters in Red Wall seats are economically to the left in that they support nationalisation and redistributive taxes, but they are culturally conservative.

Many traditional working class voters in Red Wall seats who voted Leave represent a group of less diverse voters with culturally conservative views. In an article on why Labour lost seats in the North, Ryan Swift from Leeds University, comments that "on issues such as immigration and law and order Labour appeared to be out of step with much of its traditional voter base whose socially conservative views lead them to support tighter controls on immigration and harsher punishment for offenders."[8]

The pressure group Blue Labour, set up in 2009 by political theorist and Labour life peer, Maurice Glasman, acknowledges this disconnect and argues the Labour party needs to connect with these deeply conservative socialists. Glasman argues the Labour Party must renew its covenant with these people by focusing on the family, local communities, and patriotism. The 'Blue Labour' narrative is a critique of New Labour's globalisation narrative. It argues for controls on immigration and supporting local communities through the institutions that bring meaning to people's lives, from local clubs and pubs to post offices and local hospitals.

In the run up to the 2019 election, there was a growing sense that the Labour Party was no longer aligned with the cultural values of voters in its heartland seats and this would have electoral consequences. Alex Niven argued presciently in the summer of 2019 that "Labour's relationship with the north is heading for a final reckoning. At present, the party simply does not know how to re-establish old ties with the northern territories that brought it into being in the first place."[9] This disconnect was increasingly recognised and discussed by Red Wall voters. Former Redcar MP, Anna Turley, noted that on the doorstep when campaigning in 2019 people said, "you just don't share my values."

Understanding cross-pressured voters

Working-class voters that are to the left economically and to the right culturally have been termed cross-pressured. This aligns with analysis by political sociologist Paula Surridge, who has undertaken extensive research in this area. Surridge has developed a model of analysis that replaces the traditional left-right divide with two axis or dimensions, namely an economic left-right axis and a liberal or authoritarian values axis. The authoritarian-liberal cleavage cuts across traditional left-right party lines. For example, there are Labour supporters who may be left on economic issues or at least further to the left than traditional Conservative voters but who are more authoritarian on the liberal axis than Conservative voters.

The two-axis chart developed by Paula Surridge, and shown below, reveals the average positions on the left-right and liberal-authoritarian scale of Labour Leave voters, Labour Remain voters, Conservative Leave voters and Conservative Remain voters.

Average positions on left-right and liberal-authoritarian scale of Labour and Conservative Leave and Remain voters

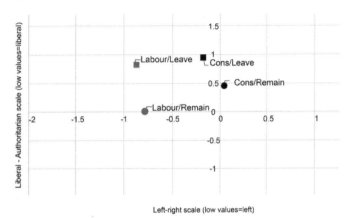

Source: Surridge, 2020, British Social Attitudes Survey (2017)

This demonstrates that Labour Remain voters were found to be lower on the authoritarian-liberal axis and have more liberal values than Labour Leave voters. They tend to support globalisation, are open to immigration, want to spend less on defence, and have more individual freedoms. By contrast, Labour Leave voters are more authoritarian on the authoritarian-liberal axis than both Labour Remain voters and Conservative Remain voters. They are actually quite close on the authoritarian-liberal axis to Conservative Leave voters. These voters can be considered 'cross-pressured' and pulled in two directions when it comes to voting in a general election.

Using data from the British Election Study Surridge has plotted the positions of voters in this two-dimensional value space according to their vote in 2017 and 2019. From this we can see that Labour to Conservative vote switchers (Lab17/Con19) are significantly more authoritarian on the liberal-authoritarian axis than Labour voters who stayed with Labour (Lab17/Lab19). They are very similar on this scale to voters who Conservative in 2017 and 2019. They are also more to the right

74

on economics than Labour voters who stayed with Labour in 2017 and 2019. Surridge's analysis shows they were actually not as far to the left economically, occupying a position between Labour voters and Conservative voters who stayed loyal to their parties across 2017 and 2019.[10]

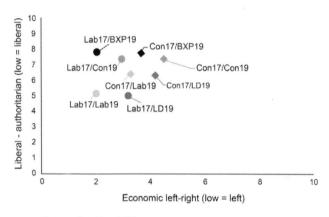

Positions of voters in value space, by vote in 2017 and 2019

Source: Surridge 2020

The values of Labour to Conservative vote switchers

Surridge's analysis reveals that Labour voters who switched to the Conservatives in 2019 are more likely to have cultural values that place a greater importance on order, security, protecting national interests, patriotism, restricting immigration, and tougher criminal sentences. They are likely to be older and to have received a lower level of formal education. These cross-pressured Labour voters are found disproportionately in Red Wall seats.

Those switching from Labour to the Conservatives are also

more likely to identify as Leave voters. Datapraxis identified a group of 'older Brexit swing voters' that split between the Conservatives and Labour in 2017, but moved more decisively toward the Brexit Party and the Tories in 2019. This group were identified as an "older, more female tribe, who lean to the left on economics but to the right on social issues."[11]

Surridge's analysis finds that Conservative voters have moved to the left on economic issues over time on the left-right axis, while Labour voters have moved to become more liberal on the social liberal-authoritarian axis. As a consequence the left-right divide economically has become less marked while the social liberal-authoritarian divide has become greater. This implies Labour will find it easier to negotiate differences amongst its electoral coalition on economic issues and harder on social issues. This is reinforced by an analysis of data from the ESRC's Party Member's Project and British Election Study by UK in Changing Europe which explored the values of 2019 Labour to Conservative vote switchers.[12] The analysis found that this group were to the right of Conservative members on social and cultural issues. It found that 88% of Labour to Conservative switchers think 'young people don't have enough respect for traditional British values' compared to just 17% of Labour members and 9% of Labour MPs. 81% of these vote switchers agree that 'schools should teach children to obey authority' compared to just 29% of Labour members and 41% of Labour MPs. 85% of these voters also support stiffer sentences, this is higher than Labour voters (53%), Labour members (25%), or Labour MPs (24%). It is also significantly higher than the public as a whole (70%).[13]

James Johnson argues that Red Wall voters who switched from Labour to the Conservatives "feel they work hard, day in and day out, and pay their taxes. But they also feel others are not paying into the system. This can be the benefit claimant who should be at work. It can be the low-skilled immigrant, who seems to get priority over them. And, often, it is big business and the super-rich, dodging taxes and not playing by the rules." [14]

There has been a growing divide on social and cultural values between Labour's older, more traditional working class voters in towns and its growing cosmopolitan membership in cities. Analysis by Datapraxis for the Labour Together review indicates this divergence on social and cultural issues is growing.[15] Surridge argues the Labour party has become "a coalition of starkly different tribes, who live in different places and have completely opposed values."[16] Managing and navigating this divided coalition is one of the major challenges for labour in creating a new strategy and new narrative.

New political tribes?

There have been many attempts to categorise or define new groups or tribes of voters who no longer align with a simple left-right model. Surridge has suggested a series of ten new political tribes or value and identity clans. David Goodhart by contrast describes two tribes in British politics that he calls the 'anywheres' (broadly 20% to 25% of the population) and the 'somewheres' (around half of the population), with the rest in between.[17] Goodhart argues the 'anywheres' are those who dominate British culture and society, are highly educated, have a degree or postgraduate qualification, and a professional career. "Such people have portable 'achieved' identities," Goodhart argues "based on educational and career success which makes them . . . comfortable and confident with new places and people." The 'somewheres' are likely to be older and less educated than the 'anywheres'. Goodhart argues that "they have lost economically with the decline of well-paid jobs for people without qualifications and culturally, too, with the disappearance of a distinct working class culture and the marginalisation of their views in the public conversation," To Goodhart the 'somewheres' are culturally conservative and these cultural views together with life experiences have become more important than former left or right political views.

Labour MP for Aberavon, Stephen Kinnock, makes a similar observation to Goodhart though in his case he refers to the two groups as 'Communitarians' and 'Cosmopolitans'.[18] Kinnock refers to 'Cosmopolitans' as younger, graduates living in major cities who are often transient and socially liberal. They feel positive about globalisation and the opportunities it creates for them. 'Communitarians', however, tend to be older, non-graduates, living in smaller towns. They feel negatively about globalisation and the impact it has had on their local industries and communities. They also have "concerns about the social and cultural impact that poorly managed immigration policies and systems can have."[19] This 'Communitarian' and 'Cosmopolitan' is replacing the redistributional left-right cleavage according to academics Koopmans and Zurn.[20] They argue 'Cosmopolitans' advocate open borders, universal norms and supranational authority whereas 'Communitarians' defend border closure, cultural particularism and national sovereignty.

Cultural realignment: the role of UKIP

Some political scientists, such as Matthew Goodwin, argue that we are seeing a realignment of cross-pressured voters, which is separate to Brexit though accelerated by it.[21] They claim that this realignment is cultural and driven by social conservatism, nationalism, social status, age, and education, which has reinforced a realignment of traditional working class voters behind the Conservatives.

In 2014, Matthew Goodwin and Robert Ford documented the loss of Labour-supporting working class voters to UKIP in their book *Revolt on the Right*.[22] They drew on Lord Ashcroft's

2012 polling of over 20,000 people and the 14 focus groups he held with UKIP voters. The findings from this research contradicted the oft-repeated claim that UKIP's appeal was mainly to former Conservative voters in the South who were middle class, Eurosceptic and right-wing. Instead they demonstrated how UKIP had growing support in traditional working class communities within Labour Red Wall towns. Professor Chris Bickerton argues that UKIP "shifted from its origins as an anti-EU party, criticising instead the government's commitment to an open labour market and its embrace of EU free movement rules. Lacking real debate within Labour, the immigration issue became a symbolic one for voters, exemplifying the detachment of the London leadership from grassroots concerns."[23] In other words, UKIP was appealing to older, white, traditional Labour voters in the North who were conservative on crime, hostile to immigration and opposed to liberal policies such as multiculturalism, climate change, and human rights.

Political realignments are generally seen as periods of dramatic rather than incremental change, as they represent turning points. A realignment is a large, and importantly, an enduring form of change in prevailing electoral patterns, with a significantly different electoral balance between partisan parties. These realignments can be exemplified by 'critical' elections when voters change their habitual voting behaviours and electoral support swings decisively in a new direction. Academics Cutts, Heath, Surridge and Goodwin argue that examples of critical elections were 1997, when New Labour won a landslide victory and the elections of 1924 and 1945 "which both represented critical turning points in the long-term party order."[24] In contrast, they suggest that the 2019 election was not critical in that it marked a turning point, but rather it was "a continuation of longer-term trends of dealignment and realignment in British politics."[25] These trends can be traced back to the period of New Labour when Tony Blair sought to appeal to more middle class voters. As set out in the previous chapter the party stopped trying to appeal to working class voters as a group. This void was filled by UKIP which arguably became the most working class party in the UK, gaining the support of many older traditional working class voters.

In 2014, well before the Brexit referendum or the election of Jeremy Corbyn as leader, UKIP came close to winning a by-election in Heywood and Middleton, a Red Wall seat held by Labour since its creation in 1983. There was an 18% swing to UKIP, which won over 38% of the vote. Labour managed to hold on, but retained the seat by just 617 votes. This was an early warning to Labour, five year before the 2019 election, that something was changing in long-held Labour seats.

In 2015 UKIP gained 3.88 million votes in the general election, representing 12.6% of votes cast. However, under the UK's first-past-the-post electoral system, they gained just one MP. The party came second behind Labour in 42 seats in the North East, North West, Yorkshire and Humberside, East Midlands and Wales.

In 2017, following the Brexit vote, UKIP were unable to hold on to their voters and their vote share collapsed to 1.8%. 45% of UKIP's 2015 voters switched to the Conservatives in 2017 and over 30% are estimated to have abstained. In 2019 it appears that many voters who previously supported UKIP and the Brexit Party, switched to support the Conservatives to 'get Brexit done'. Many UKIP members joined the Conservatives following the EU referendum. For example Mark Jenkinson, a founder member of UKIP's Cumbria branch and fought Workington for UKIP in 2015. In 2019, he won Workington as a Conservative candidate. The evidence is that, in 2019, the Conservatives gained older non-graduates from Labour while losing older graduates to the Liberal Democrats.[26]

Nigel Farage has claimed that UKIP and the Brexit Party played a key role in the realignment of voters. He argues many northern Labour voters first broke their electoral link with Labour by either voting for the Brexit Party in May 2019 or for UKIP before that, and this made it easier for them to vote Conservative in 2019.[27]

Evans and Mellon argue the new realignment that was taking place had owners and workers on one side together, and the professional, managerial, and administrative middle classes on the other side. In many ways this reflects the populist appeals of politicians such as Nigel Farage, who rail against the professional technocrats. However, Evans and Mellon note "it would be unwise to assume this new pattern is fixed."[28]

Brexit, class and voting realignment

Brexit highlighted the cultural tensions between traditional cross-pressured working class voters and the Labour Party. The Leave-Remain division cut directly across the economic left-right divide and highlighted that many traditional Labour voters were closer to the Conservatives on cultural issues, such as crime and immigration.

The Leave-Remain divide also correlated closely with class. As set out in the previous chapter there has been a decline in class based voting since 1997 and class is no longer a good indicator of Labour-Conservative voting intention.[29] However, while class is no longer an indicator of left-right voting it was a very good indicator of voting behaviour in the 2016 EU referendum.[30] The class composition of a constituency was strongly correlated with support for Brexit (r = 0.78 in England and Wales and r=0.65 across the country as a whole).[31] 57% of those in the top social classes (A,B) voted to Remain compared to just 36% in the lower social classes (C2, D, E). In short, while the middle class voted to Remain, the working class voted almost two to one in favour of Leave.

Brexit became a significant driver of voting realignment

because people held stronger views on Brexit than on party identification. Research in 2018 found that people's Brexit identities were much stronger than their party identities as shown in the chart below.[32]

Strength of Brexit and Party Identity

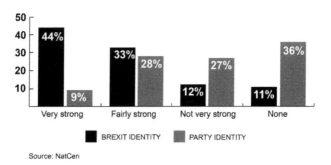

Source: NatCen

Thus being a Leave voter mattered more than a person's attachment to a political party. Brexit tapped into the cultural values that cut across the traditional left-right divide. This was significant in further severing the ties between traditional working class Labour voters who supported leave and the Labour party. Following the referendum cultural issues became more important than economic issues. This may partly reflect Surridge's analysis, that while the economic left-right divide was narrowing the social cultural divide was growing. Datapraxis argued that Brexit was the final catalyst for a change in voting behaviour, as it provided an imaginary path to national renewal and 'taking back control', splitting these voters off from the Labour Party and bringing them closer to the Conservatives or the Brexit Party.[33]

In 2017, the impact of Brexit on the election was largely

mitigated by Labour's position of respecting the referendum result. In 2019, the Labour Party adopted a new policy of a second referendum. This policy, combined with the failure to actually leave the EU in accordance with the referendum result, made Brexit a much more salient issue. Writing in the *New Statesman* in 2019, David Skelton, director of Renewal, argues the Labour Party which:

> was founded to ensure that the views of the working class was represented has, for much of the past two years, looked like it was trying to use every trick in the book to frustrate the wishes of working class voters. A second Brexit referendum was regarded as a declaration by the Labour leadership that the voters had got it wrong the first time and needed to try again.[34]

Greg Cook, the Labour Party's former head of political strategy, believes Brexit didn't cause the losses in 2019 but it did clear the path down which voters were already travelling. Gareth Snell says Brexit became an internal battle between different wings of the party and was not a conversation with the electorate. He comments that "this made us look like we were out of touch."[35] He also argues that the Party was unwilling to engage in discussions around the concerns that people had about Brexit and immigration.

Brexit reinforced two important cross-cutting cleavages

Two new key party identifiers emerged in the 2017 election – education and age. According to the British Election Study: "Labour became the party of the younger and highly educated voter, the Conservatives of older voters and those with fewer qualifications."[36] The Brexit debate appeared to reinforce age and education as two cross-cutting divides and these have become better indicators of voting behaviour than class.

Age

In reviewing the 2015 general election, Paul Hunter of the Smith Institute noted that "while Labour did relatively better in most age categories it did abysmally among the over 55s, who are the largest voting cohort."[37] Labour's falling support amongst older voters was happening prior to the 2016 EU referendum but became more salient following the referendum. John Curtice argues the 2017 election was marked by a 'new political division between age groups and generations'.[38] Older generations increasingly supported the Conservatives while younger voters backed the Labour Party. YouGov point out that "for every 10 years older a voter is, their chance of voting Tory increases by around nine points, and the chance of them voting Labour decreases by eight points."[39] The crossover point at which people were more likely to vote Conservative was 47 in 2017. This dropped eight years in 2019 to 39.

Educational divide

An educational divide has developed over the last decade, those with a greater degree of formal education are associated with supporting Labour. According to YouGov, 43% of those educated to degree-level or higher voted Labour compared to 29% for the Conservative party. By contrast, those voters whose highest level of education was GCSE or lower, have increasingly voted for the Conservatives. In the 2019 election, the Conservatives outperformed Labour in this group of voters by more than two to one (58% to 25%). Paula Surridge has noted that "Labour has become increasingly the party of the 'degree educated' class but this is not only a result of Corbyn's leadership or Brexit, it was happening before either of these."[40]

In seats such as Sedgefield, over 27% of the population have no qualifications. Those with lower levels of formal education are less geographically mobile. For example, 47% of those without education beyond GCSEs live within 15 minutes of their mother, compared to 22% of graduates. 26% of graduates live more than two hours from their mother compared to 10% of those with GSCEs.[41]

Summary

Many traditional Labour working-class voters have become cross-pressured. They are closer to Labour on economic issues but often to the right of Conservative members on cultural issues. Brexit cut across the left-right divide and highlighted the cultural differences between many working class voters and the Labour Party. Parties such as UKIP and the Brexit Party successfully appealed to these Labour voters and these parties may have acted as a stepping stone towards the Conservatives.

The increasing salience of cultural issues has accelerated a realignment of politics based on culture rather than economics. This has been reflected in new political divides, primarily age and education. This realignment was particularly significant in Red Wall seats, as these constituencies had disproportionately greater numbers of older and less educated voters.

PART II

WAR OF WORDS: NARRATIVES, CHANGE AND ELECTIONS

7

___

THE IMPORTANCE OF NARRATIVE

Narratives are at the core of the lost Red Wall story. The historic dominant public narrative in these constituencies was one of Labour towns and Labour people. Put concisely: 'Labour represents people like us'. This narrative sustained the Labour vote in the face of adverse trends such as deindustrialisation. However, by 2019 the public narrative had changed and Labour's vote collapsed.

Before we look at what happened in Red Wall seats it is useful to spend some time thinking about narratives and why they matter. This chapter sets out some of the academic thinking on the power and importance of narratives.

What is narrative?

According to Donald Polkinghorne narrative is "the primary form by which human experience is made meaningful."[1] Narratives help us to make sense of the world, as the stories we share construct our understanding of who we are, who others are and our place in society. Philip Seargeant put it well when he said, "Narrative isn't simply something that helps us make sense of things; it's the actual mechanism that structures understanding."[2]

Narrative is the primary form of commonsensical knowledge. Political narratives give people access to complex political knowledge by providing it in a simplified form. Polletta and Callahan argue:

> People's political common sense is shaped by their experience but it is also shaped by stories they read and hear on TV, stories told by friends and acquaintances, stories that substitute memory for history, stories that make the experience of others seem as if it is their own, and stories whose truth is relatively unimportant to their value.[3]

A political narrative has power when it moves out into the community to become common knowledge. These narratives can become what Gramsci described as common sense. In his view, this means a form of knowledge that people arrive at not through critical reflection or study of data, but which they encounter as something existing and self-evident. For example, the idea that 'politics is a conflict between left and right' is a common sense idea. As we have seen in the previous chapter, the reality is much more complex and nuanced, but people can make sense of politics using a left versus right narrative.

Narrative also allows us to make sense of a series of complex events and interactions. To understand an event, we place it in a narrative which links the event with previous and subsequent events in some form of coherent sequence. The narrative helps explain why an event happened. Such a narrative is retrospective giving meaning to events from the perspective of how they turned out. This meaning, often a moral or a theme, comes from the rationale of the narrative as the story is revealed.

The narrator of the story controls the selection of events and information for inclusion. This is not a transparent process. A story doesn't make explicit why it has selected certain events or left out others. The process of selection means that narratives are not neutral, they communicate a particular perspective of what happened, they seek to persuade an audience through the process of narration. Truth is relatively unimportant to the value and effectiveness of a narrative.

Stories help us to define ourselves, but they also build connections with others. Marshall Ganz argues one important story is 'a story of us'.[4] This is a collective story that focuses on how a challenge is addressed, how a choice is made, and how the outcome is achieved. 'A story of us' demonstrates the shared purposes, goals, and vision of a community. It also invites others to be part of the community. A 'story of us' is also part of our own personal story and our place in the community.

James Carville, who oversaw Bill Clinton's presidential campaign in 1992, argues that politicians need to develop a political narrative. He says, "we could elect somebody from the Hollywood Hills if they had a narrative to tell people about what the country is and where they see it."[5] Barack Obama has said that his biggest mistake was not telling enough stories during his early years in office. Obama says about the Presidency:

The nature of this office is also to tell a story to the American people, that gives them a sense of unity and purpose and optimism, especially during tough times. ... In my first two years I think the notion was, "Well, he's been juggling and managing a lot of stuff, but where's the story that tells us where he's going?" And I think that was a legitimate criticism.[6]

Drew Westen, a professor of psychology, very much agrees with Obama's perspective: "The stories our leaders tell us matter, probably almost as much as the stories our parents tell us as children, because they orient us to what is, what could be, and what should be."[7]

Key narrative elements

According to American academic Gerald Prince: "A narrative is the representation of at least two real or fictive events or situations in time sequence, neither of which presupposes or entails the other." [8] The traditional concept of narrative is that it must have three essential elements: events, sequence, and plot.[9] In a narrative, events are selected and configured into a plot which structures them into a meaningful sequence.[10] In this way narratives create a coherent story out of discrete events that give a broader meaning to the whole.[11] Thus, narratives perform a powerful function, they are a way to make meaning out of events and human actions.[12] The value of narratives is that they "create coherent stories out of the complex and messy reality of human life."[13] Mark Laity, Strategic Communications Officer at NATO, refers to narrative as 'a story of stories'.[14]

According to Israeli academic Shaul Shenhav, the key elements of narratives are:

- **story**: what is being told, the events in the world of the narrative.
- **text**: the mode of the communication and

representation of the story, often referred to as discourse. The use of words is important as the use of one term over another can represent a whole worldview, a form of shorthand for a narrative. For example, using words like 'elite' or 'mainstream media' may reference or reinforce a populist view of the world.

- **narration:** the act or process including who the narrators are and the co-creation process that takes place.
- **multiplicity:** stories are told in many ways and through different media and narrators. This process of repetition and variation shapes social narratives.[15]

We can break down the narrative concept into three elements:

1. Events, characters, and background. This element includes all the events covered by the narrative, the main characters, and the geographical, social and historical space.
2. The sequence of events.
3. Causality. This element is about the attribution of cause and effect, which exists in most political narratives.

Narratives and social practice

Life operates through a collective process of storytelling which is a social process. By definition, storytelling involves a narrator and an audience. Narratives need an audience, a community of people that listen, interprets what they are hearing and then go on to retell the stories. Every audience member can also be a narrator. With social media this narration role has arguably grown, albeit it has had to adapt to the digital world with increasing use of images, symbols, icons, and concise language. The process of retelling stories is not a direct transmission of a message through a story but a creative act by the listener who interprets what has been said.

Cultural theorist Stuart Hall argued that the audience has an active role in decoding messages in a way that makes sense to them in their social context.[16] This decoding or interpretation influences the retelling of stories by people to new audiences. Narratives may connect and resonate with the audience but they are also open to interpretation.

It is the audience that makes sense of the story, that fills in the details, that recognises characters or themes based on their own experience or understanding of events. Wolfgang Iser argues it is only through omissions that a story gains dynamism with the audience, it avoids detailing everything and leaves space for the audience to fill in the gaps.[17] Thus, the audience is engaged and participates in the co-creation of the story. The narrator seeks to provoke an audience response. The narrator intends the audience to share their "wonder, amusement, terror, or admiration of the event. Ultimately, it would seem, what he is after is an interpretation of the problematic event, an assignment of meaning and value supported by the consensus of himself and his hearers."[18]

Narratives are also constructed and reinforced through collective performance. This performance could be remembrance days or collective acts of protests such as Occupy Wall Street events.

Storytelling is not a static process as stories are reshaped and co-created through listening and retelling. In this way, social narratives are co-constructed through dialogue, interpersonal interactions, and the perceptions of those who surround us. Consequently, social narratives are fluid in that they are composed of discourses and can change over time.

Narratives are not neutral

The most important defining feature of a narrative is that it is necessarily the product of a particular perspective. No individual or political actor can faithfully represent the 'reality' or 'truth' of complex situations. A narrator selects events that they consider important in order to create a coherent story. It is simply not possible in a short narrative to accurately portray all events and the linked consequences in a complex and interconnected world. Thus, narratives are not true in this sense, even though they may aim to provide an explanation that helps people to make sense of the world.

Narratives do, however, have to resonate with people's perceptions of reality or risk being rejected. Audiences make critical assessments of narratives based on their perceived coherence and fidelity. Does the story hang together as a whole, does it resonate with their experience and does it reflect something that could be reality? According to Joseph Davis, a professor of sociology, to be persuasive, narratives must "appeal to what audiences think they know, what they value, what they regard as appropriate and promising."[19] Narratives must refer to the same framework that their constituents see as the 'political reality', even if this is not an objective reality. In the same way to be effective an imagined future must seem feasible, even if it is not.

The complex nature of reality means stories will always be a heuristic, a shorthand way of explaining something in a way that can be understood in everyday discussion. Therefore, they are more likely to resonate with audiences if they align with narratives that they are familiar with and their broad perceptions of reality. It follows that political narratives may be powerful even if they don't reflect reality, as long as they align with the audience's perceived reality.

According to educational scientist Frederick Mayer, persuasive storytellers draw on themes that are familiar to their audience such as historical, religious, or ideological themes, and on audience perceptions of reality, to create narratives that resonate.[20] Steve Rathje observes that the human mind is not "a machine, engineered to behave entirely rationally. Instead, like a work of art, the mind thrives on metaphor, narrative, and emotion – which can sometimes overtake our rationality."[21]

When it comes to political narratives Donald Tusk, the former President of the European Union, observes that "perception can be more important than fact."[22] American cognitive linguist George Lakoff, has argued that this was something the Democrats failed to understand in the 2016 presidential election. He says they simply thought "that if you just tell people the facts, they will all reason to the right conclusion. That's why they keep coming up with fact after fact after fact."[23] He argues that this misses the importance of a story that frames a worldwide view as people with different views will reason to different conclusions.[24]

To Hannah Arendt, whether a story is 'good' or 'bad' was not based on whether it reflected a truth or conveyed true knowledge but on the effects of the story. Thus, a story that was not based on truth but communicated such things as democracy and equal rights could be seen as 'good'.

The imagined future

Powerful narratives connect the past with the present, but they also contain stories about the future. By their very nature, these future narratives do not exist, but are imagined. We have all imagined narratives, the stories we tell ourselves about the future, whether it is about our future children, careers, or retirement.

The concept of imagined futures brings to mind Benedict Anderson concept of imagined communities.[25] To Anderson, a nation "is imagined because the members of even the smallest nation will never know most of their fellow-members, meet them, or even hear of them, yet in the minds of each lives the image of their communion." Yet despite this people can feel a deep connection and comradeship with this imagined community.

In Anderson's view, imagined communities are not just nations. He argues "all communities larger than primordial villages of face-to-face contact (and perhaps even these) are imagined."[26] The traditional industrial working class might be seen as an imagined community which no longer exists, at least not in the way it did previously. An imagined community, where there is deep comradeship with other members, that they may have never met, but to which they feel enormous loyalty and commitment. To Anderson, imagined communities were made possible using the vernacular, the language of everyday speech. Imagined political narratives are made possible in a similar way, they are understood, discussed, and retold using everyday language. It can be argued that simpler narratives are more likely to resonate as they can be grasped quickly, discussed, and easily shared.

Narrative and identity

Children in all cultures are raised with stories. These stories explain how the world works, they engage with and play on their emotions, and clarify their place in the society. Dan McAdams argues that "identity is a life story."[27] Martin Potter argues that "humans cast their identity in some narrative form in all cultures, and so storytelling is at the core of describing both individual and collective experience."[28] Narratives can create a sense of collective identity. The repeated telling of stories reinforces and sustains a collective memory and community allegiance. Thus, a collective identity can be constituted by stories.

In Red Wall seats there was a historical and deeply felt narrative about the collective identity of industrial working families and how they were Labour communities and Labour people. These were rooted in tales from the early twentieth century of how the Labour movement, both the Labour Party and the trade unions, protected and represented industrial workers and their families. The interpretation and retelling of such stories shape a community's collective memory, its identity and its politics.

Lisa McKenzie has argued that "narratives, and storytelling, are important in working-class lives. It is how we explain ourselves, how we understand the world around us, and how we situate ourselves in a wider context. We learn to make sense of what sometimes seems senseless through narratives."[29]

Narratives configure our perceptions of belonging and identity "by shaping the relationship between individuals and the collective."[30] We represent our own sense of identity to others through the stories we tell about ourselves and our communities. We locate ourselves in relation to others, we may identify as part of a community or as separate from it, but it is often defined in terms of the relationship. It is also the case that through stories, people's sense of personal experience may encompass experiences that are not actually their own, they may be experiences suffered by others in their perceived community or experienced by say their parents or grandparents. These stories also create social pressures.

In the case of Red Wall seats, the historic stories of Labour and community solidarity created their own social pressures, such as a taboo on voting Tory. These social pressures were reflected repeatedly in focus groups and interviews. For example, in a focus group in Bury South one voter said their family, including their mother, would disown them if they voted

Conservative.[31] In Bolsover, another voter commented "If I voted Tory, my dad would've shot me."[32] An observer of a focus group with northern voters commented "for many the social shame and embarrassment of voting Tory was evident."[33]

In helping us make sense of the world, narratives also help create and reinforce our identities and our place in this world. Graef *et al* argue "we live in a storied reality .... by organizing and synthesizing multiple and scattered events in time and space, human beings 'come to know, understand and make sense of the world' around them, and constitute their social identities ....narratives are tools to understand, negotiate, and make sense of situations we encounter."[34]

Narratives go to the core of our identity. As Hammack observes "the narrative *is* our identity, and it provides the lens through which we justify our actions, to both ourselves and others."[35] This relationship between narrative and identity is important. If a story is to be persuasive and readily accepted by an audience, it must confirm how the audience thinks about themselves, about their collective and individual identities.

Narratives and behaviour

Narratives are powerful in that they not only shape our understanding of the world and our identities; they can also influence our behaviour. There is much debate about the causal effects of narratives. In his recent book, *Narrative Economics*, Shiller argues that narratives can persuade people and cause changes in their behaviour that result in economic events.[36] He argues that the power of narratives to influence behaviour is much broader and deeper than contemporary economics allows for. He also argues that this is not a one-way process, and that events can also change narratives. Thus, there is an ongoing interaction in Schiller's view between events and narratives.

As people understand the world through stories, they can be more powerful in persuading people than statistics or cost benefit analysis. Robert Cialdini says, "People don't counter-argue stories... If you want to be successful in a post-fact world, you do it by presenting accounts, narratives, stories and images and metaphors."[37] Hammack argues that "the primary role of narrative in political life is to motivate the political behaviour of individuals."[38]

Stories are powerful spurs to political action as well as economic action. They can cause behavioural change amongst groups of people. As Frederick Mayer observes: "it is no accident that stories are so often involved in group mobilisation. Shared stories are humanity's essential tool for overcoming the obstacles to collective action, because they help people forge common interests in a collective goal."[39] Thus, the shared nature of stories can lead to changes in group behaviour.

Powerful narratives pull the audience onto the stage, they make people aware that their choices will determine whether the collective drama will end in triumph or tragedy. The audience can become heroes or villains in the unfolding story. Powerful stories cause people to question the actions they take. Mayer makes the following critical point in relation to stories.

Powerful story wielders compel each individual to confront the question, 'What did you do when history called?' They make participation in collective action the dramatic imperative, a fundamental test of character, a necessary expression of identity.[40]

This is why narratives are used by social movements to frame grievances and mobilise support. They also recognise the importance of discourse in the framing process and building of collective identities through 'collective action frames'.[41] Social movements seek to attract others by aligning their movement frames with personal experiences, beliefs, and interests of people. They seek to foster a link between personal identity and collective identity, and to get people to take action.

Summary

Narratives help us to make sense of the world by creating meaning out of wide ranging and complex events. They link the past with the present and create an imagined future. Importantly, narratives are not neutral, the selection of events and stories is always from a particular perspective, and a powerful narrative does not have to be true.

There is a strong relationship between narrative and identity. Stories help shape both individual and collective identities. Storytelling is also a social process. It involves an audience that gives a story life through its retelling. In this way stories are reshaped and co-created by the audience. Finally, narratives not only help us to understand the world, they can also shape our behaviour.

8

POLITICAL AND PUBLIC NARRATIVES

The success of recent political campaigns from Brexit to
Trump to Orbán owes much to their storytelling, their ability
to create political narratives that resonate with people and
that shape the public narrative.

Philip Seargeant [1]

Following the US presidential election of 2016 there has
been renewed interest in the concept of political narratives and the power of storytelling. A political narrative is both
a theoretical concept and a device used by political strategists
to influence how people view their environment and their
community.[2] One of the main aims of a political narrative is to
shape the public narrative, namely the stories that people share
about themselves, their communities, and what needs to be
done. The transmission of stories, the political storytelling, is
only the first step. The real power of political narratives resides
in their retelling.

This chapter sets out the importance of public narratives

and the approach to analysing these narratives in Red Wall seats. The chapter also identifies what makes an effective political narrative, highlights the power of concise narratives such as 'take back control', and sets out the key elements they require if they are to shape the public narrative.

Public narratives

Public narratives are the narratives that people share publicly, typically with more than one other person. Each person has their own public narrative. It is the story they share with others in their own words, their own use of everyday language. The story may be shared in a social setting such as over a drink in a bar or equally in a focus group or in response to a question from a journalist. There will be many different public narratives but some narratives will come to dominate. These narratives, the ones that become familiar and influential, are the narratives repeated the most often. They are the narratives that resonate with people.

Why are some narratives more powerful than others? Harvard's Marshall Ganz, who was credited with the grassroots organising model for Obama's 2008 presidential campaign, has researched the links between public narratives and their ability to influence others. Ganz argues that powerful public narratives bring together three stories namely, a story of 'self', a story of 'us' and a story of 'now'.[3] The story of 'now' frequently takes the form of what needs to be done, what action needs to be taken given where we are, to achieve a desirable future. Ganz has developed the concept of public narratives as a leadership technique whereby leaders can better connect with and persuade others through their own public narratives.

For the researcher there are many challenges in capturing public narratives. Ideally a researcher would be able to track people sharing their stories, monitor those that get frequently repeated, and identify the common themes. In practice this is difficult. Public narratives get shared all the time in a great many settings, including social, work and family environments. They get expressed increasingly through public social media and through private group messaging apps. Public narratives can also take the form of media interviews conducted by the local newspaper, radio and TV. How does a researcher select which discussions to listen to and assess public narratives? How do they design a representative methodology for particular constituencies or communities? The challenge becomes even greater when looking back at a particular period. The researcher needs to identify if, and where, public narratives were captured, documented and recorded during the period of interest.

During elections one possibility is to analyse the public narratives through the lens of focus groups and media interviews, where the stories shared by the public are recorded in their own words. During elections journalists interview many people in constituencies to get a feel for the public narratives.

After Brexit and the election of Trump many journalists felt they had missed the public narratives in post-industrial towns. Both in the UK and the US, journalists acknowledged that they had underestimated the scale of anger that existed, the scale of the desire there was for change[4] and "how upset people were with the elites."[5] As a consequence, after 2016, there were more forays by city based journalists to post-industrial towns to seek out and to report public views. This often raised the hackles of local and regional journalists who had been reporting on local public narratives for many years.

A group of northern UK journalists from regional papers such as the *Manchester Evening News*, *The Yorkshire Post*, *The Liverpool Echo* and others, created their own podcast 'the North Poll' to report on local political developments in the north during the 2019 election.[6] The podcast covered public narratives in post-industrial towns with episodes such as 'word on the street' where journalists reported on their discussions with voters.

As a consequence of these developments there were many journalist reports of public narratives in post-industrial towns during the 2019 General Election. These reports set out the journalist's perceptions of local narratives based on their assessment of what they had heard and discussed. They also frequently included selected quotes from members of the public, though they rarely provided transcripts of the interviews. Journalists and polling groups also reported on focus groups held in particular constituencies. There were many instances of the media setting up their own focus groups to seek out the views of voters in specific areas. The reports of these focus groups often contain extensive quotes and in some cases, audio or video of the sessions were made available online.

The public narratives shared through these focus groups, vox pops and local interviews may not be representative but they are amplified through the media. This may give them greater weight or influence, enabling some to become symbolic of a wider public narrative.

Of course the use of contemporaneous public narratives reported through the media is not unproblematic. They are often selected for their newsworthiness, and both vox pop interviews and focus group findings are frequently reduced to short soundbites. Interviews and quotes are frequently selected to support a particular view or particular story. Vox pops are often criticised as lazy journalism and for not being representative. It is certainly true that vox pops are not representative though some organisations such as the BBC have taken inspiration from focus groups and use private companies to help pull together representative panels. Despite these developments, as a general rule individual exemplar viewpoints are unlikely to be representative and there is no scientific base for generalising from them.[7]

Despite these issues, the public narratives reported through the media matter as they have a significant influence on voter perceptions of public opinion even though they are not representative. People are influenced by what they believe other people think and research has consistently found that media presentations of statements by individual voters have a stronger influence on how voters judge the opinions of others, and the overall climate of opinion, than polling data reported by the media.[8] This may be because individual stories connect with people in a different way. They connect at an emotional level and are easier to understand than movements in polling data.

Recent research found these effects exist regardless of the introduction and format of reports and vox pop statements.[9] Thus even when journalists provide context, explicitly stating that vox pops are not representative of the population, this does not seem to reduce the influence these public narratives have on voters' perceptions of public opinion. The same research also found that not only do vox pop viewpoints influence perceptions of public opinion, "they also directly influence people's own opinions."[10] These effects exist in other spheres such as healthcare. Research has found that "when presented with health data and stories of individual patients, they (the public) find anecdotes more compelling and memorable."[11] In summary, individual stories reported in the media tend to be more influential than data and raw numbers.

John Harris and John Dokomos, who have conducted hundreds of vox pop interviews over ten years for their *Guardian* video series, *Anywhere But Westminster*, also claim that such interviews "can tell you things that opinion polling and election data still can't."[12] The value of these vox pops does not come from being representative. For example, a poll may tell us that the majority of people are uneasy with immigration but it doesn't provide us with the public narrative: the language people use, how they express themselves, or the concise way they lay out their story of themselves, their community and what needs to change.

Media narratives

Media narratives matter as they can frame issues and set the political agenda. The political bias of newspapers can lead them to focus on some stories rather than other stories, to promote information which supports their political view and to ignore arguments that run counter to their point of view. These narratives may not directly determine public narratives, but they clearly have a role in framing the debate. A great deal of discussion in the media, even in social media, is in relation to issues highlighted by mainstream media content.

Research has found that national narratives are often quite different and distinct from local narratives.[13] For example, Local newspapers give a relatively high degree of coverage to local politicians and local issues. While many in the media would argue they seek to reflect rather than shape the public debate, others would acknowledge that they can and do seek to influence public narratives in a particular way.

Competing political narratives

Political narratives are designed to influence both media and public narratives. Political actors engage in narrative competition to shape and re-imagine the world and their place in the world. In their book *Narrative, Political Violence, and Social Change*, Graef *et al* argue that "social and political change is connected to actors' struggle to formulate and tell their stories and, perhaps even more importantly, to have them heard."[14] The narratives that dominate are likely to be those that resonate with the audience and which are are shared and retold the most often.

In the political arena, a narrative is not simply a practice to make sense of the world, but rather a strategic tool for legitimising particular political views or actions. Political narratives are not neutral, they emerge from a particular perspective on the world and how it should be. According to Shenhav political narratives "do not just spring into being; they are created in the course of political action."[15] They are created to shape our understanding of the world and directly connected to questions of social and political power.

Political narratives provide value to people by helping them make sense of complex political events. They act as a heuristic, rather than necessarily uncovering the truth of the political situation.[16] Political narratives seek "to shape the present in light of lessons learned from the past."[17] They seek to shape our understanding of history and to create 'deep stories'. For example, in America, it has been argued that the appeal of modern conservatism is due to a 'deep story' that many Americans believe describes their lives. A story where hardworking citizens struggle and are penalised by high government taxes.[18]

It is often claimed that all stories conform to a limited number of specific archetypes. In essence, stories become familiar because they follow the same basic structures. Kurt Vonnegut identified eight archetypal structures[19] while Christopher Brooker identified seven basic plots[20] including 'the quest' and 'rags to riches'. One of the core plots in politics is Brooker's 'overcoming the monster' where a community is threatened by some monster or evil force. For example, a core populist narrative is to defend the nation by giving voice to the people who are suffering from the contempt of an evil corrupt elite. Another core plot, which Robert Shrimsley argues is currently effective, is "the tribune, a Roman concept of a people's champion, sent to vanquish a powerful establishment that is denying decent citizens the life they deserve, need or perhaps think they used to have. There is always a problem, there is always a community betrayed and there is always a saviour."[21]

Former presidential advisor Mark McKinnon says that when it comes to political communication, voters favour the presidential candidate who has the best overarching narrative. The core of Bill Clinton's narrative was economic growth, while Obama's core narrative was a story of hope and change. For McKinnon, effective political narratives have an emotional appeal based around either hope or fear.[22] Obama's appeal was hope, the title of his 2004 address to the Democratic National Convention was 'The audacity of hope'. By contrast Donald Trump sought to appeal to both fear and hope: the fear and threat of external forces and the opportunity to make America great again.

Successful political campaigns create a narrative architecture with a single overriding story. A story that embraces others to make complex issues and events easily understandable and to frame what the election is about. The reality of course is that there is never a single story. To fully engage with the world, you have to engage with complex multiple stories and contradictory stories. There are many dangers in a single story.[23] However, the fundamental nature of elections is one of competing political narratives that seek to ensure their story, their view of the world, is the one that dominates the public narrative.

Concise political narratives

The journalist Ezra Klein argues that one of the biggest divides in politics is between the informed and the uninformed.[24] With the rise in digital media, it has never been as easy to become politically informed. However, the abundance of choice and access has also been accompanied by the ability to opt out of political news. Previously with 'linear media' such as the radio or TV, the audience might hear or watch news between sports or entertainment programmes. With 'on demand' media such as the internet, Netflix, Spotify or podcasts, the audience can decide to not listen to political news. The key factor which drives political knowledge is not access but interest, and many people are simply not interested.

Obama's former campaign manager Jim Messina famously argued that the average person spends just four minutes a week thinking about politics.[25] It follows that one of the key challenges for those developing political narratives is creating a concise narrative. Former US presidential communications adviser David Gergen says that you not only need concise narratives, you need to repeat them constantly. He comments: "For a narrative to work, a president has to be extremely repetitive."[26] There is a psychological benefit to repetition as the more people are exposed to something, the more they see it as true. Research has found that the number of times a person sees something is one criterion they use to assess whether a plausible statement is likely to be true.[27]

Concise narratives become very powerful in the context of public narratives i.e. the stories that are shared. It is not easy to comprehend or share a long and complex story. People need to get the essence of a narrative very quickly, to understand what it means and how it relates to their own experience. Concise narratives are easier to repeat and to share, which is why campaigns seek to create slogans that summarise their narrative.

'Make America great again' is a classic political narrative that tells a story. In very few words, it appeals to a particular perspective on history, that America was once successful, that it has declined and needs to rise again. This has echoes of the 'take back control' narrative of the Leave campaign in the 2016 European referendum. This narrative implies there was a time when people had more control and creates an imagined future where this control can be reinstated. These political narratives carry a moral stance and purpose. There is no need to expand on the moral of the story, it is implicit in the narrative. Thus, it is right to 'make America great again' or to 'take back control'.

In 2019, 'get Brexit done' was a concise narrative and resonated with many people, not simply Leave voters. Conservative strategists say the phrase emerged from focus groups and was the language voters used themselves. The phrase connected the past, the vote to leave the European Union with a perception of the present, namely that Brexit was being frustrated by Parliament and there was a deadlock causing ongoing delays. It also created an imagined future where Brexit would be done quickly if the Conservatives had a majority. It was a concise and easily understood narrative even if the reality was far more complex, it also resonated with what many people perceived to be the reality and their desire to 'get on with things'.

Narrative arc and multiple stories

While powerful political narratives have an overall narrative arc, which can be represented in a concise form, it is also important to recognise that effective narratives have many multiple stories that each reinforce the overall arc. A powerful political narrative is like a rope, it has many strands or stories that combine to give it strength. A good narrative plays to an overall arc that people recognise, it leverages trends and existing perceptions of reality. The persuasive power of an overarching narrative lies in embracing or calling up multiple compelling stories that each resonates with audience. According to Polletta and Callahan: "Donald Trump did not win the election because he told a single story that knitted together Americans' fears, hopes, and anxieties in a compelling way. Rather, the stories he told, along with the arguments he made, slogans he floated, and facts he claimed all drew on and reinforced already existing stories of cultural loss."[28]

It is rarely a single narrative that causes social or political change but rather a confluence of narratives: an overarching narrative that is supported by many stories that are mutually reinforcing and which resonate with existing trends and perceptions. These stories often use phrases or concepts that act as heuristics to summon up and support the overall narrative. In the case of Trump these might include the 'liberal media', 'fake news', 'crooked Hilary', 'drain the swamp', and 'countries have taken advantage of us'. These all support Trump's overall narrative arc and the need to 'Make America Great Again'. David Gergen, who advised four US presidents on communications, says there must be a larger story. He uses the analogy of a clothesline, "you adopt your clothesline, and then you hang all your policies from it."[29]

New narratives

New political and media narratives can be created but are highly unlikely to be influential unless they chime with people's perceptions of reality or contextual trends. However, new data and information can help to create new narratives. One of the big drivers of new political narratives is polling data, which plays into journalistic tendencies to report on politics as if it were a horse race: who is ahead, who is gaining ground, and who is going to win. New polling data can shape and influence public narratives. This is particularly the case at a constituency level as this book shows in Chapter 13 on the changing public narrative in Leigh.

The media plays an important role in facilitating new political narratives and reinforcing existing narratives. There are always multiple stories, but the media select stories to fit with particular narratives. Social media also facilitates the distribution of new narratives. Following the 2016 US presidential election, there has been an increased focus on the role of social media in facilitating political narratives. In an increasingly interconnected world with mass use of social media, it is potentially much easier for new narratives, including fake news, to spread and take hold.

Summary

Political narratives provide people with access to political knowledge. These narratives are not neutral; they are intimately connected with questions of power and of legitimising political viewpoints. There is intense narrative competition that seeks to shape politics by persuading an audience of a particular perspective. Narratives do this by selecting and configuring events to support a particular interpretation of developments. At its core, political narratives seek to shape public narratives, the stories people share about themselves, their community, and their vision for the future.

Political narratives can include emotional appeals and be more powerful in persuading people to change their behaviour than presenting them with statistics or cost benefit analysis. However, narratives are not simply transmitted to the audience, as outlined in Chapter 7 they are interpreted by the audience in a creative process that includes the retelling of these stories. Importantly, political narratives do not need to be true to persuade others of their narrative, but they must align with themes the audience is familiar with and their perceptions of reality.

From the research it is clear that for a political narrative to be powerful and persuasive it should:

- Reflect themes and narratives the audience is already familiar with.
- Connect the past and the present with an imagined future.
- Align with the audience's perceptions of reality.
- Be capable of being understood, discussed, and retold in everyday language.
- Enable the audience to identify with the narrator or the story.
- Confirm rather than negate the audience's sense of collective and individual identity.
- Support the overall narrative arc by combining multiple stories that are mutually reinforcing.
- Be capable of being conveyed as a concise narrative.

9

UNDERSTANDING SOCIAL AND POLITICAL CHANGE

"I never thought I would see a Tory win here. They didn't use to count the Labour vote, they weighed them."

Keith Ritson, retired, Blyth Valley[1]

The 2019 general election results in Red Wall were remarkable and inconceivable a few short years ago. These were long-held, historic labour seats that had never fallen to the Conservatives in a general election before 2017. In seats such as Mansfield, Bassetlaw and Great Grimsby the Conservatives didn't simply win, they won majorities of over 20,000. The scale of the social and political change is difficult to overstate.

It is important to understand what was happening in Red Wall seats prior to the 2019 election from a social and political change perspective. This chapter provides an overview of how rapid social change happens and then looks at how Labour's growing disconnect with its traditional working class voters was creating a new public narrative and increasing the potential for rapid change in Red Wall seats.

How rapid social change happens

Rapid social change may appear to come out of nowhere, like a thunderstorm or sudden earthquake. The reality is that there are underlying trends in social and political conditions that combine to create the potential for rapid change. It is a dialectical process where small quantitative changes may get to a point where they produce a qualitative change or upheaval. Hegel used the example of water to explain this process:

> The temperature of water is, in the first place, a point of no consequence in respect of its liquidity: still with the increase or diminution of the temperature of the liquid water, there comes a point where this state of cohesion suffers a qualitative change, and the water is converted into steam or ice.[2]

Quantitative changes over time may be visible as individual social, economic, and political trends and these may increase the potential for qualitative change. However, just because there is potential for such a change does not mean it will happen. Where conditions for change exist Cass Sunstein points to three factors that can cause rapid and unexpected change to take place.[3] These are:

- Preference falsification.
- Diverse thresholds and cascade effects.
- Interdependencies.

Preference falsification

Sunstein points out that when certain norms or taboos are in place, people tend to falsify their preferences or remain silent about them. This is because people don't generally want to be viewed as outliers in their social group and have a tendency to falsify their preferences to fit in. In some communities there are views that are taboo and therefore, people who hold such views do not share them publicly. If we take a simple example, a person who voted Brexit might conceal this from their social group if the group as a whole has expressed strong support for Remain and hostility to Leave, and this has become the norm. It might equally apply to views on religion, race, sex, gay marriage, or immigration. According to Jon Elster social norms are "shared by other people and partly sustained by their approval and disapproval. They are also sustained by the feelings of embarrassment, anxiety, guilt, and shame that a person suffers at the prospect of violating them."[4] These social pressures may lead people to express false preferences i.e. views that they state publicly which they do not hold privately; or alternatively they may choose to remain silent.

The difficulty with preference falsification is that if people hide their preferences then by definition they are not easily identified. Thus, it is very difficult to gauge to what extent preferences are being concealed by people and you cannot accurately know people's true preferences. However, what we can say is that where there is the widespread concealing of true preferences amongst a group, there is also the potential for rapid social change. This is because if the existing social norm is based on false preferences it is likely to be discarded quite quickly when people's true preferences are revealed.

Social change does not always require there to be false preferences. Social change can also occur when what people believe changes. For example, people may be persuaded to change their minds but persuasion can take time and therefore the social change may not be rapid. By contrast, if large numbers of people are concealing their true preferences it is possible for very rapid social change to occur as old norms can be dropped and exchanged for new norms that reflect already existing, but hidden, preferences.

However, even in communities with widespread preference falsification, there is no guarantee that true preferences will be revealed and hence, there may be no social change. Widespread preference falsification creates the conditions for change but is not sufficient in and of itself to cause change. Rapid social change depends on a complex process of events, thresholds, cascades, and interdependencies which are discussed below.

Diverse thresholds and cascade effects

If people are concealing their preferences within a group, what might cause them to speak out and reveal their true preference? Cass Sunstein argues that "Our own willingness to say or to do something is highly dependent on what other people are willing to say or do."[5] Some people may have a low threshold and always speak out even if they are the only one and it risks them being seen as someone who is difficult or an outlier in the group. Others who share the same view as the person that speaks out, may remain silent. They may not be happy to share their views until a threshold has been met, say when three or four others have also shared the same view, as they may feel there is safety in numbers. Each of us has a different threshold.

A theory of threshold levels for collective action was developed by Schelling and Granovetter in the 1970s. The theory hypotheses that individuals take into account information about the size of the group sharing particular views before deciding to participate or voice their own opinions.

Diverse individual threshold levels can create cascade effects as once three or four people speak out, that may meet the threshold for others to speak out which in turn will meet the threshold for others. It is like the famous scene in Spartacus where one after another people stand up in turn to defend the hero declaring "I am Spartacus."

A classic example of a cascade which is continuing to change social norms is the MeToo movement, where women began to speak out about sexual harassment. Alyssa Milano tweeted using the #MeToo hashtag on 15th October 2017. The hashtag had been used previously but, in this instance, it aligned and resonated with a social and political context that led to a rapid online mobilisation as woman after woman also spoke out. The hashtag quickly moved from one network, Twitter, to another network, Facebook, where it was used by 4.7 million people in the first 24 hours.

The MeToo example demonstrates how, albeit on very rare occasions, digitally mediated cascades can scale very quickly. Margetts *et al* argue that in an online world of rapid communication it is possible for mobilisations to spring from initial individual actions such as that by Alyssa Milano, as they are facilitated by technological platforms, rather than requiring organisational support. Also with social media it is possible to can see how many people have liked or retweeted a particular viewpoint. Thus it may be easier for individuals to assess the level of public support and whether it meets their own threshold. As the support for a particular view increases it may trigger a rapid cascade effect.[6]

By their nature, cascades are unpredictable, they depend on the circumstances. For example, will those with low thresholds be aware of what is happening, will the circumstances meet their thresholds for participating, will others with higher thresholds be aware of this increased participation and will they participate in turn, for example, how will they assess the perceived risks and benefits of participating?

In summary, while there is the potential for rapid change in communities where there is large scale preference falsification it requires a catalyst or an event that reveals people's true preferences. If the scale of false preferences is large enough it may trigger a cascade effect. A cascade is also more likely to happen when there is "a growing sense that an existing norm is vulnerable."[7] This may encourage people to challenge the norm and when a growing number of people challenge a norm this can create an undoing or an unravelling of preference falsification. When norms start to collapse, when something is no longer taboo, people become free and able to say what they believe and state their personal preferences. What was once unsayable becomes said. Classic examples include repressive states where people have been afraid to speak out until the regime has changed. New information can also cause people to speak out as this information can be the spark that reveals the scale of true preferences leading to a cascade and a collapse of existing norms.

Interdependencies

Social change is unpredictable as not only do we not know whether people are concealing preferences, there are also interdependencies that we are unable to predict. Social conditions create or restrict how preferences are revealed. We may or may not meet a person who publicly shares our view. They may well express a view similar to our own, but we may not be around at the time of the discussion. If we had perfect information, we would know how many people have shared similar opinions to our own, but we are dependent on being present or coming to hear of such views maybe via social media. Alternatively, we may gauge support from other sources of information. For example, when it comes to political views we may review polls, public opinion surveys or interviews conducted by journalists. Recent behavioural research has found that perceptions about public opinion can have a marked influence on behaviour. According to Sunstein, "if people are told there is a new or emerging social norm for example on healthy eating or sustainability then the likelihood that they will behave in accordance with the emerging social norm jumps a lot."[8]

People are influenced by other people both directly and indirectly. It is possible that people may come to support something just because they are told large numbers of other people believe it. However, it is more likely to happen if they actually see or hear others supporting the new norm, in simple terms if they see evidence that the change is real. For example, if the new norm is to stop smoking and people see lots of other people stop smoking, they are more likely to feel that the new norm is valued by others, that it matters to their social group or community. In this way the change becomes compatible with their social identity. Finally, if they see others doing it, they may feel they can also stop smoking. This is what behavioural scientists call the demonstration effects hypothesis.

The communication and demonstration of emerging changes in social norms is important to achieve behavioural change but this is very difficult to predict due to the interdependencies. It is a bit like trying to predict how a virus will spread. However, research has found that social influence and contagion increasingly shapes peoples' behaviours, tastes and actions. This social influence and contagion is "likely to become increasingly evident as our society becomes more interconnected."[9] This can be seen in social media and online shopping sites which provide indicators of social popularity such as the numbers of likes, shares, reviews and ratings. There is evidence that popular things become even more popular.[10] People don't just buy a product; they buy into conformity or to be part of the ongoing conversation. The connectivity provided by the internet and applications such as social media may increase the opportunities for people to see and hear evidence of emerging changes in their social group.

Change through persuasion

As noted above, change does not always come about through the revealing of false preferences. There are times when some people are also persuaded to change their opinions or views. There have been decades of research exploring the issues of persuasion and attitude change, and a great many books written on the principles of persuading people, whether for marketing or political purposes. Many of these books draw on the six principles of persuasion developed initially by Robert Cialdini.[11] It is worth outlining Cialdini's thoughts on persuasion as the Tory Party campaign strategists in 2019 specifically claimed to have designed their campaign based on Cialdini's thinking about persuasion.

Cialdini on persuasion

Cialdini's original six principles of persuasion were:

- **Authority:** people are more likely to listen and give weight to the arguments of those in positions of authority, including experts in certain fields.
- **Commitment:** if people commit to do something, they are more likely to follow through.
- **Consensus:** people take cues from those around them and their decisions are influenced by the views of other people.
- **Liking:** if people like someone they are more likely to agree with them or do something they ask.

- **Reciprocity:** people reciprocate such as supporting people who have supported them.
- **Scarcity:** the rarer something is, the more people tend to want it. Thus, demand can go up if a product is more exclusive or hard to get.

In 2016, Cialdini added a seventh principle, which he called the unity principle. This seventh principle is related to our social identity. He argues the more we identify with other people, such as those in our community, the more we are influenced by these people.[12]

In 2017, Cialdini also provided advice for persuading people in a world of competing facts on social media. He says, "People don't counter-argue stories ... If you want to be successful in a post-fact world, you do it by presenting accounts, narratives, stories and images and metaphors."[13] This is significant when we consider the concept and power of public narratives.

Changing attitudes

One of the key findings by psychologists is that changing attitudes can be a result of two different processes, often called the dual process theory. As Richard Lau has identified there are "two different paths by which persuasion can occur, one a central route based on a relatively deep, systematic, conscious processing of the arguments in a persuasive message; the second a peripheral route based on more shallow, heuristic, and sometimes almost automatic processing of a persuasive message."[14]

People use the first method, thinking carefully and weighing up arguments where they are highly motivated and can access and process information. By contrast, when people are less motivated, they spend less time thinking about the issues and use shortcuts or heuristics to make their decisions and judgements. On this basis, we might expect those who are more interested and motivated by politics to spend more time considering and evaluating their options in line with rational choice thinking. They may invest time reading about policies, watching political debates and make a final evaluation on the information they have gathered. However, those less interested in politics may invest significantly less time in gathering and processing information. These people may be more likely to take their cues from their friends and family, and to think more quickly and emotionally when coming to a judgement.

Despite the extensive research on effective persuasion methods psychologists have found that once people hold a certain view or attitude it is very difficult to persuade them to change their minds. We instinctively seek to defend our existing beliefs which can lead us to discard or ignore information that might challenge these beliefs through a process that psychologists call motivated reasoning. Ryan Cotter, in the *Oxford Handbook of Electoral Persuasion* comments:

> Motivated reasoning in defence of one's belief system appears to be the default response when faced with contrary evidence. This stems from a deep, primal, existential need to maintain one's worldview, which has derivative consequences for how we process the more mundane issues we encounter in politics.[15]

A rational strategy for changing a person's beliefs is providing them with new information such as new facts and figures, combined with authoritative expert views, in the expectation that the person's evaluation of the issues will change through a more informed understanding of the issues. However, this approach may have a lower chance of success with those that are less motivated to understand the issues. For these people, an emotional appeal that fits with their perceptions of reality may be more persuasive than new information.

In either case, whether using new information or emotional appeals, research on motivated reasoning over tens of years has found that "citizens routinely place a higher priority on defending their preexisting beliefs than on updating them in response to new and conflicting experiences."[16] Ziva Kunda argues that "we give special weight to information that allows us to come to the conclusion we want to reach."[17] In simple terms, we are more likely to filter out information that doesn't fit with our views and place more emphasis on information that aligns with them. This is known as confirmation bias, where we select information that supports our existing views or biases. Renowned investor Warren Buffett was referring to confirmation bias when he said, "there's no question that what human beings are best at doing is interpreting all new information so that their prior conclusions remain intact."[18]

John Curtice surveyed Leave and Remain voters to see if their views had changed in the light of new information that emerged in the two years after the referendum. He found people interpreted information to fit their referendum choice, almost a definition of confirmation bias. He commented: "the partisan lens through which they see the world helps ensure that the 'facts' of that debate do not disturb their commitment to the choice that they have already made."[19]

In addition to the barriers erected by motivated reasoning and confirmation bias, researchers have also found that new information that contradicts a person's existing beliefs can create potential backlash effects. This is where new information that counters or challenges a person's existing beliefs creates a strong adverse reaction to the new information and can even cause people to double down on their existing beliefs.

In summary, persuasion is difficult. Changing people's beliefs and attitudes is not simply a rational process of providing new information. Dual processing means that many people do not make decisions based on careful consideration of new information but on short cuts or heuristics, and emotions. Even where people do consider information, they instinctively resist information that challenges their pre-existing beliefs.

So, what makes an effective persuasion process? Based on an examination of thousands of studies, recent research suggests "that effective persuasion begins by understanding and accepting the receiver's underlying feelings—it does not try to dismiss them as irrelevant or abolish them outright."[20]

To craft persuasive messages, you must understand and connect with the emotional concerns of those you are seeking to persuade. While for some people processing new information may be a primary route for reconsidering their views, for other's the primary route may be a narrative that connects with their perceptions of the world and provides evidence of what other people that they identify with, are thinking.

Understanding social change

As noted above, it is difficult to know the scale of concealed preferences when they are, by their nature, concealed. It is also difficult to gauge individual personal thresholds and whether these have the potential to create cascades. Furthermore, it is hard to anticipate the social interactions that will take place and their impact on revealing false preferences and triggering thresholds.

When it comes to change through persuasion rather than revealing false preferences, we can observe that this may take time to achieve as people are more likely to engage in motivated reasoning and confirmation bias to resist changing their views. Despite these difficulties, theories of social change and persuasion provide us with a set of tools and a lens for analysing the processes of political change. The next section discusses the growing potential for rapid change in Red Wall seats from a social change perspective.

The growing potential for rapid political change in Red Wall seats

Matt Cole, an historian and expert in British party politics at the University of Birmingham comments:

> There is a cultural, generational sense of loyalty to the Labour Party even today ... British voters used to be more like supporters of football teams; you don't choose it, you inherit it by geography, or family, or friendship group, and you never leave it, not with any respectability anyway. It doesn't matter that the owner is a crook, that the manager is an idiot or the players are lazy. You might not go to as many matches or always turn out, but you never support another team - and that spirit of consistent loyalty and unwillingness to support the opposition remains strong in a very large number of Labour seats.[21]

The act of voting Labour was a core part of people's identity, confirming their commitment to their community. Paul Mason, who grew up in Leigh, commented that people in the community voted Labour as "an elementary act of solidarity with each other."[22] As discussed earlier in this book there was also a strong historical antipathy to the Tories that was passed down through families. To vote Conservative would be seen as an act of betrayal in these communities. As recently as 2015 and 2017, people taking part in focus groups in Red Wall constituencies said their families would disown them if they voted Conservative. Despite these social pressures there is evidence that things were changing in Red Wall seats. However, the strong community hostility to the Conservatives will have led many people to conceal their preferences. Many of those considering switching their vote are likely to have kept their counsel as social pressures made many people unwilling to admit to even thinking about voting Conservative.[23] Where there was discussion it was often couched in terms of regret that Labour had changed.

There is evidential support for people concealing their preference for the Conservatives. Polling companies have referred in the past to 'shy Tories'. This referred to people who voted Conservative despite saying to pollsters that they would not.[24] In communities where it was not socially acceptable to vote Tory, many voters not only hid their true preferences from their friends and community, they also hid them from pollsters.[25] This was despite polls being anonymous. The social pressure was such that people were still reluctant to reveal their true preferences. Recent research from the University of North Carolina has found that conservatives are more likely to self-censor their views than liberals in environments that may be perceived as hostile to their views and hence not reveal their true preferences.[26]

The contextual trends identified earlier in this book, such as deindustrialisation, economic decline, regional inequalities, left behind communities, Labour's focus on a new electoral coalition, and the growing disconnect between Labour's cultural values and the values of the former industrial working class, particularly older, white, and less educated voters, all combined to make people question their commitment to Labour. Despite Labour's support being undermined by a growing disconnect between the party and Red Wall voters, Ben Houchen, argues people were still reluctant to voice support for the Tories.[27] The historic 'Labour towns and Labour people' narrative with its strong social antipathy to the Tories, led to people concealing their changing views and preferences.

Widespread preference falsification is by its nature very

difficult to prove but ostensibly the conditions that encourage preference falsification existed in Red Wall towns. The scale of the switch to the Conservatives, once preferences were revealed, lends further support for the thesis of concealed preferences. For example, in 2017, the Conservative scraped home in Mansfield beating the Labour Party by 46.6% to 44.5% and revealing a preference for the Conservatives for the first time in a hundred years. Just two years later, in 2019, the Conservatives won 63.9% of the vote to Labour's 30.8%. A swing of over 15%.

An analysis of focus groups and voter interviews prior to the 2019 election reveals that the public narrative in traditional Labour seats was changing. People were becoming more confident and outspoken in their criticism of Labour. From a social change perspective the conditions for rapid political change were building and by 2019 Red Wall seats were at a tipping point. On issues such as patriotism, the EU, immigration, and crime many people no longer felt aligned with Labour. Worse, was the sense that Labour actually looked down on the values they held. These public narratives fuelled the sense of loss, grievance, and anger.

Summary

Red Wall seats were not immune from the wider economic, social and political trends taking place. Deindustrialisation, economic decline, regional inequalities, increased political volatility, growing numbers of cross-pressured voters and Labour's increasing disconnect with its traditional voters were all undermining Labour's support. The party was increasingly reliant on the historic narrative, on loyalty to the party, and on the hostility to the Conservatives.

The social pressures and 'never Tory' narrative caused many voters to keep their counsel and to conceal their growing preferences for the Conservatives. However, as support for

Labour steadily declined, people who were previously unwilling to reveal their preference for the Conservatives were becoming more confident. They were increasingly willing to speak out albeit they couched their views in a language of regret, talking of heavy hearts, and that Labour was moving away from them.

The potential for political change was building in Red Wall constituencies but there still needed to be a catalyst or a series of events to reveal the scale of true preferences and to create a cascade. Chapters 11 to 14 set out how a series of events, including Jeremy Corbyn's response to the Salisbury poisonings, Labour's adoption of a second referendum policy and the publication of individual constituency projections based on MRP polling, combined to reveal the scale of support for the Conservatives and create a cascade that caused a collapse in the Labour vote.

10

DEVELOPING AN EFFECTIVE ELECTION CAMPAIGN NARRATIVE

S uccessful campaigns understand the trends, stories and issues that precede elections and weave a narrative around them. According to Mark McKinnon they develop an overall narrative architecture that ties complex events and trends "together into something meaningful and coherent."[1] Through this political narrative they seek to position themselves advantageously and to influence and shape the public narrative.

Before we look at the election campaigns of 2019, this chapter provides an overview of what makes a successful campaign and in particular what makes a successful campaign narrative, one that resonates and shapes the public narrative.

The second half of this chapter provides an overview of the academic research on campaigns, including how voters decide and evidence about the impact of political campaigns. This second half can be skipped by those that already familiar with the core political theory or those that don't want to read this more academic and theoretical content.

What makes a successful campaign?

A clear strategy is the core element of any successful election campaign as it provides consistency and underpins all campaign actions and messaging. The strategy must be based on a clear narrative, as this allows the campaign to develop very clear messages that are aligned.

It has been argued that Labour's failure to craft a clear message in the 2015 general election campaign was due "to the party's lack of a clear narrative prior to the election."[2] Without a clear political narrative it is difficult to influence and shape public narratives, the stories that people share and retell in their communities.

Leadership is critical in an election campaign, but the right strategy is key. Spencer Livermore, former Director of Strategy to Tony Blair, argues that a successful leader cannot win an election with a bad strategy whereas a poor leader can win with a good strategy. Livermore argues a good campaign is based on:

- A vision, a coherent imagined future for the country that resonates with voters.
- Having a clear economic narrative and establishing your credibility to manage the economy.
- Having a clear narrative on the big issues of the day, which in the case of 2019 was Brexit.
- Having a core leadership narrative that aligns with the overall narrative. One which is viewed as authentic and establishes the leader's credibility as a potential Prime Minister.
- Framing the key question that will define the election, the core thing that voters will be thinking about when they enter the polling booth.
- An organisation that will translate support into votes, such as knowing where your voters are,

targeting them and having a strong 'get out the vote' operation.

Core to developing a successful strategy is understanding the electorate and current trends better than the opposition. Through this understanding, campaigns can position themselves to take advantage of the situation. They can craft a core overarching narrative and clear messages that resonate with trends and voter perceptions. Dominic Cummings often makes the case for an overarching narrative and a focus on the key questions being posed by the electorate. He argues "figuring out the answers to a few deep questions is much more important than practically anything you read about technology issues like microtargeting."[3] In summary, individual policies and tactics are no match for an overarching narrative.

Developing a strategic campaign narrative

Successful political campaigns require the development of "an overarching narrative that identifies problems, interprets events and invokes values in a way that mobilises public support."[4] The eight stages of developing an effective strategic campaign narrative are:

1. Identify the challenge set by the electorate. It is critical to understand that the basic elements of public opinion are fixed, parties must tap into current trends as they can rarely change them. Parties must therefore seek to leverage current trends and narratives, creating a story of events that frames issues in a favourable way. This involves listening carefully to polling and focus groups.

2. Understand your opponent's competitive narrative,

what is their critique of you, how does their
economic and leader narratives compare?

3. Develop a clear overall narrative that connects the
past and the present with a desirable imagined
future. A narrative that leverages current trends, that
is perceived as realistic (it may not be) and which
can shape voter perceptions.

4. Identify the multiple stories or strands that will
combine to reinforce your overall narrative.

5. Explain your narrative in everyday language. For
example, Thatcher used simple language such as
'you cannot spend what you haven't earned' to
reinforce an overall narrative about controlling
public spending.

6. Craft a concise narrative that summons up multiple
stories. Much of the power of stories comes from
their retelling and it is essential that voters can
identify with and retell your narrative.

7. Articulate your narrative and supporting stories in
your campaign messages consistently across all
channels such as traditional media, digital, social
media, debates, direct mail, and advertising.

8. Long term planning. Successful strategies and the
development of associated narratives are long term
projects. Labour's Philip Gould says, "You cannot
win a campaign in four weeks, but only in four
years."[5] The narrative of New Labour did not emerge
during the 1997 election campaign. It was crafted
over the four years preceding the election itself.

Regional and constituency narratives

There has been an historic view that local constituency
campaigning has little impact on general election results due to

the dominant nature of the national campaign and party leaders. Former Labour MP for Great Grimsby, Austen Mitchell, once referred to constituency campaigns as an "arcane irrelevance" compared to the national narrative.[6] However, there is growing evidence that regional and constituency campaigns can have a significant impact, particularly in terms of mobilisation and turnout. Weaker party loyalties, increasing voter volatility and more 'late deciders' may all increase the importance of constituency campaigns to election results.[7]

In 2019, there was a specific narrative taking hold in Red Wall towns. This was based on multiple stories, for example: Labour was taking people for granted, not respecting their views and their values, and betraying them on Brexit. These were stories of towns being left behind, failing local Labour councils, and that Labour, as the party of cosmopolitan cities, no longer cared about them.

At a constituency level it is particularly important for those seeking to unseat an incumbent to create a challenger narrative, namely a story that they can realistically win the seat. Fundamentally, they have to create a narrative of viability to persuade voters that it is worth taking the time to vote or to switch votes. Green MP for Brighton Pavilion, Caroline Lucas, argues it is critical to create a narrative in the constituency that provides people with the sense you can win and to give people the confidence to vote for you.

Chapter 13 explores how individual constituency projections based on MRP polling gave added momentum to challenger narratives in Red Wall constituencies.

The role of focus groups

Focus groups have become increasingly important to developing campaign narratives that resonate with voters, particularly the use of language and the crafting of concise stories.

Focus groups "are small groups of representative citizens, who discuss and explain what they feel about political issues."[8] Focus groups were pioneered by Philip Gould and New Labour in Britain, and by Bill Clinton's presidential campaign in the United States in the 1990s. According to Philip Gould "the most important thing a party must do in a campaign is listen to what the voters are saying."[9] To Gould there is no mystique to focus groups he says, "they are simply eight people in a room talking" but their importance is that they enable politicians "to hear directly the voters' voices," to hear the public narratives they are sharing and importantly the language they use. Gould commented: "I never went to a focus group where I didn't get some sort of insight which was useful."[10]

Dominic Cummings strongly agrees with Gould and argues that focus groups have become essential tools in election campaigns. Cummings was regularly seen watching live streams of focus groups in 2019. The Conservative team recognised the importance of focus groups, not just for understanding voters but for finding the voters they could persuade and the right language that would resonate with them. As detailed in the next chapter, the 'get Brexit done' message emerged from focus groups as it was a public narrative, a phrase that participants used repeatedly in discussions. One of the criticisms of the Remain campaign in 2016 was its reluctance to spend the time and resources on focus groups required analyse, hone and test key messages.[11]

News management

News management is important in election campaigns, specifically when seeking to set the agenda in terms of the topics or stories being discussed. Mainstream media remains the primary force in setting news agendas. Focus groups undertaken for the Labour Party in 2017 found older voters were more likely to be influenced by mainstream media than social media.[12] However, social media activity can influence and occasionally set the mainstream media agenda. This is particularly so if campaign activity gains large volumes of engagement on social media. Legendary campaign strategist, Jim Messina, has argued that mainstream journalists are influenced by content on Twitter and that you can predict the topics that will gain media attention by tracking Twitter discussions.[13]

It can be difficult for the Labour party to influence the issues that the media decide to focus on. However, the campaign messaging can be used to consistently reinforce an overall narrative. The party can also decide when and how to deploy messaging through funded channels such as advertising. Dominic Cummings believes this messaging is most important in the last week as there are more late deciders and the Conservatives held back much of their advertising until the last week of the 2019 election campaign. However, campaigns also need to have momentum throughout the campaign. Philip Gould commented that "in politics either you have momentum, or you are losing momentum, there is no middle way."[14]

Academic research into voting and campaign effects

The rest of this chapter covers some of the core academic theory on how voters decide, the implications for political campaigns and evidence of campaign effects on voting. This section can be skipped by those that already know the core theory or are less interested in the academic research.

How voters decide

There are three broad academic schools of thought on how voters decide who to support in an election. These are:

- Rational choice.
- Cleavage voting.
- Political Psychology.

Rational choice

Rational voting theories suggest that voters weigh the benefits of policies and the costs when making a voting choice and they are utility maximisers.[15] Hence, they will choose a party closest to their preferences. This model's weaknesses include assumptions about perfect information and that voters understand the impact of the various policies. It can also be argued that since an individual vote typically makes no difference to a result it is rational to not to spend a lot of time trying to understand political positions and to abstain. A counter argument is that voting makes you feel good, that it is part of your public duty, and hence voting provides a utility in this way. Under a rational choice model political parties should focus on communicating their policies to the public.

It can be argued that the decision of many voters to cast their ballot for the Conservatives for the first time in 2019 was based on rational considerations, such as weighing up the policy proposals of the political parties, particularly their policies on Brexit. In Leigh, 42 year old police officer Dave Trownson, 42, had supported Labour all his life but turned to the Conservatives out of frustration at the long Brexit impasse. He commented to the BBC "it just felt like the logical thing to do. People want to get Brexit done and move on, and they were the only people offering that."[16] Johnson's campaign slogan to 'get Brexit done' may have persuaded voters like Dave to vote Tory based on a rational choice of supporting a policy that most aligned with their priorities.

Cialdini's principles of persuasion, cited by Tory campaign staff, include rational choice arguments but they also highlight the power of consensus and how people look to the actions and behaviours of other people to determine their own behaviour. In his book *Influence*, Cialdini describes 'social proof' as a powerful weapon: "We view a behaviour as more correct in a given situation to the degree that we see others performing it."[17]

Cleavage model

This model conceives of partisanship as the expression of underlying social conflicts. These cleavages may be urban/rural, employer/worker but importantly political parties come to reflect and represent these cleavages. Thus, cleavages ultimately shape the party system and the competition between parties.

In the cleavage model, choice is based on partisanship and identity. Thus, voters are influenced by their friends and family, their community, and therefore, identify as a Labour voter rather than evaluating parties on a rational basis at each election.

This model would suggest that political campaigns have limited impact in terms of persuasion if a voter's choice is determined by long term social and identity factors. This model suggests change comes from voters and underlying social trends rather than political parties as such. Under this model the focus of a political campaign would be on getting supporters to turn out to vote.

The danger for parties is that a shock such as austerity or Brexit may create realignments and new cleavages. These shocks and cleavages may give rise to new political parties that challenge existing parties and create intense tension within political parties on how to respond and adjust.

As noted in Chapter 6 Brexit appears to have crystallised a new cleavage which David Goodhart has defined as being between the 'somewheres' and the 'anywheres'.[18] Some have referred to this new cleavage being between open and closed people or liberals and authoritarians. Others have put a greater focus on cleavages around education and age, which also reflects cleavages between cities and smaller towns. These new cleavage, however they are defined, cut across traditional left-right traditional party cleavages as discussed in Chapter 6.

Hooghe and Marks argue there is also a new transnational cleavage.[19] For example, in Europe there are those that support transnational bodies and the pooling of national sovereignty and those who wish to "defend national culture, language, community and national sovereignty against the influx of immigrants, against competing sources of identity within the state, and against external pressures from other countries and international organisations."[20] The losers of globalisation "resent the dilution of the rights and protection of citizenship by a global élite that views national states and their laws as constraints to be finessed or arbitraged."[21]

Declining party identification does appear to have lessened the impact of left-right party cleavages and past voting has become a less reliable indicator of future voting.

Political psychology model

This model assumes that voters change their minds based on information they are exposed to. It assumes campaigns do have an impact in terms of influence and persuasion, albeit this may be over a longer period. The model also brings in aspects of personality, memory, and emotion. An increasing number of electoral scholars have found affective states, emotions, and feelings can influence voting behaviour. These may include fear, anger, pride, and anxiety. This contrasts with the cognitive process of maximising utility under the rational choice model. In this model voters often rely on heuristics or cues.

In the political psychology model campaigns matter but in terms of setting the agenda and framing the narrative. Thus, coverage in mainstream media and other forms of media is important, as is information and feedback from polls and surveys. Using emotional appeals is of particular importance in campaigns.

Under this model campaigns need to focus on a range of matters:

- Framing the issues.
- Knowledge gain.
- Perception change.
- Mobilisation.
- Emotional appeals.
- Persuasion.
- Conversion activation.
- Reinforcement.

Campaign effects

Research from the 1940s onwards has argued that political campaigns have 'minimal effects'[22]. This 'minimal effects' theory is challenged by other scholars who point to evidence that shows campaigns matter in limited but significant ways, such as mobilisation and increasing turnout.[23] These two broad schools reflect the academic debate on the effects of election campaigns.

The traditional theory is that election campaigns have minimal effects. This started in the 1940s with research by Lazerfeld which supported the cleavage model, namely that voting was strongly influenced by social, cultural, and economic factors. The importance of deep, long term factors was also highlighted by Campbell *et al* in 1960.[24] They used data from the 1956 US election to show how identity strongly influenced voting and argued a person's social and family environment led them to identify with a particular political party and these affiliations largely determined their voting behaviour. The emphasis on these long-term factors leaves little scope for short term campaigns to change voting behaviour beyond reinforcement and activation. This view indicates that campaigns can influence voting behaviour, but this is secondary to influences such as identity and also to issues such as the economy and the performance of the incumbent.

More recent studies have sought to use experiments to test the impact of campaigns. A meta-study of 49 field experiments by Kalla and Broockman found that direct contact and advertising employed by campaigns had no direct persuasive effects on voters thus supporting the traditional 'minimal effects' theory.[25] However, they were careful to note that this didn't mean campaigns don't matter. They specifically noted that campaigns can change the media narrative and increase turnout. There are two specific campaign effects that have been observed, persuading undecided or swing voters to support your candidate and ensuring your supporters actually turn out to vote.[26] These campaign effects may be limited, but Jacobson argues they can be decisive during close elections.[27] Jacobson also makes the case that campaigns matter more for new or challenger parties as they need to build brand awareness.

Campaign effects may also be underestimated by estimating them across the whole electorate when they may only concern a minority of voters such as 'late deciders', those who make their final voting decision in the period between an election being called and the day of the election. These 'late deciders' are more likely to switch parties between elections than other voters, for example in the 2005 Danish national election they were more than five times as likely to switch parties compared to non-late deciders.[28]

There is some evidence that political campaigns are becoming increasingly important for election results. In simple terms, campaigns have more potential to influence voters when there is turbulence than when there is stability.

In Europe, weaker party loyalties, increasing voter volatility, better targeting of 'get out the vote' campaigns combined with closer elections, an increase in insurgent parties and more turbulent societal changes all contribute to political campaigns becoming increasingly important to election results.[29] Dealignment matters as the stronger people identify with parties the less scope there is for campaigns to have an impact. Also, the closer an election the more important campaigns are likely to be as a small number of votes may be enough to determine the outcome. The better a campaign can identify and target its own supporters, the more it can run an effective 'get out the vote' campaign to mobilise these supporters and maximise its vote.

Election campaigns are not simply the period of weeks or months immediately prior to an election, which can be defined legally through campaign finance rules or purdah rules. Philip Gould believed the 1997 Labour election campaign started almost immediately after the party's defeat in 1992 and was a five-year transition to New Labour without which the party could not have been successful.[30] In many ways, the Conservative Party campaign of 2019 began much earlier and has its roots in the 2016 Vote Leave campaign.

In periods of declining party loyalty and identification, with an increasing proportion of swing and 'late decider' voters, and an increasing number of new parties, campaigns are increasingly likely to be important to election results. The lower levels of party identification increase the potential opportunities for campaigns, particularly as more voters in Europe change their party allegiances between elections.[31] People who decide who to vote for during a campaign are less committed to a political party.[32] Declining party identification can therefore be expected to result in an increase in the number of swing voters and late deciders.

There is evidence in Europe of more voters switching parties between elections. In the 1960s only ten percent of Swedish voters switched parties between elections, this figure has risen to thirty percent.[33] The position is similar in the UK, where the recent elections have seen the highest voter volatility since 1931.[34] Of the 30 million people who voted in 2015 UK general election, 10 million changed their votes, or did not vote, just two years later in 2017.[35] Thus a third of voters switched between elections just two years apart.

Opinion appeared to shift significantly during campaigning for the 2017 election as measured by opinion polling. The Labour party started the campaign with an average standing in the polls of just 26%. By the end of the campaign their poll average was 36% and they achieved 40% in the actual vote.

The decline in party identity, increased volatility and more cross cutting cleavages also potentially opens the door for new political parties. Dalton observes "the emergence of Green or New Left parties in Europe during the 1980s and extreme right parties in the early 21st century is likely linked to a larger number of unattached voters."[36] In Europe, from 2015 to 2017, thirty one new political parties gained seats in national parliaments across 23 EU member states.[37] Many new parties have also become significant players in a very short period of years such as Podemos in Span, Syrizia in Greece, Five Star in Italy and En Marche in France. Campaigns are much more important to new parties as they help establish brand awareness.[38]

One of the most observed campaign effects is voter turnout. Studies have shown that face-to-face contact can increase turnout by as much as 9%.[39] Research shows that other methods such as telephone canvassing and reminding people to vote can all increase the overall turnout. Facebook advertising has been shown to increase turnout but closer to the 1%

level.[40] The key is being able to target your own supporters as you do not want to mobilise the supporters of opponents. The professionalisation of campaigns combined with new data practices means that political parties are increasingly able to identify and target their supporters. Better data on supporters has led campaigns to move from a 'media logic' of mass audiences to a 'marketing logic' of tailored audiences that are reached through individual targeting, microtargeting, direct email and text messages.[41] Thus, campaigns have greater potential to specifically increase supporter turnout as voter data becomes more accurate though it has to be leveraged effectively. Of course, it is also possible that parties cancel each other out if both sides are equally effective at increasing turnout.

Summary

Successful political campaigns develop a core overall narrative which links the past and the present to an imagined future. This core narrative is developed over many years not simply during an election campaign. Key elements include a vision for the political economy and the big issues of the day. They also include a leader narrative which must align with the overall narrative. The aim of the narrative is not to change public views as such but to frame grievances, interpret events, and appeal to cultural values in a way that mobilises public support for the party. This involves listening to the electorate and focus groups very carefully. Narratives should be crafted to reflect the language voters use and ideally a concise narrative should be developed which can be easily understood and shared by voters. While the overall national narrative remains critical, there is evidence to suggest that regional and constituency level narratives are increasingly important in influencing voters.

Historically academic studies have consistently found that

political campaigns have limited persuasion effects, particularly on opposition party voters. Consequently, much political campaigning orthodoxy suggests campaigns should focus less on persuading opposition voters and more organisational tasks such as getting out your core vote. This orthodoxy downplays the importance of campaigns and political narratives in influencing voters.

PART III

THE RED WALL COLLAPSE

11

THE 2019 ELECTION: AN OVERVIEW OF THE MAJOR PARTY CAMPAIGNS

"Get Brexit done and unleash Britain's potential"
Conservative Party 2019 election slogan

"It's time for real change"
Labour Party 2019 election slogan

∾

This chapter provides an overview of the Conservative and Labour 2019 election campaigns. It particularly focuses on the political narratives that were crafted to influence and shape the national media and public narratives. This analysis highlights the major differences in the main party campaigns, and in particular, the weaknesses of the Labour campaign.

∾

The Conservative campaign

The Conservative campaign was headed by Isaac Levido, who had run the successful campaign for the Australian Prime Minister Scott Morrison. Boris Johnson recruited Levido to run the Conservative campaign very shortly after he became prime minister, suggesting that he'd anticipated calling an early general election.

Levido's team included Lee Cain, Johnson's director of communications, who previously ran communications for the Vote Leave campaign, and Dominic Cummings, Johnson's most senior adviser. Levido was given the authority to run the campaign and make key decisions. Cummings focused on strategy in the run up to the campaign and he developed the 'People vs Parliament' narrative during the autumn Brexit debates. Paul Stephenson, who ran the Vote Leave campaign with Cummings, was also recruited to support the campaign, and it was his company, Hanbury Strategy, that supplied the seat-by-seat polling that underpinned the Conservative Party's targeted Red Wall approach.

The Conservative strategy and narrative

Led by Levido, the team focused on unifying the Leave vote as their path to victory. This made sense, as the Leave vote was more efficiently distributed across the country and there were far more Leave-leaning seats than Remain seats. They crafted a very clear Conservative campaign strategy, namely "to identify 50 marginal seats the Conservatives wanted to capture and 50 others the party needed to defend. Most of the targets were seats in leave-voting areas of the Midlands and the north of England."[1] Thus, from the very outset, the Conservative campaign was focused on winning sets which had voted Leave, where residents were culturally conservative and where the

Labour vote appeared artificially high relative to the constituency's demographics. These were characteristics that defined Red Wall seats.

The previous chapter provided an overview of academic research which has found campaigns have limited persuasion effects (i.e. they are not often successful in persuading a voter to switch from Labour to Conservative). This research has often led campaigns to focus on maximising the turnout of their party's core vote rather than trying to persuade people to switch party. However, the 2019 Conservative campaign strategy had a strong focus on persuading Red Wall voters to switch their loyalty from Labour to the Conservatives. The team claimed that they designed their persuasion campaign using Robert Cialdini's principles of persuasion, outlined earlier in Chapter 9.

Cummings has long been persuaded by the importance of 'cross-pressured' voters and does not believe in the significance of the 'centre-ground'. For example, he believes that many traditional working class voters support much tougher policies on violent crime and terrorism than most Tory MPs but also much higher taxes on the rich than Labour centrists. Cummings saw the failure to implement Brexit as an opportunity to persuade cross-pressured Labour voters to switch directly to the Conservatives by playing on their frustrations. Prior to the election, Cummings wrote about the importance of tapping into public feelings and leveraging existing contextual trends. He believed that political campaigns could ride waves and trends but almost never create them.[2] Matthew Goodwin has argued that it was easier for the Conservatives to appeal to cross-pressured voters by moving to the left on economic issues than it was for Labour to move to the right.

The Conservative campaign was very cognisant of the gains they had made with cross-pressured voters in Red Wall seats in 2017. In the run up to the 2019 election, one Conservative official who had worked on both the 2017 and 2019 campaigns commented "We are targeting fewer seats this time ... There is a clearer dividing line on Brexit and we got close in many seats last time. Now there is something to build on."[3]

Targeting Brexit voters

The core Conservative strategy was to target Leave voters. The core message they developed to appeal to these voters was to 'get Brexit done'. Ivan Levido explained that the slogan was not something thought up by Dominic Cummings or their team, but rather something that emerged from extensive focus groups. He says, "It was what people were saying to us."[4]

Following the 2016 referendum, Dominic Cummings wrote that the foundations for the Vote Leave success in 2016 came from "listening very hard" to people and that future campaigns should "invest time and effort in researching public opinion."[5] The Conservative campaign invested heavily in listening to voters in Red Wall seats. Denis Staunton, London editor of *The Irish Times*, notes that "intensive polling and focus groups in these seats helped the Conservative team to target messages to each constituency."[6]

The 'get Brexit done' slogan was tested extensively in focus groups and was found to be an extraordinarily effective campaign message. The Conservative team found it appealed strongly to those wanting to Leave but also to those who were fed up about the whole process and debate. This message was also reflected in focus groups run by Public First for *The Times*. For example, Emma, 50, from Bristol said: "I would absolutely not be voting for Boris Johnson if this wasn't purely to get this thing done and the country back to start looking at other priorities. I'm not saying Brexit is right—I didn't vote for it—but it's got to be done now." Another voter Shannon, 24, from Plymouth, said: "It's just got to be done now."[7]

Levido wanted to present voters with a choice between getting Brexit done and more dither and delay. Levido says, "When someone walks into a polling booth they're answering a question" and "the successful campaign frames the questions that voters are asking."[8] In the Conservative case, the answer to the question voters were asking was 'get Brexit done'.

For those that follow politics messages such as 'get Brexit done' are repeated ad nauseam. It was repeated at every opportunity by Boris Johnson and his team. However, politicians are conscious that most people spend very little time listening to news about politics. As noted in Chapter 8, Barack Obama's campaign manager, Jim Messina, famously said voters only spend four minutes a week thinking about politics. Politicians constantly repeat their core message as they want to make sure it gets into that four-minute window.

According to the YouGov public model, 5% of the electorate in 2019 was composed of those who voted Leave in the 2016 referendum but who stayed at home in 2017 and didn't vote. This equated to over two million people, including many people who typically do not vote. The Conservative campaign, like the Vote Leave campaign before it, was concerned to maximise the turnout of these voters. The turnout in the 2016 referendum was 72.2%; higher than the 2015 general election which was 66.2%. The Leave campaign was effective at reaching those who sat out the 2015 general election. The 'get Brexit done' message was designed to appeal to those same voters that had turned out to vote Leave in 2016. It was framed as a way to finish what they had started. The election review by Labour Together claims "the Conservatives succeeded in turning out 2 million previous non-voters, accounting for two thirds of the increase in their vote share."[9]

'Workington man'

Workington is a town in Cumbria which elected its first Labour MP in 1918, and until 2019 had never returned a Conservative MP in a general election. Only in 1976 for a brief period following a by-election had the Conservatives held the constituency. Workington represented the type of Red Wall seat that the Conservatives aimed to win in the election.

In the run up to the 2019 election the think tank Onward created a persona of the type of voter the Conservative party would have to win over in the election. The persona became known as the 'Workington Man.' The profile was a northern man over the age of 45 without a university degree, a rugby league fan, a person that traditionally supported Labour but voted to Leave in the 2016 referendum. In simple terms a cross-pressured older voter with less formal education, a stereotypical Labour voter who might swing to the Conservatives in Red Wall constituencies.

Customer profiles or personas have long been used in marketing and have also been frequently used in politics. Tony Blair had previously targeted the 'Mondeo Man' (a Ford family car). Tony Blair described this man as "his dad voted Labour. He used to vote Labour, too. But he'd bought his own house now. He'd set up his own business. He was doing very nicely. His instincts were to get on in life."[10] Personas have been described as semi-fictional in that while they combine characteristics into a single character, they are based on research data. These personas act as a heuristic or guide when creating content designed to appeal to a target audience.

Robert Crampton, writing in *The Times*, said that he met dozens of voters on his four-day tour of northern Labour heartland seats and commented: "If I fed their characteristics and conversation into a computer to come up with an archetype, it would yield a person in his or her mid to late sixties, white, working class, ancestrally Labour but detached—or about to be —from that party, angry about Brexit not happening and utterly scornful of Jeremy Corbyn."[11]

The 'Workington Man' persona was heavily criticised. For example, Miranda Green in the *Financial Times* said, "'Workington Man' is just the latest depressing political caricature."[12] The former Labour MP for Workington, Sue Hayman, said her constituents felt belittled and that the electorate could not be put into cliched groups. *The Sun* ran a series of vox pops in Workington where local residents criticised the persona as a nineteen seventies cliche and a "patronising stereotype".[13] Many commentators thought that the 'Workington Man' persona would damage the Conservatives in the constituency, not least by ignoring the opinions of women. Tim Burrows in *The Guardian* went further and claimed that "the persona "was a Frankenstein monster, a shorthand stereotype, that held the electorate in contempt and denied the complexity and vitality of local issues."[14]

Despite these criticisms, and claims the persona would damage the Conservatives in the constituency, the party won Workington by over 4,000 votes. This was the first time they had won the seat in a general election in over one hundred years.

Local candidates

National narratives dominate general elections, but the quality and nature of local candidates can also influence voters. The narrative that Labour 'no longer represents people like us' was partly reinforced by criticism many Labour MPs representing Red Wall constituencies were professional politicians not local people. As noted in Chapter 5, there was a growing general antipathy to the notion of professional MPs.

The Conservative Party stressed that its candidates in 2019

would be more locally representative and played down the notion of professional MPs. Despite this, 20% of the 107 new Tory MPs elected in 2019 previously worked for an MP. In many Red Wall seats though, Conservative candidates did stress their local connections, their working class roots, and their ability to represent the area. For example:

- In Leigh, James Grundy stressed he was a lifelong resident of Leigh, who went to the University of Central Lancashire.
- In Stockton South, Matt Vickers highlighted he was born in Stockton and worked locally in retail and construction.
- In Redcar, Jacob Young, was profiled as an industrial worker who studied at the local college and university, and who had lived in Teesside since birth. Young was profiled in the *Financial Times* as "part of a new-look cohort of Tory MPs."[15]

Detaching voters from Labour

The Conservative Party specifically sought to create a narrative that would detach culturally conservative voters from the Labour Party. The Conservatives pushed a series of messages designed to resonate with the narrative that Labour no longer represented these voters. These messages included Labour's lack of aspiration for local areas, the poor performance of Labour councils, Labour taking voters for granted and, importantly, betraying them on Brexit. The Conservatives also pushed the line that the priority for the country was getting Brexit done, and for those that retained an antipathy to the Conservatives they could lend their vote to the party to achieve this. The Conservatives were very conscious of the historic antipathy towards them in Red Wall towns and were making the point voters didn't need to be Conservatives to vote for the party.

The Labour Party campaign

In contrast to the Conservatives, the Labour Party did not employ high profile private consultants to design and manage its election campaign. The Labour campaign chair was John McDonnell, the Shadow Chancellor, and the election campaign chief was Karie Murphy, the Labour Leader's former chief of staff and former union official.

Labour went into the campaign with a number of weaknesses, particularly around leadership and credibility, but also on specific issues, especially Brexit.[16] Tony Blair's Institute for Global Change highlighted five areas of weakness that the national Labour campaign had to address:

- Leadership.
- Brexit.
- Extremism.
- Security and patriotism.
- Economic credibility.[17]

The Labour Party was also on the back foot in terms of the UK's electoral geography. 60% of constituencies voted Leave in 2016, giving the Conservatives, with their clear Leave policy, a built-in advantage. In electoral terms, the Leave vote was spread more efficiently than the Remain vote.

The other challenge for Labour, as noted in chapters 5 and 6, was trying to hold together a coalition with a wider spectrum of views than the Conservatives. Labour risked alienating some of its culturally conservative voters with some of its policies but if it moved towards them it risked alienating both its more liberal voters and its socially liberal membership.[18] Matthew

Goodwin argues that Labour was struggling with this dichotomy, namely how to keep its growing support among the liberal metropolitan middle-class while at the same time retaining the support of a declining traditional working class.[19]

Labour strategy and narrative

The Labour strategy was to build on its gains in 2017 and to focus on public services. The party's campaign slogan was 'It's time for real change'. In support of this narrative the party developed a wide range of major policies. Some of the key policies were as follows:

1. Nationalise the big six energy firms, National Grid, the water industry, Royal Mail, railways, and the broadband arm of BT. The latter was linked to a promise to provide free Broadband.
2. Increase NHS funding.
3. Hold a second referendum on Brexit.
4. Build 100,000 council homes a year.
5. Provide £58bn compensation to 3 million women affected by increases to the state pension age.
6. Increase the minimum wage.
7. Abolish universal credit.
8. Stop state pension age rises.
9. Introduce a national care service.
10. Bring forward net zero carbon emissions target date.
11. Abolish private schools' charitable status.
12. Provide free bus travel for the under 25s.
13. Give EU nationals the right to remain.
14. Increase the length of statutory maternity pay from nine months to a year.

Labour's wide range of major policy initiatives was in stark contrast to the Conservative campaign which had a clear focus on Brexit, the dominant issue of the day. Labour sought to drive the national narrative away from Brexit to issues such as the NHS. For example, the party argued that the election was about saving the NHS. To support this strategy, they released documents which they claimed showed that the Conservatives were putting the NHS up for sale.[20] However, the scale and breadth of Labour's proposed policies meant that it was always going to be hard to get across a coherent and simple narrative.

Labour's election grid for the campaign deliberately avoided Brexit. A draft copy of Labour's election grid, leaked to *Sunday Times* journalist Gabriel Pogrund, revealed that only two days were set aside to discuss Brexit.[21] Instead the grid was designed to highlight a different Labour policy each day. The leaked draft grid is set out below.

Day 1 Launch
Day 2 Brexit
Day 3 NHS funding
Day 4 National Education Service
Day 5 High St
Day 6 Dentistry, extension of free dental care
Day 7 Taxation
Day 8 Animal welfare
Day 9 Low pay
Day 10 Rail tickets
Day 11 WASPI generation
Day 12 International
Day 13 Education
Day 14 MANIFESTO LAUNCH
Day 15 No Deal: attack
Day 16 Constitution day
Day 17 Regional manifesto(s)
Day 18 Social security intervention
Day 19 Government that works for you

Day 20 Social care
Day 21 Climate chaos
Day 22 Cycling + walking
Day 23 Energy for all
Day 24 Race & Faith
Day 25 Housing
Day 26 Crime and justice
Day 27 Culture

The draft electoral grid covered a mass of major policies. This is despite the evidence that most people spend very little time focusing on politics and certainly would not recall all of these major policies. Labour's slogan, 'it's time for real change', did seek to bring these policies together under an overall narrative of change but this wasn't used consistently. Even Labour supporters failed to remember this core narrative. The Labour Together review conducted 50 interviews with party figures and supporters and found "very few" could spontaneously recall that this was Labour's core message.[22] One of their 11,000 survey respondents commented that 'time for real change' failed to set out what Labour stood for and what kind of change it wanted.

While Labour's policies taken together did represent significant change, for the public the message was confusing and more importantly the scale of policies undermined their credibility. Paul Williams, who lost Stockton South for Labour, commented: "There was also a sense that Labour's election promises were 'all over the place' and didn't add up to a simple and coherent narrative. Labour were perceived as being too much 'in the past' and people didn't hear messages from Labour painting a vision of a positive and dynamic future for our country."[23] One of the participants in Lord Ashcroft's focus groups after the election agrees. "They kept chucking in crazy ideas like free broadband. Nobody was sure what he was doing. He (Corbyn) was all over the place."[24]

General elections are about key questions. In 2019 the key question was Brexit. Labour's campaign strategy sought to make the election about other issues, but the campaign's lack of focus meant this was never going to be successful. Following the election Issac Levido commented "What was the question that Labour was asking?"[25]

The submission by Progress to the Labour Together election review argued that "the party lacked a strong narrative arc, either to combat the Conservative's mantra, 'get Brexit done', or provide a positive, optimistic set of reasons to vote for us." Following the election Labour's Deputy Leader John McDonnell also commented "I don't think our narrative was good enough – or simple enough."[26]

Credibility

To Labour strategist and pollster Philip Gould the critical issue when developing manifesto policies "is not the promise, but making the promise credible."[27] Gould believed that people want smaller promises they can believe in, not larger ones that seem incredible. This was advice that the Labour Party ignored when formulating its manifesto in 2019. Eric Shaw, from the University of Stirling, observed that: "A policy will be credible to the extent it is seen as affordable and deliverable. Labour seemed to have problems grasping this."[28]

While many of the party's policies were individually popular, they lacked coherence and credibility and people simply didn't believe that collectively they were credible. 57% thought Labour would likely lead Britain into recession (39% for Conservatives), and 67% thought Labour's policies would require tax increases (46% for Conservatives). The party's proposals included nationalising Royal Mail, water companies, energy companies, train operators and the parts of BT that own and maintain the UK's internet infrastructure, the most significant of which is Openreach. The Institute for Fiscal Studies estimated this would increase publicly owned assets by over £200 billion and increase the number of public sector workers by 310,000. In addition to whatever sums were agreed to compensate the current owners of the companies to be nationalised, the proposals would also bring £150 billion of debt onto the public balance sheet.[29]

Labour seemed to believe that the scale of their policy offers, their generosity and radicalism would enthuse voters despite focus groups demonstrating time and again that voters were deeply sceptical about the party's ability to deliver on these promises.

Labour's Brexit policy

The Labour Party's 2017 policy on Brexit was to respect the result of the referendum. In 2019 this policy changed under pressure from Labour members who voted overwhelmingly to Remain. On 23rd September 2019, the Labour Party conference agreed it would negotiate a new deal with the EU, and then hold a referendum with two options: Remain or Labour's deal. On the 17th October 2019, Jeremy Corbyn said, for the first time, "the best way to get Brexit sorted is to give the people the final say in a public vote."[30] He subsequently confirmed the party would "immediately legislate" to hold a second referendum if it won the election.

However, it was not clear what the referendum question would be or what Labour's stance would be. Labour stated they would negotiate a credible Brexit option that protected jobs and the economy with the European Union but the leadership was unclear if they would then campaign for the deal.[31] Prominent Labour MP, Emily Thornberry, appeared on BBC Question Time in September 2019, and stated she would negotiate a Brexit deal with the EU, but then campaign for Remain— against her own deal.[32] Within the party, Corbyn fought to retain a neutral stance on a future referendum, saying repeatedly that he personally would remain neutral and that the Labour Party's stance would be decided at a later date. However, high profile front bench spokespeople such as Emily Thornberry and Keir Starmer were clear in saying they would campaign to Remain in a second referendum.

Labour's approach to Brexit was designed to appeal to voters in its new heartlands, in cities and in Remain seats in the South such as Canterbury and Putney. It was also designed to deal with the threat of losses to the Liberal Democrats.

However, the effect in Red Wall seats was catastrophic. The traditional 'Labour towns and Labour people' narrative was already being undermined by a growing disconnect between the party and its traditional voters. The adoption of a second referendum policy, and the public stance of high profile Labour frontbench spokespeople that they would campaign to overturn the result of the first referendum, combined to reinforce the narrative that Labour no longer represented traditional voters in Red Wall towns.

The change in policy acted as a catalyst for voters who felt their vote to Leave was being ignored by Labour, and they were being asked to vote again to achieve the 'right' result. In Workington, Will McCall, a 71-year-old lifelong Labour voter, who switched to the Conservatives, summed up the views of many when he commented "They (the Labour Party) were trying to weasel out of giving us Brexit."[33] In Redcar Grandfather Jed McMahon, 60, commented: "Labour stuck two fingers up at 17.4 million who voted to Leave ... They ignored us, they wouldn't listen."[34]

The Labour Party wrongly anticipated that many Labour Leave voters had nowhere else to go. They believed the historic

'Labour towns and Labour people' narrative, combined with antipathy to the Tories would continue to shore up their vote. This was a serious error. The party failed to understand how far the public narrative had shifted and underestimated the willingness of voters to switch from Labour to the Conservatives. One northern Tory MP commented the Labour Party "seemed blissfully unaware of how much they had alienated their core vote."[35]

Leadership

Research on persuasive communication suggests that the view that voters have of political leaders is influenced by two factors, firstly, whether they seem trustworthy and secondly, whether they have the personal qualities and competence to lead.[36] Jeremy Corbyn fared badly on both. Going into the election campaign, 76% of people were dissatisfied with how Corbyn was doing his job, this was much lower than his rating in 2017. He also had the worst 'net satisfaction' ratings of any opposition leader since polls began. Only 16% of people trusted Corbyn to run the economy compared to 34% for Johnson.[37]

Corbyn's personal politics and persona did not appeal to traditional working class voters in Red Wall seats. He was seen as not being patriotic and not being tough on crime or terrorism. When former Labour voters were asked by YouGov why they were no longer backing labour in 2019, the most commonly stated reason was Jeremy Corbyn (35%). Brexit was second (19%) and lack of economic competence was third (16%).

Interestingly, Jeremy Corbyn's favourability ratings were higher than Theresa May's following the 2017 general election, though both were negative. At the end of January 2018 Corbyn still held a twelve point lead over Theresa May. This changed in March 2018 when the Salisbury poisonings took place. Corbyn failed to condemn Russia for the poisoning of former

Russian spy Sergei Skripal and his daughter, Yulia. This contrasted strongly with May's condemnation of Russian actions and caused fury amongst Labour MPs who condemned the attack.[38] For example, Yvette Cooper, then chair of the Home Affairs Select Committee, said the poisoning should be met with "unequivocal condemnation."[39] By the end of March Corbyn's ratings had fallen markedly and May had a better favourability rating than him for the first time since the 2017 election; leading by ten points. Writing about Consett in County Durham in the *New Statesman*, David Skelton says "many of my friends from school in the town served in the armed forces and they, as well as their friends and family, were repulsed by Corbyn's response to the Salisbury poisonings and his perceived sympathy with the IRA."[40] Corbyn's response to the poisonings highlighted the gap between his worldview and values and those of many Labour voters.

As in 2017, Corbyn got a very rough ride from the media. However, in 2017 the public knew less about him and were prepared to give him the benefit of the doubt. This did not apply in 2019.

Labour's negative media coverage

The Labour Party's raft of individual policies struggled to get airtime in an election that was dominated by Brexit. However, when Labour's policies were covered in the national media they were overwhelmingly portrayed as negative. Much of this coverage was focused less on individual policies, many of which were individually popular, and more on the proposed scale of Labour's proposals and its ability to deliver.

The level of negative coverage that Labour received in the media was demonstrated by analysis of the election campaign undertaken by Loughborough University.[41] The stark difference between the coverage that Labour and the Conservatives received is set out in the chart below.

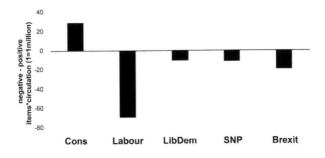

Overall evaluations of parties in newspapers weighted by circulation

Source Loughborough University, 2019.

The key findings from Loughborough University's analysis were as follows:

- The unweighted results show that only the Conservative party received more positive than negative coverage across all newspapers.
- The positive Conservative coverage reflected the strong editorial support provided by the newspapers with the largest circulation, particularly the Daily Mail and the Sun.
- Labour had a substantial deficit of positive to negative news reports in the first formal week of the campaign.
- Some Labour politicians had more coverage in the national press than Conservative politicians, but a large proportion of this was negative.

Labour's lack of economic competence

Any party seeking to form a government must convince the public they are competent to run the economy. This an area where Labour has traditionally trailed the Conservatives and is why Tony Blair and Gordon Brown focused so strongly on proving their economic competence. In 2019, the credibility of Labour's economic proposals came under intense scrutiny. The nationalisation proposals, combined with other major spending pledges, such as compensating women who lost out on pension changes at a cost of £58bn, were seen by many as exemplifying Labour's lack of economic competence and credibility. According to a YouGov poll more than half of voters (57%) thought the country would go into a recession within a couple of years if Labour won the election.[42] One man from Worksop agreed saying, "now some of the policies that the Labour people want, and they are advertising is you know, you'll make the country bankrupt. How is he going to pay for all of this?" The same thoughts were echoed by a woman in Walsall. "Where are they going to get the money from? Are they going to print it out the bank? It's like Monopoly money."

The IGC report on Labour's loss noted that in their focus groups a constant refrain was 'where is the money coming from?' The report argued that Labour's wide ranging policies "underpinned the electorate's disbelief on the credibility of Labour's spending programme."[43] A Datapraxis analysis of YouGov data found that many voters "came to the conclusion that the manifesto as a whole was unrealistic, risky and unlikely to be delivered. This undermined the positive response to individual policies, making them seem less credible."[44]

A Lord Ashcroft poll carried out immediately after the election found that 62% of voters who switched to the Conservatives, supported the statement: "I did not believe Labour would be able to deliver the promises it was making." A typical example is this comment from a man in Bishop Auckland. "As this campaign goes on, it seems ludicrous, the sorts of things that he's (Corbyn's) offering. I'm not saying they're not good things.....but there are other things he just keeps coming out with...Now it just seems too many, it just seems ridiculous."[45]

Many voters also felt that Labour's tax policies would damage the economy. One Red Wall voter on taxing the rich commented: "We need clever, innovative millionaires in this country. We need a welfare state, but you've still got to reward people for doing well. They're very blinkered, they don't see the big picture."

The one policy that did cut through was free broadband but this only added to questions about Labour's credibility. Voter comments from Lord Ashcroft's focus groups with former Labour voters included:

> When they said they were going to give everyone free broadband, I thought, 'what are you talking about? That money could be going towards the police, or nurses.' That was a red flag moment for me. I thought, I don't trust a word you say anymore.
>
> We don't need free wifi, for heaven's sake. It costs £20 a month. I can afford it.[46]

These negative narratives about Corbyn and Labour's economic competence were leveraged by the Conservative campaign but also by many on Labour's right wing. Several former Labour MPs went as far as saying people shouldn't vote Labour.[47]

Labour's failure to deal with antisemitism

A major political and media narrative before and during the election was Labour's failure to deal with antisemitism within the party. While close to three quarters of Labour Party members believed antisemitism in the party was created, or at least exaggerated, by the mainstream media and opponents of Jeremy Corbyn, they also felt the party had not done enough to respond to the concerns raised.[48]

In focus groups former Labour voters lamented the failure to get to grips with antisemitism. One participant commented: "Why couldn't he say, 'yes we've got a problem and I'm dealing with it and I'm sorry'? Why couldn't he say that?"[49] It was not clear that they felt this was a widespread problem or that Jeremy Corbyn was antisemitic, but they did believe his inability to respond firmly to the issue was an indictment of his leadership.[50]

Targeting strategy and resource allocation

Under the UK's first past the post system not all votes are equal in terms of winning seats. Where you win your votes can be just as important as how many votes you win. For example, in 2019, Labour gained more votes than it achieved in Tony Blair's 2005 election victory. However, Labour's votes were inefficiently distributed, while it piled up votes in some constituencies, it lost votes in key Red Wall seats resulting in a net loss of seats.

In a UK General Election, it is critical to target resources efficiently, which means allocating them to those seats you need to defend and those that you can gain. The 2017 election results, subsequent local election results, and feedback from local Labour Party members and MPs, all pointed to Labour being vulnerable in Red Wall seats. However, there is no evidence that Labour nationally recognised its vulnerability in these traditional Labour seats and allocated resources accordingly. On the contrary, it appears that the party embarked on an offensive campaign to attack Tory seats.

Labour developed a list of target seats that it believed to be winnable. These seats benefited from extra support and campaign activity including "direct mail, digital advertising, newspaper advertising, staff support, shadow cabinet visits and mobilisation of activists."[51] According to a source that spoke to the *Sunday Times*, Karie Murphy's targeting strategy devoted 80% of Labour's resources to "attack" seats that they believed they could win from the Conservatives.[52] This was confirmed by senior figures in the Labour Party that spoke to the *Financial Times*.[53] Though it was later disputed, it was even claimed that Murphy had said that 'every single seat is there',[54] citing the surprise results in 2017.

Subsequent leaks suggested that Labour targeted 60 Conservative held seats, including former Red Wall seats such as Mansfield and Stoke-on-Trent South. *Sunday Times* journalist Gabriel Pogrund described the targeting as a "deranged" offensive campaign focused on Tory Leave seats.[55] In addition to the 60 Conservative seats targeted, there were 27 targeted as defensive seats. These included just three Labour held Red Wall seats: Bishop Auckland, Penistone and Stocksbridge, and Barrow and Furness. This target list has been disputed by those within the Labour campaign such as Steve Howell, who says there were initially 66 offensive target seats and 30 defensive seats. In either case, the party strategy was clearly to fight an offensive campaign, which ran the risk of neglecting vulnerable seats in the North and Midlands.

During the campaign Tim Waters, Labour's director of data and targeting, left his role amidst allegations of fierce disputes about campaign targeting and the allocation of resources. After the manifesto launch, and based on polling data, Steve Howell says Labour belatedly added sixteen further defensive seats and then a further twenty-one, including the two Red Wall seats of Bolsover and Stoke North. The impact of these later additions on resourcing decisions is disputed by Labour activists. For example Phil Brickell says, "in Leigh the Saturday before the election. There were fewer than 15 activists out across the constituency, with everyone encouraged to go to Bolton West, which we didn't win."[56] According to a Labour Party staffer there were people in the Red Wall seats of West Bromwich and Ashfield "saying they are getting no manpower, no leaflet budget, and it's all being ploughed into seats up the road which we've got no chance of winning."[57]

Sienna Rodgers, commented on the differences in the allocation of campaign resources.

> My mid-campaign trip to a Leave-voting Midlands constituency also brought into sharp relief the differences in Labour's ground game across the country. On a weekend in London, literally hundreds of supporters would turn up to a single canvassing session in Kensington or Chingford. But a 'Super Sunday' in a so-called Red Wall seat? Around forty, maybe.[58]

The Labour Together review of the 2019 election notes that "of 27 Labour-held seats lost narrowly to the Conservatives, 21 were not on an initial list of seats to be defended. The Tories won all of these by fewer than 700 votes."[59] Labour lost Red Wall seats by slim margins which arguably could have been retained with more targeted campaigning. For example, Labour lost Bolton North East by 378 votes, where they sent activists instead to campaign in Bolton West in an attempt to win the seat back from the Conservatives. Labour also lost Bury North by 105 votes and High Peak by 590.

In Blyth Valley, Conservative councillor, Helen Welsh, commented: "Labour rested on their laurels. I didn't think they put the effort in that we did. They believed that because it had been Labour so long it would stay Labour forever."[60]

Labour's belated change of strategy

As the campaign progressed it was becoming clear that the Labour Party had underestimated the willingness of Leave voters in Red Wall seats to switch to the Conservatives. Hence, the addition of more seats to the list of defensive seats outlined in the previous section. The YouGov MRP poll at the end of November revealed that hundred of thousands of Red Wall voters were likely to abandon Labour for the Conservatives. This was a critical poll, which acted as a catalyst in revealing the scale of concealed preferences for the Conservatives and is discussed in more detail in the next chapter. The poll also reinforced the feelings of many that Labour was struggling in Red Wall seats.

In desperation Labour was forced to adopt a new communication strategy, prompting the BBC's Iain Watson to comment that, "in the next two weeks, if you live in a Leave area, you are likely to see a very different style of campaign."[61] For the final few weeks of the campaign Labour gave a higher profile to senior figures that supported a Leave deal rather than Remain. They also organised a tour of Leave areas by Ian Lavery who supported a Leave deal, moved more activists to Leave seats, and focused more on basic policy issues such as crime and buses, and sought to argue that the second referendum policy was about offering people a genuine choice rather than seeking to stop Brexit.

The reality is that it was too little, too late.

The Liberal Democrat campaign

Many traditional Labour supporters were clearly disillusioned with the party, and had an historic antipathy to the Conservatives. This raises the question why these voters did not switch to the Liberal Democrats. There are a number of reasons but the most significant was the party's Brexit strategy. The party decided to ignore Leave voting areas of the UK and seek votes in Remain voting areas with what some saw as an extreme Brexit position. The party's election slogan was 'Stop Brexit' and the policy adopted was to ignore the 2016 EU referendum result and revoke Article 50 to stop the Brexit process with no further public consultation beyond the election. Given that many traditional Leave Labour voters felt betrayed by Labour's policy of a second referendum, it is fair to assume these voters would have been incandescent at the Lib Dems proposal to simply ignore the referendum result.

Red Wall seats had also never been targets for the Lib Dems. In seats like Leigh, Bolsover, Workington, Sedgefield and West Bromwich East they barely gained a thousand votes in previous elections and often not even a thousand votes. There was simply no real Lib Dem ground campaign or operation in most of these seats. The party's 2019 election campaign strategy was described as a car crash by an internal party review conducted by the Lib Dem peer Dorothy Thornhill. The review concluded that the party's Brexit policy 'effectively ignored' the majority of UK voters.[62] Therefore while the Lib Dems might have previously been a home for disillusioned Labour voters, in 2019 their Brexit policy, lack of local resources and campaign strategy effectively ruled this out.

The presence of Brexit Party candidates

The presence of the Brexit Party in pro-Leave seats does appear to have an impact on the Labour vote. Cutts *et al* show that Labour's support declined more significantly in pro-Leave seats when there was a Brexit Party candidate than when there was none.[63] It is not possible to conclude from the data that Labour voters switched directly to the Brexit Party. However, Burn-Murdoch *et al* in the *Financial Times* argue that, "where the Brexit party contested seats, they took more votes from Labour than the Tories, and Labour suffered greater losses on average where the Brexit party stood than where it did not" and this was most evident in the region of Yorkshire and the Humber where the Brexit party had their best performances.[64]

In Don Valley, the Brexit party picked up 15% of the vote as Labour's share fell by 19 percentage points."[65] This was significant and unseated Labour's Caroline Flint. In 2019, the constituency elected a Conservative MP for the first time since the election of local miner, Thomas Williams, as its Labour MP in 1922.

The Brexit Party gained over 20% of the vote in some Labour Leave seats, for example:

- Barnsley Central (30.44%).
- Barnsley East (29.19%).
- Blaenau Gwent (20.57%).
- Doncaster North (20.38%).
- Hartlepool (25.84%).

Labour managed to hold on in all five of these seats. However, in several other seats, which were lost by the Labour party, the number of Brexit Party votes was higher than the Conservative majority. These are shown below.

Constituencies where Conservative majority was smaller than Brexit Party vote

Constituency	Brexit Party Votes	Conservative Majority
Blyth Valley	3,394	712
Bolton North East	1,880	378
Burnley	3,362	1,352
Delyn	1,971	865
Don Valley	6,247	3,630
Durham North West	3,193	1,144
Heywood & Middleton	3,952	663
Leigh	3,161	1,965
Stoke Central	1,691	670
Ynys Mon	2,184	1,968

Source: House of Commons Library

It is not possible to say that all of the Brexit Party voters came from former Labour voters but in some seats it does appear that a significant number of Labour voters switched to the Brexit Party. For example, if we look again at Don Valley, the Conservatives won with just a 1.4% increase in their vote share. The big shift in votes was between Labour and the Brexit Party. Labour's vote share fell from 53% to 35% while the Brexit Party won 14% of votes. This does lend some support to Nigel Farage's claim that by standing in Labour constituencies the Brexit Party may have offered a home to Labour voters who felt unable to switch to the Conservatives and disproportionately damaged Labour's vote.

However, in other Labour constituencies, some Conservative candidates have claimed the Brexit Party split the Leave vote and prevented them from winning. For example, in Wentworth and Dearne the Labour Party won with 40.3% of the vote, the Conservatives came second with 35.1% and the Brexit Party was third with 16.9%.

Overall, it appears that the Brexit Party's decision not to stand in Conservative held seats but to stand in Labour held seats was a significant factor in the election.

Tactical voting campaigns

Tactical voting is a specific form of constituency campaign where voters are persuaded it is in their best interest to vote for a less preferred candidate. Stephen Fisher defines a tactical voter as "someone who votes for a party they believe is more likely to win than their preferred party, to best influence who wins in the constituency."[66]

Studies using the British Election Survey typically find that around 5% to 10% of voters cast their ballot strategically. Fisher, for example, estimates that around 5% in 1987, 7.7% in 1992 and 8.5% in 1997 voted insincerely.[67] In 2010, 8% of respondents to the British Election Study indicated that they really preferred another party but it stood no chance of winning in their constituency, and a further 8% claimed that they voted tactically; summing the two suggests that 16%, just under one sixth of all respondents, were tactical voters in 2010.[68]

In 2019, most tactical voting campaigns were designed around Brexit and sought to mobilise the Leave or Remain vote in a particular direction in specific constituencies. The main tactical voting campaigns were designed to mobilise the Remain vote. These included Remain United, organised by Gina Miller; the People's Vote campaign; and Best for Britain, a civil society campaign launched in April 2017 to stop Brexit and continue the UK's membership of the EU.

Initial analysis of the 2019 General Election results by Chris Hanretty suggests that recommendations by tactical voting sites had a significant impact on the Liberal Democrat vote share in constituencies. His analysis shows "the estimate of the effect on the Lib Dem vote share of being endorsed by Best for Britain is around 5 percentage points (95% CI: 4 to 6 percentage points). The equivalent figure for Remain United is smaller (2.6 percentage points), but significantly different from zero (95% CI: 1.1 to 4.1 percentage points)." In summary, he believes that, "tactical voting can have a significant impact in elections, particularly where the recommendation goes to a smaller party which otherwise struggles to demonstrate local viability."[69]

Summary

What stands out from the analysis in this chapter is the weakness of the Labour campaign. This led not only to the Conservatives fourth successive election victory, but also the fourth successive increase in the Tory vote share. The election was called as a referendum on Brexit and yet the party failed to develop a coherent story or position on this key issue. The Conservative campaign had a clear strategy, namely targeting Labour Leave voters in Red Wall seats with a concise narrative that was designed to resonate with their frustrations about Brexit. By contrast the Labour campaign lacked both focus and a clear overarching narrative. The scale and magnitude of the policies the party proposed only added to the sense of Labour's lack of economic credibility. Jeremy Corbyn's personal ratings never recovered from their fall after the Salisbury poisonings in March 2018, and fell to an historic low in 2019 as he failed to act decisively on issues such as anti-semitism.

In terms of Red Wall seats the party did not fully appreciate the growing disconnect with traditional working class voters and how far the 'Labour towns and Labour people' narrative had been undermined. The party's adoption of a second referendum policy was a final straw for many. The leadership's assumption that these voters would never vote Tory was badly misplaced. As a consequence the party failed to develop the aggressive defensive campaign required across the 41 lost Red Wall seats and it failed operationally to allocate resources which might have helped save a number of these seats.

12

RED WALL PUBLIC NARRATIVES AND THE LABOUR PARTY IN 2019

"I come from a mining family. My dad and my granddad were miners. It goes back centuries. But I think we're all voting Conservative now."

Yvonne Chapman, 74, Bolsover[1]

This book has set out how the historic 'Labour towns and Labour people' narrative in Red Wall constituencies was being undermined by a series of contextual trends and by Labour's growing disconnect with its traditional working class voters. This chapter examines the public narratives about the Labour Party in Red Wall communities in 2019, and particularly during the election campaign.

The analysis is based on a thematic review of the public narratives communicated directly by Red Wall voters in focus groups and interviews undertaken with thousands of voters in these constituencies. The focus groups were commissioned and run by a wide range of organisations. These included Hanbury, J&L Partners, Fabian Society, Demos, Edelman, IGC, Public

First, Deborah Mattinson, and Lord Ashcroft. The Lord Ashcroft focus groups over the last decade have been conducted with tens of thousands of people, providing very useful insights into the changing public narrative. The analysis is based on public reports of these focus groups and where available, on analysis of videos and transcripts. The interviews and vox pops analysed were conducted by a wide range of media organisations including the *BBC*, the *Guardian*, the *Times*, *Huffington Post*, *New York Times*, the *Sun*, *Daily Express*, *Channel 4*, *ITV*, *Sky News* and many others. The analysis also reviewed reports of public narratives in the 41 lost Red Wall seats by by journalists, particularly local journalists.

This approach is not unproblematic. The quotes from interviews for example, have been selected by journalists and may have been used to support a particular viewpoint or to add drama and colour to a story. It is rare to have access to the full interview that a journalist conducted or even knowledge of those that were interviewed but whose accounts were not published. In the case of focus groups there is generally more to work with, as there are more detailed reports and some are made available in full as videos, audio and transcripts, However, in many cases only summaries or selected quotes are published from focus group discussions.

Despite these limitation this analysis does allow us to capture part of the public narrative, and importantly the public narratives that were represented through the media. While these may not be representative, statements by individuals in the media have the potential to become symbolic of the wider public narrative. Research has consistently found that statements by individual voters reported or broadcast in the media have a strong influence on how voters evaluate the opinions of others, and how they assess the overall climate of opinion, much more so than representative polling data.[2] For those interested in ethnographic research in these communities, Lisa

McKenzie has been undertaking critical, public and political ethnography in communities, such as North Nottinghamshire mining towns, for 20 years. Her publications include *Getting By* and *The Class Politics of Prejudice*.[3] Deborah Mattinson's book *Beyond the Red Wall* also reports on the findings of focus groups and ethnographic interviews in seats such as Workington, Don Valley and Redcar.

The analysis below identifies the narratives that were being constantly repeated and that appeared to be resonating with voters. It pays particular attention to the language that voters were using and the concise narratives they used. To provide a good feel for the public narrative in Red Wall seats this section extensively uses direct quotes from voters taken from focus groups, interviews and vox pops.

The analysis in this chapter reveals that Labour's growing disconnect with traditional working class communities was undermining the historic public narrative of 'Labour towns and Labour people' in Red Wall towns. People were increasingly sharing stories of disillusionment with the Labour Party and Labour councils. They shared stories of being left behind, of being taken granted, of not being respected and of being betrayed. They told stories of Labour not respecting their values, for example not being patriotic and of Labour being primarily interested in cosmopolitan cities and global issues rather than local issues in their communities. The following comment from a focus group participant sums up the way the public narrative was changing: "My parents voted Labour, so then we voted Labour and I think that we have started to rethink it now."[4]

The Labour Together report comments that "many traditional Labour voters started moving away from the Party around two decades ago." The analysis reveals that this disconnect was increasingly being reflected in Red Wall seats through multiple, mutually reinforcing public narratives:

- "Labour takes us for granted."
- "Labour is not patriotic."
- "We have been left behind by Labour."
- "Labour looks down on us."
- "We need to get Brexit done."
- "Labour has betrayed us."
- "We don't trust Jeremy Corbyn."
- "Labour has no aspiration for our area."

In 2019, these multiple narratives combined to form an overarching new narrative in industrial working class communities: 'Labour no longer represents people like us.'

Examples of each of the narratives and how they were expressed by former Labour voters are set out below.

"Labour takes us for granted"

"Jeremy Corbyn is a clown. He and his party took us for granted." John Brown, McDonald's worker, Bishop Auckland.[5]

"Labour have taken us for granted. They haven't done anything for us in 60 years. I don't know if Boris is the answer, but I'm prepared to give him a chance and see what he's got. We need something – we need a change." Chris Barnes, former fisherman, Blyth Valley.[6]

"They take our votes for granted and think we were born yesterday." Focus group participant.[7]

"I don't think they get out and listen to people like they used to. They used to be part of the local community, but they became complacent. They thought 'whatever we do we're going to get the votes off the local people, especially in the North,' but it didn't work like that." Focus group participant.[8]

The idea that Labour was taking Red Wall towns for granted wasn't just being voiced by voters. Labour MPs made similar observations. Labour MP, Lisa Nandy, speaking in 2018 commented:

> Town voters have been taken for granted for a very long time. There was an assumption that in the south of England people in towns would vote Tory and in the north of England they would vote Labour.[9]

"Labour is not patriotic"

The following comments about Jeremy Corbyn were made by former Labour voters in Ashcroft's focus groups in 2020.

> He is not patriotic. He meets all those terrorist parties. You want someone with good old values.

> His sympathies with Hezbollah and the IRA and all these different groups. He empathises with everybody.

> That woman who moved to ISIS, he said she should be let back into the country. That was a turning point for me.

There is a deep sense of patriotism in traditional working class communities and frustration that the country has become less patriotic. The following comments came from Demos focus groups in 2018.

> For some reason, you can make lots of money out of St

Patrick's Day, but when you celebrate St George's day you're a racist.

My husband's got a van and it's got an English flag and [...] he's been doing this business for 40-odd years and he actually got pulled up the other day by somebody, and they said why have you got an English flag on your van?

That's the way it's gone unfortunately, where we can't be proud of our own flag.

Corbyn's views on internationalism caused many to question the Party's patriotism and its support of an English identity. After touring northern Labour seats Robert Crampton in *The Times* commented:

The northern working class is also, I was reminded time and again, deeply, sincerely patriotic. They don't like being told what to do by foreigners and they didn't much fancy voting for a man who seems to prefer any foreign country over his own.[10]

Traditional Labour voters simply did not believe the party was patriotic according to former Labour MP for Sedgefield Phil Wilson.[11] This was reflected in the experience of former Red Wall MPs. Former Labour MP, Ruth Smeeth, said that daily on the doorsteps, voters criticised Labour for not supporting the UK's armed forces. Former Labour MP, Melanie Onn, who lost Grimsby to the Conservatives said Jeremy Corbyn's lack of support for the armed forces was "a kick in the teeth for working class towns."[12] She added, "There is a big ex-armed forces population in Grimsby and people felt that he was standing up for other people and not standing up for them."[13] Caroline Flint commented that when she was canvassing, armed forces families were consistently concerned about Jeremy Corbyn and his views.[14]

The English Labour Network argues that "Labour has resolutely refused to recognise the salience of England and English identity" despite all the warning signs of the power of national identity and patriotism.[15] Their analysis found that the Conservative 2019 victory was due "almost entirely" to voters that identify as more English than British, and who "are very patriotic, both about England and Britain." In 2015, the Conservatives won 21 votes to every 10 won by Labour in this group of voters. This fell in 2017 when the Conservatives won 17 to every 10 won by Labour in this group. In 2019, the gap increased, and the Conservatives won 27 votes to every 10 won by Labour. The ELN estimated that "the Conservatives gained the support of an additional 1.625 million 'more English than British' voters between 2015 and 2019."[16]

The ELN note the idea of national identity is very closely tied to an "attachment to particular places and the people who live there" and "fits the profile of many of the voters we have been losing since the early 2000s including the Red Wall seats in the most recent election."[17] This aligns with David Goodhart's concept of the 'anywheres' and the 'somewheres' outlined in Chapter 6.[18] The English Labour Network argues that "unless Labour now responds and gains significantly more support from voters who emphasise their English identity, the path back to power is blocked."[19]

"We have been left behind by Labour"

"Stoke has always been Labour but it hasn't done us any favours. If you walk round, some of it is quite scary. It was voted the 9th worst place to live." Focus group participant.[20]

"We have had 50 years of Labour and we have been standing still for years. This place is neglected, I would like change and investment in Blyth Valley." Lifelong Labour voter, Blyth Valley.[21]

"All the funding just goes to Wigan." Gail Robinson, first-time Conservative voter, Leigh.[22]

"The council has been Labour all my life and they are shocking. Fly tipping is awful." Focus group participant.[23]

A YouGov study in January 2020 examined the views of voters who switched from Labour to the Conservatives and noted: "There is a real feeling among these voters that the Labour Party has left them behind."[24]

Most Conservative gains came from Leave-voting towns on the edges of more successful larger cities. Voters outside these areas felt increasingly left behind, both from London and from larger cities in their region. Dehenna Davison, the new Conservative MP for Bishop Auckland commented:

In our parts of County Durham people say we are a long way from Westminster, well as far as County Durham goes our communities feel a really long way from Durham itself. It feels like all the investment goes straight into Durham, the jobs go there, all the focus is on Durham City itself, so the communities that Richard (Richard Holden, Tory MP for North West Durham) and I represent feel very left behind.[25]

This view is backed various research reports. The Joseph Rowntree Foundation and UK in a Changing Europe which found that in "towns overshadowed by larger cities, there was a sense of losing out twice – first to London then again to their larger neighbour."[26] Research by the Centre for Towns found that nearly 70% of people felt "politicians don't care about my area."[27] Such voters were also unhappy with decisions made by their regional and local Labour parties.

Melanie Onn, the former Labour MP for Grimsby, commented that "Labour's decision to ignore millions of its Leave-supporting voters was reflective of its transformation towards becoming more closely aligned with the politics and character of Britain's metropolitan cities."[28] Glen O'Hara commented that the Labour Party's stance on Brexit and the election of Corbyn as leader "'spoke to London' and ignored millions of others."[29]

For many voters in Red Wall towns, there was a sense of despair. Those who conducted research in these towns reveal how voters were distressed at the aesthetics of their areas and would describe unprompted their boarded-up high streets, litter and disrepair. Jo Platt, says, "for years Leigh has been neglected, ignored and betrayed. People there feel anger and resentment, and a lot of it is directed at Labour."[30]

Former Labour candidate Rachel Burgin, who lives in Copeland argues that "in places like West Cumbria, it is Labour who are the establishment–and it was Labour councils tasked with making savings. And hence it was Labour who shouldered a lot of the blame for much of the austerity at a local level."[31] It does appear that many voters blamed the local council and the local MP for the conditions in their constituency and being left behind.

"We need to get Brexit done"

"I've always voted Labour before, but I'm pleased we have a Conservative member of Parliament because now we can get on with Brexit." John Puntis, lifelong Labour voter, Bolsover.[32]

"Many people are looking to the Tories. It has been three years, it should have been done and dusted by now." Ed Renyard, 27 year-old former Labour supporter, West Bromwich.[33]

"It (voting Conservative) just felt like the logical thing to do. People want to get Brexit done and move on, and they were the only people offering that." Dave Trownson, 42 year-old police officer and lifelong Labour voter, Leigh.[34]

"We're a mining community and we were born to vote Labour. But Labour have had it. We voted to leave Europe in the referendum and if Labour get in, we'll never get out." Wayne Kissane, former miner, Bolsover.[35]

"I'm an ex-miner and worked at Warsop Main Colliery for nearly three decades. But I'll be voting for the Tories in December because we need to get Brexit done. It will be a tough thing for me to do. I've been a member of the Labour party for donkeys' years and it goes against my principles. It will go against the grain." 75 year-old pensioner, Bolsover.[36]

"If you go to work in overalls then you vote Labour. But I voted Conservative for the first time in 50 years because they were the ones who could give us Brexit. It was a really big deal for me to change my vote. Corbyn is the biggest idiot ever to lead the Labour Party." Harry March, 73, Bishop Auckland.[37]

"I have always voted Labour. Over the past four years their approach to Brexit has really frustrated me and I'm at the point now where there's no chance of me voting for them again." Bethany, 24, Grimsby.[38]

The core national narrative in the 2019 election was about

Brexit. After all, it was the reason Boris Johnson gave for calling the election. In October 2019, Johnson called for an election to break the Brexit deadlock. He argued that whilst no one wanted an election, it was necessary as "our MPs are just refusing time and again to deliver Brexit."[39] Johnson's political narrative framed the election as the opportunity to 'get Brexit done'.

Many Remain supporters also saw the election as an opportunity to elect a government that would stop Brexit and groups such as the People's Vote, Best for Britain and Remain United called for tactical voting to elect Remain supporting MPs. It was therefore no surprise that one of the key media narratives in the 2019 election was Brexit and the election became framed by many as a rerun of the 2016 referendum debate. Despite attempts to focus attention on public services the Labour party was unable to shift the media narrative away from Brexit.

The Labour party had no convincing counter narrative to the Conservative's 'get Brexit done.' The Tories convinced 74% of Leavers to back them while Labour only convinced 49% of Remainers to back them. In simple terms the Tories were better at consolidating the Leave vote than Labour was at consolidating the Remain vote.

The 'get Brexit done' narrative resonated strongly in seats that had voted heavily to leave the European Union, which included every one of Labour's lost 41 Red Wall seats. This was reflected in the public narratives expressed in focus groups and interviews. Labour List editor Sienna Rodgers wrote about how the "get Brexit done" narrative was resonating with voters during the campaign.

So many people in Dudley North quoted the Tory slogan at me when I knocked on their door convinced me that the seat was a goner, and the chances of similar seats being lost on the same basis started to seriously worry me.[40]

Deidre Campbell, the wife of the former Blyth Valley MP, Ronnie Campbell, said Labour had been "at war with the people over Brexit. I went to houses where there was poverty but they were going to vote Tory. It was like they were on some kind of drug."[41]

Traditional working class voters who had supported Brexit felt their views were being ignored by Labour, particularly when it adopted a policy supporting a second referendum.

"Labour has betrayed us"

"Labour stuck two fingers up at 17.4 million who voted to Leave." Will McCall, 71-year-old lifelong Labour voter, Redcar.[42]

"They were trying to weasel out of giving us Brexit. Sue Hayman (former Labour MP) especially was trying to stop it. She's been punished for that." Jed McMahon, 60, Redcar.[43]

"I felt let down. 17.4 million people voted leave, and we're supposed to be a democracy. They threw spanners in the works and did everything they could to stop it. It was arrogance. They were no longer listening to the people." Focus group participant.[44]

"When your own MP votes against her constituents, you lose faith." Focus group participant.[45]

"They assumed we would back Labour because we always have" but "for the last three years the will of the people has been blocked." Juliet Metcalfe, 56 years-old, hairdresser, Bishop Auckland.[46]

Brexit led to a greater emphasis on cultural values and highlighted the differences between Labour's core Remain membership and industrial working class Leave voters. These value differences were exacerbated when Labour decided to support a second referendum. For many people they suddenly felt as if their views didn't matter. Correctly or incorrectly they felt their vote didn't count and they were being asked to vote again. They felt betrayed.

Eyal Clyne, a Labour canvasser who campaigned in eight marginal constituencies in the north west of England, commented:

> For Leave voters, Brexit now symbolises the way in which their voices were being ignored, repeatedly and undemocratically, by the losing Remainers, who are also associated with other classes and more privileged groups... As far as they are concerned, Labour (and others) did not fully respect the will of the working class, and a democratic result. They feel betrayed.[47]

"Labour looks down on us"

> "It goes back to Gordon Brown calling that woman a bigot. He tarred her with the bigot brush rather than listening to what she had to say. It's the same with Brexit." Channel 4, Focus group participant.[48]

Many Labour Brexit voters felt that the party looked down on them as bigoted and less educated. Robert Langley recalls how his grandfather was ridiculed, undermined and called racist and stupid for voting Leave from people on the left.[49]

Some voters felt the Labour party not only abandoned them but showed nothing but contempt towards them. Since the millennium there has been a general hostility in the media towards the poor white working class. Claire Ainsley refers to the linguistic denigration of the white working class poor with terms such as Chav.[50] Owen Jones in his book 'Chavs: The demonisation of the working class' argues that after the turn of the century the hatred of working class people became socially acceptable.[51] Many traditional poor working class communities felt as if politicians of all parties looked down on them and ignored them. This was reinforced after the 2016 EU Referendum. The prevailing narratives shared by Remain supporters of the left was that Leave voters were uneducated and simply didn't understand the consequences of their vote.

Following the 2019 election, there has been further anger and contempt aimed at those in Red Wall seats on social media. A particular theme has been a critique of working class Tories and their stupidity for voting against their own interests. After the 2019 election, Paul Mason declared the result "a victory of the old over the young, racists over people of colour, selfishness over the planet."[52] Former Labour MP, Gareth Snell, acknowledges that such an approach is counter productive and says Labour must try to understand and win back these voters rather than criticising them or even worse calling these voters stupid or traitors.

"I don't trust Jeremy Corbyn"

"I've always voted Labour all my life, always voted Labour. I will not vote Labour this time, I will only vote Conservative and that's because of the party leadership. I could never vote for Jeremy Corbyn. I just couldn't do it." Male participant, IGC focus group, Worksop.[53]

"I thought Boris was going to get more done, he made a lot of sense – even though he is a bit of an idiot – and he had to be given a chance. I just hope he doesn't forget the North East. I didn't like Jeremy Corbyn, I just didn't–the way he comes across, I just don't like the man." Barbara Haslin, 72, Sedgefield.[54]

"My family has voted Labour for 100 years – they were dustmen, coalmen. But there's no way I can vote for Jeremy Corbyn ... Unless someone knocks on my door from Labour then...actually no, no....even then I just don't think I can. I will vote Conservative." Lorraine Lloyd, Vale of Clywd.[55]

"I voted Labour until Jeremy Corbyn became leader. Last night I voted Conservative. We have former soldiers on the streets in Blyth, men who fought wars for us, who are homeless and sleeping rough." Chris Barnes, Blyth Valley.[56]

"I don't trust a word he says." Channel 4 focus group participant, Birmingham Northfield.[57]

The leadership of Jeremy Corbyn highlighted the differences between the values of the Labour Party and those of its traditional industrial supporters. Corbyn was widely disliked and went into the election as the most unpopular leader since surveys began.[58] Many people, including Labour supporters, vocalised their dislike of the Labour leader. In 2017, Corbyn's commitment to implementing Brexit may have been enough to convince many he was still 'on their side'. This was not the case in 2019.

Tim Bale, professor of politics at Queen Mary University, commented before the election that "although people talk about Brexit as being a problem for the Labour Party, I don't think it is anywhere near as much of a problem as Jeremy Corbyn."[59] He added that some ex-Labour voters were "coruscating" in their assessments of the leader: "They see him as unpatriotic, weak, unlikeable, indecisive and incompetent ... almost any kind of negative you can come up with, that's what they will say about him."[60] Corbyn was widely disliked even within the party, and many members viewed him as extreme. For example, former Labour MP John Woodcock claimed that Corbyn "would pose a clear risk to UK national security as prime minister."[61]

As noted in the previous chapter, in early 2018 Corbyn actually had higher favourability ratings than Theresa May but these collapsed after his response to the Salisbury poisonings. By 2019 Corbyn had become a major problem for Labour in Red Wall seats.

"Labour has no aspiration for our areas"

"We have had Labour in control here as long as I have been alive, but you see the town centre and you can see they do not do a lot for the area ... I do not think they try hard enough for us and Bishop Auckland is a prime example to me of Labour doing nothing." Stephen Nicholson, painter and decorator, lifelong Labour voter, Bishop Auckland.[62]

In Sedgefield, former Labour MP, Phil Wilson, says the Labour hierarchy failed to understand working class aspiration. He believes "the bedrock of Labour politics is aspiration – to improve the lot of working people." He added, "When I was 16 my dad said to me, 'You can do whatever you want, son, but you're not going down the pit' .... he worked down the pit the best part of 40 years. What he wanted was better for me than he had himself."[63] Robert Langley agrees that Labour failed to grasp the ambition of many in the working class "to make their own lives better while promoting the overall wealth of a country that they love and call home."[64] Former Redcar MP, Anna Turley, says Labour never spoke to the pride of local areas. Former Stoke-on-Trent Central MP, Gareth Snell, agrees, arguing that too often Labour were saying "isn't it awful here." By contrast the Conservatives were transforming the local narrative and using Facebook ads to "pump out success stories."[65]

An analysis of focus groups does show that working class voters were becoming increasingly frustrated at the erosion of opportunities for social mobility. Focus groups run by Demos revealed a frustration with a system that many saw as increasingly "rigged against ordinary workers."[66] Participants in these focus groups commented:

> I think there was more opportunities. You started at the bottom and you worked your way right up to the top [...] Now what they're doing, even in the police, they're fast-tracking them. They're fast-tracking people to management.
>
> [In the past] you could start out and think, actually in 17 years, I can be a manager, whereas now that's just not the case.

"Labour left me"

> "I feel dirty for doing it but, aye, I voted Tory. Labour has taken us for granted for too long. They thought they could ignore us and we'd keep voting. Well, now, they know they can't .. but it's the party that moved away from me. Not me from it. They forget the grassroots. They forgot who they are supposed to stand up for." David Dixon, a steelworker for 40 years and a Lifelong Labour voter, Workington.[67]

In the Scottish referendum many Labour left-wing defectors to the SNP repeated a quote attributed to Jimmy Reid, a Scottish trade union activist, "I didn't leave Labour. Labour left me." This feeling was echoed during the 2019 election campaign. The BBC's Sarah Smith asked voters in former Labour strongholds in Scotland why they left the Labour Party. She observed that "they almost always reply: 'I didn't—the party left me.'"[68]

In 2019, many Red Wall voters also felt that Labour had left them. Labour MP, Lisa Nandy commented that voters in Wigan told her "I didn't leave the Labour party, Labour has left me."[69] Whether it was on Brexit, on patriotism, or on investment in the local area many former Labour voters felt it was the party that had changed not them. This is evidenced in the stories people shared and in the results of six focus groups conducted by IGC. In these focus groups there was a common feeling that Labour was no longer on the side of traditional working class voters. The report's authors commented that people "were angry that Labour had moved so far away from them."[70]

In Grimsby, Christopher Barker, the local Brexit Party candidate, sought to leverage this narrative in his campaign materials and claimed he heard the same phrase all the time, namely that "I didn't leave Labour — Labour left me."[71]

"The Labour Party no longer represents people like us"

What flowed from all of the public narratives above was a growing sense in traditional working class communities that Labour no longer represented people like them. This was reflected in focus groups and interviews, for example:

> "It used to be Labour was very much for the working man and I was always Labour as a young lad. But the last few years they have gone away from their root values and I do not think

they stand for the working man." Stephen Nicholson, a painter and decorator, Bishop Auckland.[72]

In Derbyshire, Mary, a 78-year-old retiree, said in an interview she had always voted Labour because she was brought up to believe that Labour were 'for the working class people'. However, she felt this was no longer the case as "over the past few years Labour hasn't 'been how they should be'."[73] The person who interviewed Mary commented that she left the interview with a "distinct sense that she (Mary) no longer feels the Labour party is on her side."[74]

In Stoke-on-Trent, Michael, a 63 year old care worker said Labour was no longer 'trying hard enough' and no longer cared about working class voters because they have gathered enough support elsewhere: "I feel as the Labour party is like 'we're all right Jack, sod you lot'."[75]

According to a YouGov study in January 2020, 74% of Labour to Conservative vote switchers agreed with the statement "Labour used to represent people like me, but no longer does."

In total, just 12% of Lab-Con switchers thought the Labour Party was close to people like them.[76] In a panel discussion where Labour members discussed the collapse of the Labour vote, one participant commented: "People in northern seats just didn't trust the Labour Party to represent their values."[77] Former Redcar MP, Anna Turley and former Sedgefield MP, Phil Wilson, commented that voters turned away from the Labour party because they "no longer thought it was for them."[78] After her election loss, Ruth Smeeth, the former Stoke-on-Trent North MP, said simply "we don't represent the people we were created to represent."[79]

For voters, the question of whether a party is perceived to 'stand up for them' is vital—more so than politics or ideology.[80]

Labour voters in Red Wall seats no longer felt that Labour was on their side.

In her ethnographic research, Lisa McKenzie observes that in traditional working class communities there was a sense Labour had failed them. "The Labour Party, that they thought once was supposed to represent working–class people had failed, the employment available offered nothing in hope or self–respect and the people here were barely meeting the bills."[81] McKenzie highlights the perception in these communities that Labour no longer stood in solidarity with them, that there was no longer a common interest or support from the party. She argues it was the absence of solidarity that caused these communities to look to the Conservatives, not because they believed things would be better but to try to change things.

A poll conducted after the election found the third most important reason Labour voters gave for deserting the party (after Jeremy Corbyn and lack of credibility and competence) was "the Labour Party no longer seems to represent people like me."[82] This was ahead of Brexit in the reasons for switching their vote.

"I am lending my vote to the Tories"

A further narrative specific to 2019 was one of vote lending. The Conservative campaign appealed to Labour Leave voters to set aside their differences in 2019, and lend their vote to the Tories to get Brexit done. The notion of lending votes to achieve Brexit provided a way for people to feel better about voting Conservative i.e. they were not really a Conservative they were just supporting Brexit. This appeared to resonate with voters. Deborah Mattinson ran a large workshop of undecided voters from around the country for the BBC in December 2019, and reported that she found "an increasing number (of voters) were, pragmatically, willing to 'lend their vote' to Johnson as the least-worst option, without feeling that it meant they were now Tory."[83] This was reflected in numerous interviews and focus groups.

"I don't see it as a vote for the Conservatives, I see it as a vote for Brexit." "It's the first time I've done it. My dad was a miner, and his dad was a miner, and I've always voted Labour." Retired woman, Conisbrough, Don Valley constituency.

"I will vote Conservative purely because I want us out of the EU ... I have no particular love of Boris Johnson or any politicians." David Hamilton, retired marine engineer, Leigh and lifelong Labour supporter.[84]

"I've always voted Labour since I was 18 because it's a working party for the working people, and that's just what you voted. But I voted Conservative this time because Boris wanted to Leave. Labour's core values are for the working people, but this time Brexit was more important." Carrie Mekins, 42, a mental health nurse, Sedgefield.[85]

"When I found out the other day that our MP has stood in the way of Brexit on every single vote, despite the fact that the majority of people round here voted Leave, that really annoyed me. So potentially I will vote Conservative. It would be a one-off, to get Brexit done." Ashcroft focus group participant.[86]

"I'm not saying I would never go back to Labour. I'm voting Conservative on Thursday and it's the first I've ever voted Conservative." Male voter in IGC focus group, Bishop Auckland. [87]

The notion of vote lending allows people to say they haven't changed, that they are still Labour people.

The notion of extensive vote lending to 'get Brexit done' might superficially seem to be good news for Labour. However, it is essential that Labour does not rely on this, or again take voters for granted. Labour will need to actively work to persuade voters to return. Once the narrative that 'we always vote Labour' is broken, it loses its power, and there is no guarantee that people will revert back. For example, there is evidence from tactical voting studies that once someone votes for a party, albeit tactically, they then hold a more favourable opinion of that party. This makes sense psychologically as if you voted for a party you may need to convince yourself it was not a bad choice. This gives rise to the possibility that those that have lent their vote to the Conservatives will look more favourably upon them next time.

Summary

The analysis of Red Wall public narratives reveals multiple, mutually reinforcing stories of disillusionment, and particularly disillusionment with the Labour Party. These stories undermined the historic 'Labour towns and Labour people' narrative. For many traditional working class voters the combination of Brexit and Jeremy Corbyn reinforced the growing disconnect between themselves and the Labour Party. This became reflected in a new public narrative: 'The Labour Party no longer represents people like us'.

A NEW CHALLENGER NARRATIVE IN RED WALL SEATS

"Leigh and Bury South could both go Tory... says shock new
poll"
Manchester Evening News[1]

The nature of the British electoral system means that people are conscious of wasting their vote. This can create a major obstacle for those seeking to unseat incumbents. To win seats political parties have to create a challenger narrative. In essence a narrative that it is worth voting, and potentially switching votes, as the challenger has a very realistic chance of winning in a specific constituency.

Traditionally to evidence their chances of winning, and to support their challenger narrative, parties have drawn upon a range of information sources. This has included previous general election results, local election results, canvassing returns, local news, ground campaigns, and visible support such as numbers of posters.

It has been difficult for parties to use opinion polls as part of a constituency challenger narrative, primarily because these tend to report the national vote share of each party. It can be helpful for campaigns to be able to point to national poll swings but circumstances may vary significantly in specific constituencies or regions. As we saw in Chapter 2, there were wide regional variations in party support with Labour's vote share falling over 12 points in the North east but less than 6 points in the South West. There were much larger variations when it came to individual Red Wall seats.

It has always been possible to conduct constituency level polls to better understand the state of play in specific seats but such polls are expensive, hence, they have typically been limited to a number of marginal seats or target seats. This all changed with developments in multilevel regression and post-stratification polling (MRP) in 2017. Suddenly there were relatively accurate projections for every constituency in the country.

MRP polling and constituency projections

Three pollsters (YouGov, Ashcroft and Hanretty) used MRP techniques in 2017 to produce estimates of the outcome for individual constituencies. These were derived from aggregate level survey data combined with constituency level covariates. This allows an MRP poll to provide a relatively accurate voting projection for a constituency, despite not being a constituency poll i.e. it is not based on interviewing people in the constituency. Instead an MRP poll is based on a large national survey sample (say 20,000 people) and imputes a result, and a projection for each constituency, based on the constituency's characteristics. In 2017, YouGov's MRP model correctly forecast the winning party in 93.3% of the 631 constituencies in Great Britain, and it correctly predicted which party would have the largest vote share in 68 marginal constituencies.

The relative success or accuracy of MRP constituency projections means they have become an important source of information for local parties, campaigns, media, and voters about the state of play in a constituency during a General Election. Johnston *et al* argue the influence of such constituency projections "will be profound."[2]

The value of MRP constituency projections has become more valuable in a world of voter volatility and voter realignments, as previous election results are a less reliable indicator of the state of the parties in a constituency. MRP projections provide a new source of constituency level information that can shape:

- Campaign strategies, including the resources dedicated to local campaigns, the messages to focus on and materials produced, motivation of staff, deals with other parties across seats etc.
- Local and national media coverage of the local campaign.
- Decisions by tactical voting campaigns. For example, Best for Britain changed 83 constituency voting recommendations based on updated MRP data.
- Assessments and decisions by individual voters.

The 2019 general election saw an increased use of MRP techniques to produce estimates of opinion for individual constituencies. This extended far beyond vote share. For example, the website UnHerd, in partnership with Focaldata, commissioned a large survey of more than 20,000 people for their views on specific issues, and then used an MRP model to map them to individual constituencies. They identified strong social conservatism in specific constituencies. For example, in Hayes and Harlington, they found only 33% residents believed that "immigrants should be free to move to Britain and work" whereas in Battersea the figure was 63%. Such information can be utilised by local campaigns to develop specific constituency messaging.

The potential impact of MRP polling on constituency electoral contests

The constituency level projections produced by MRP polling can have a number of potential effects on electoral contests, including:

- Increased tactical voting, where people are persuaded that one party is in a clear second place and/or where it is worth turning out to vote as their vote may count in a close contest.
- Bandwagon effects, where people align behind the perceived winner which provides them with increased momentum.
- Social persuasion effects, where evidence about how a community is voting may persuade other people to also vote the same way. This is based on Cialdini's consensus and unity principles of persuasion.
- The revealing of concealed preferences. The nature of MRP polling means that the projection may reveal the true scale of support for a party.
- The creation and reinforcement of challenger narratives. Unexpected constituency projections can create new challenger narratives, and also reinforce views that a shift in support is taking place.

The impact of YouGov's MRP poll on 27th November 2019

The YouGov MRP poll published on 27th November 2019, was particularly significant in the context of Red Wall seats. The poll revealed for the first time the level of concealed preferences in these constituencies. It disclosed that hundreds of thousands of Labour voters were switching directly to the Conservatives. This provided evidence that the Tories could realistically win in these former heartland Labour seats, which many commentators and voters had considered out of their reach.

In 2019, the idea that many Labour voters were considering voting Conservative for the first time was gaining ground before the publication of the YouGov MRP poll. Academics were making the case that Brexit was accelerating a longer-term realignment in British politics and reshaping the country's political geography.[3] More people were also prepared to challenge the taboo of voting Conservative and openly discuss voting Conservative as highlighted in the previous chapter. However, while the idea of former Labour voters switching to the Conservatives was increasingly discussed and seemed plausible, there was no evidence that the scale of vote switching was sufficient for Conservatives to win many Red Wall seats. That evidence was supplied by YouGov's MRP poll, as it revealed for the first time at the level of individual constituencies the potential scale of vote switching.

The MRP poll created a powerful and new challenger narrative in Red Wall constituencies. This narrative had multiple threads:

- People are switching to the Conservatives for the first time.
- Labour voters are lending their votes to the Conservatives.

- UKIP/Brexit Party voters are tactically voting Conservative.
- The scale of these developments means the Conservatives can win here.

The MRP poll potentially increased the level of strategic/tactical voting by UKIP and Brexit Party supporters. The tactical voting calculus being that the Conservatives were not only well ahead of the Brexit Party, but had a very good chance of winning. Hence, UKIP and Brexit Party voters could make the difference.

The poll gave many Tory candidates the confidence that they could win these seats, some for the first time in almost one hundred years. This poll may also have given many voters the confidence that a Conservative vote would not be wasted. This new challenger narrative was essential to the Conservatives winning these seats. People must believe you can win a seat to be encouraged to cast their vote for you.

Fundamentally, the poll reinforced the public narratives that Labour no longer represented these communities and perceptions that the tide was shifting. Johnston *et al* conducted research using BES wave data in 43 Labour seats in the North and Midlands that were lost to the Conservatives. They found that local voters "were aware that the tide was turning against Labour."[4] People were increasingly seeing local people on television and in newspapers publicly voice their discontent with Labour and sharing stories that aligned with their own views. Public statements of Conservative support might have been couched carefully in terms of disappointment, heavy hearts, regret that Labour has moved away from them or lending their vote just to get Brexit done, but there was visible and growing public support for the Tories.

Those voters who were concealing their preferences for the Conservatives due to social pressures, suddenly found that far from being an outlier or socially isolated, they might be in the majority. In these circumstances the sense of risk and potential loss of voicing your support for the Conservatives would be reduced as it became clear many people had a similar view. Robert Langley says, "supporting the Conservatives would have once seen you exiled from certain communities in the north. No longer."[5]

Cialdini and Sunstein both reference the power of social persuasion. People are influenced by other people and the evidence that many people in the Red Wall communities were switching to the Conservatives increased the likelihood that other voters would be persuaded to do the same. As the campaign progressed, voters in Red Wall seats became less sure that Labour would win. Interestingly during the campaign the largest decline in local voters' views on Labour's likelihood of winning was in its safest seats.[6] This reveals a significant change in voter assumptions about what was happening in these previously long-held Labour seats.

The section below explores the example of Leigh and shows how the MRP poll acted as a catalyst and triggered a new challenger narrative in the constituency.

～

New challenger narratives: A case study of Leigh

In the general election of 1922 Henry Twist, a former miner, was elected to represent Leigh. For the next 97 years the constituency returned Labour MPs to Parliament.

When the 2019 election was called, most commentators believed Labour would win again in Leigh. In the run up to the election, the Tory candidate, James Grundy, made it clear he also expected Leigh to remain a Labour seat and anticipated he would make gains but "lose with dignity."[7] The belief that

Labour would win was understandable. Labour had repeatedly won the constituency since 1922. In the four elections from 1992 to 2005 Labour won between 61% and 69% of the vote.

However, things began to change in 2010, when the Labour vote fell to less than 50% for the first time since 1923. In 2015 UKIP also won 19.7% of the vote. It seemed many former Labour voters were switching to UKIP. Despite these developments Labour still held a strong lead in the constituency. Labour won 54% of the vote in 2015 and 56% in 2017.

Leigh was still seen as a Labour town, populated by Labour people. Paul Mason, who grew up in Leigh, commented that people in Leigh vote Labour as "an elementary act of solidarity with each other."[8] In this community there had previously been a strong antipathy to the Conservatives, and social pressures meant that many people would have been reluctant to express support for the Tories. Given the nature of concealed preferences, it was not possible to gauge how many voters might be considering abandoning Labour and switching their votes to the Conservatives in 2019. The previous election provided some evidence for growing Conservative support. The party's vote increased from 22.6% in 2015 to 35.8% in 2017. However, Labour's vote also increased in 2017 to 56.2% from 53.9% in 2015, maintaining a healthy twenty point lead over the Conservatives.

On November 27th, 2019, YouGov published their shock MRP projection for Leigh, which had the Conservatives winning by 1%. This came as a major surprise to many, including the Conservative candidate James Grundy, who posted on Facebook the day after the poll was released: "I'm taking nothing for granted, but this is astounding news."[9]

The MRP poll challenged previously held assumptions about the opinions of people in Leigh and the number of people thinking of switching to the Conservatives. The MRP projection for Leigh was big news and influenced the media narratives both locally and nationally. Local newspapers were quick to run with the story that Leigh voters were turning to the Conservatives. The *Manchester Evening News* included the MRP projection on their website just hours after the poll was released. The headline ran:

> "*Leigh and Bury South could both go Tory in a fortnight's time, says shock new poll*"
>
> *Manchester Evening News*[10]

On the 28th November, the poll was also headline news in the local Leigh Journal.

> "*Leigh could vote in Tory MP, says YouGov MRP poll*"
>
> *Leigh Journal*[11]

The MRP projection created a new challenger narrative. A respected poll, which was one of the most accurate in 2017, projected the Conservatives were going to win Leigh, despite being 20 points behind at the previous election. The challenger narrative was accompanied by a local media narrative along the lines that things were changing in Leigh. Local newspaper headlines now read: "I'm voting Tory for the first time."[12]

On the 30th November 2019, an article in the Leigh Journal headed 'Leigh constituency election portrait' talked of "a clamour for change" and it specifically noted that "for some this will be the first time in their lives that they will be placing an X next to another party's name in the election booth on December 12." The article commented "more than a few Leythers have seen it coming" and "the word change is on the lips of many Leythers – and it's just possible change will be what they'll get."[13]

Importantly the article reinforced this perspective with public narratives in the form of vox pops, for example:

His (Boris Johnson's) pro-Brexit stance has won admirers in leave-voting Leigh, including mum-of-two Carla Bassett. 'I'll be voting Tory for the first time in my life.'[14]

The notion of vote switching was gaining ground. It was a similar story in Bolsover, Yvonne Chapman, 74, commented:

I come from a mining family. My dad and my granddad were miners. It goes back centuries. But I think we're all voting Conservative now. I don't even know the name of their candidate. I've never needed to know until now.[15]

The projection of large scale of vote switching, directly from Labour to the Conservatives, was also becoming part of the national media narrative. Just a few days after the poll was published, on 2nd December 2019, Channel 4 ran a report on two focus groups of Leave supporters in Birmingham Northfield. In the introduction, Channel 4's chief political correspondent, Gary Gibbon, introduced the video commenting:

Is something shifting? .. Tory strategists say they weren't expecting many Labour voters who backed Jeremy Corbyn in 2017, to come direct their way in this election, but they think that there could be quite a lot of them considering doing just that... maybe more than a million of them.[16]

Channel 4 broadcast a video of participants in the focus groups sharing their own views and stories.[17] In the first focus group, none of the eight participants were considering voting Labour again and all said they were thinking of voting Conservative. In the second group of eight, seven were thinking of voting Conservative. The videos show participants commenting:

My parents voted Labour, so then we voted Labour and I think that we have started to rethink it now.

I don't know what the Labour Party stands for anymore, they used to be the working person's go to party but now I don't really know what they stand for

The narrative of Labour voters abandoning the party for the Conservatives was also reinforced by national newspapers, for example:

"Labour CRUMBLES in North "First Time I'm Voting Tory!'
Heartland voters ABANDON Corbyn"
Daily Express[18]

The paper quotes the article from the *Manchester Evening News*:

In Leigh, 'an impenetrable Labour stronghold for almost a century', voters look set to put an X next to another party's name for the "first time in their lives.[19]

The MRP poll also influenced the local public and political narratives. The Labour Party ran a Facebook ad in Leigh, with the headline 'Only Labour can stop the Tories in Leigh' with a graph of the MRP poll showing the Conservatives ahead. This may have unwisely drawn more attention to the fact people were switching the Conservatives and that they could realistically win the constituency. It was also a negative message, calling on people to vote Labour to stop the Conservatives. The advert sought to appeal to the traditional antipathy to the Tories in the constituency, not recognising the public narrative had shifted. The advert simply reinforced the fact people were switching to the Conservatives and further undermined the narrative of 'Labour towns and Labour people'.

The MRP constituency projection for Leigh was the trigger behind public and media narratives that people were switching in large numbers to support the Conservatives. Previous assumptions that people would vote Labour in the constituency were undermined by credible data that the Conservatives had more support in Leigh than the Labour Party. This was backed up with articles in the press, vox pops and information from the political parties.

The new narrative may have benefited the Conservatives in several ways. First and most importantly it revealed the potential scale of true preferences. From social change theory, discussed in Chapter 9, we know the revealing of true preferences is often the trigger for a cascade where more and more people feel able to reveal their views freed from social pressures to conceal them. Those people previously nervous of expressing support for the Conservatives would have felt more comfortable in doing so. This would be reinforced by the vox pops of voters saying they were switching their vote. As outlined in Chapter 8, research finds that people are strongly influenced by media presentations of statements by individual voters and this affects how voters judge the opinions of others and the overall climate of opinion.[20]

The new challenger narrative may have encouraged former UKIP and Brexit Party voters to switch to the Conservatives as the most credible Brexit supporting party. In 2015 19.7% of voters supported UKIP in Leigh and while many of these had switched to the Conservatives in 2017, there were still many that hadn't.

At 1.56am on the morning of 13th December 2019, the result of the Leigh constituency was announced. James Grundy had narrowly won the seat for the Conservatives with 45.3% of the vote compared to Labour's 41.1%. He had a majority of just under two thousand on a 12% swing away from Labour. The BBC called it a "seismic shift." One man in Leigh interviewed by BBC breakfast after the election commented: "I'm the son of a miner. My Dad was called a tunnel rat, that's what he did, he put up steels in the tunnels. People will say he'd turn in his grave at me voting Tory, but I'm so glad I voted for James Grundy and not Joanne Platt."[21]

14

SUMMARY: THE PERFECT STORM WHICH BROUGHT DOWN THE RED WALL

Why did large numbers of Labour voters in Red Wall constituencies switch to the Conservatives in 2019, many voting Labour for the first time? What were the dynamics that led to such a sharp and dramatic switch whereby hundreds of thousands of people in these seats switched directly from voting Labour to voting Conservative?

This summary chapter brings together the material set out in this book to explain the collapse in the Labour vote in the 2019 General Election. The core argument is that despite unfavourable economic and demographic changes, a powerful 'Labour towns and Labour people' narrative kept the Labour vote disproportionately high in Red Wall seats. This narrative with its strong antipathy to the Tories led many people to conceal their real preferences which, when revealed, led to the rapid breakdown of previous norms and the collapse of the Labour vote.

The historic public narrative was undermined over twenty

years by long term trends including deindustrialisation, declining party loyalty, Labour's focus on a new electoral coalition and an increasing number of cross-pressured voters. The growing disconnect between Labour and its traditional working class voters in these seats was accelerated by Brexit and Jeremy Corbyn. An analysis of hundreds of focus groups and interviews reveals how multiple stories shared by Red Wall voters plaited together over many years to create a new public narrative that 'Labour no longer represents people like us.'

It is difficult to point to a single trigger that caused the Labour vote to collapse in 2019 but there were a number of key events. The first was Jeremy Corbyn's response to the Salisbury poisonings in March 2018. As discussed in Chapter 11, this caused his favourability ratings to plummet and highlighted the disconnect between Labour's leader and traditional working class Labour voters. The second was Labour's adoption of a second referendum policy in September 2019. This was viewed as a slap in the face for Labour Leave voters who felt the party was ignoring them. The third was the publication of YouGov's MRP poll in late November 2019. This poll revealed for the first time the scale of support for the Conservatives in Red Wall seats.

Despite these factors it may have still been possible for Labour to hold to a number of the 41 lost Red Wall seats they ultimately lost. However, Labour's election campaign lacked focus and a concise narrative. The myriad of policies put forward to deflect from Brexit only added to the sense of Labour's lack of credibility. The party failed to understand the degree to which the public narrative had shifted and the very real risk to Red Wall seats. As a consequence it did not allocate its resources effectively as part of a defensive campaign.

Contextual trends undermined the Red Wall narrative

The historic dominant public narrative in Red Wall constituencies of 'Labour towns and Labour people' was steadily undermined over twenty years. Four of the key trends undermined the principal foundations of the narrative:

- Increasing political volatility, weaker party identification and more cross-pressured voters.
- Deindustrialisation and economic decline in towns, which reduced the number of industrial working class voters and associated institutions.
- Labour's focus in the 1990's on a new electoral coalition, and declining traditional working class support for the Party.
- Cultural realignment of cross-pressured voters, Labour's increasing disconnect with traditional working class values and growing Conservative support in Red Wall seats, albeit much of this support was concealed.

Growing potential for rapid political change

The political and social conditions in these seats, including the historic hostility to the Conservatives, created the potential for rapid political change. Labour's traditional industrial working class base was steadily declining and people were becoming less attached to political parties. Many voters increasingly viewed the Labour Party as taking them for granted, and being more interested in a new electoral base in the Cities. Many voters any also felt the Labour Party no longer represented their views on issues such as crime and immigration. Demographic changes further weakened Labour's vote, as these constituencies became older and younger people moved to cities for work. However, social pressures including a taboo about voting Conservative and the belief that they were Labour people and Labour towns combined to keep Labour's vote artificially high.

Many people that were thinking about supporting the Conservatives concealed their preferences to avoid being viewed as outliers in their social group or being ostracised. Given most people thought the Conservatives couldn't win these seats, there was little to gain by voicing support for the Tories. Revealing your true preference would be all risk for no potential gain. Thus, many former Labour voters concealed their true preferences to fit in with their perceptions of the community's preferences. The growth of these concealed preferences created the potential for rapid political change.

Rapid change requires a catalyst that reveals concealed preferences, and creates a cascade effect. The cascade is caused by threshold levels. People are influenced by the views and actions of other people. They may not act on their personal preferences if they feel that would make them an outlier but if they see evidence that other people share their views this may reach a threshold where they are prepared to take action and reveal their own preferences. Everyone has a different threshold level, a person might be prepared to say they are thinking of voting Conservative if two of their friends express this view, for others their threshold might be four friends or six friends. Differing threshold levels can create cascades, as two people expressing support for the Conservatives, might cause two more to express support and these four people might cause two more people to express support and so on.

Warning signs and 2019 narratives

Prior to 2019, there were a number of warning signs for Labour. For example, there was growing support for the Conservatives in both national and local elections. In the 2017 General Election, the Labour Party lost seats such as Copeland, Mansfield, Middlesbrough SE and Cleveland, Stoke-on-Trent South, and Walsall North. There was also the highest ever recorded level of Labour to Conservative vote switching. There was also a shifting public narrative. For those listening, voters were increasingly sharing stories of discontent with Labour.

In 2019, MRP polling created and reinforced a powerful challenger narrative that the Conservatives could realistically win Red Wall seats for the first time. This development gave more voters the confidence to reveal their previously concealed preferences for the Conservatives. This created a cascade effect in Red Wall seats, leading hundreds of thousands of former Labour voters to switch their votes to the Conservatives.

Confluence of long-term trends and narratives

Political narratives must resonate with people if they are to influence the public narrative. They have to chime with perceptions of reality if they are to shape the stories people share of themselves, their communities and their desired future. Powerful political narratives leverage existing trends. They tell a story that makes sense of the trends taking place. In the case of Red Wall seats the combination of long-term trends, political narratives, media narratives and individual stories combined to create an overarching new public narrative amongst traditional working class communities, namely 'Labour no longer represents people like us.'

Political change is rarely about a single narrative but rather a multiplicity of mutually reinforcing narratives. People are reluctant to change and rarely is an individual narrative going to be powerful enough to shake people's beliefs, a combination of trends and stories is required. Long term trends such as economic decline, loss of manufacturing jobs, declining party identification, and Labour's focus on a new electoral base were chipping away at the foundations of the party's support. A combination of Brexit and Jeremy Corbyn were accelerating the disconnect between Labour and its traditional working class voters. This disconnect was further reinforced by Labour's adoption of a second referendum policy. In 2019, national narratives such as 'get Brexit done' and Labour's lack of economic credibility were resonating in Red Wall seats. Focus groups and interviews show that voters were increasingly confident to share stories such as Labour having no aspiration for their area, Labour taking them for granted, Labour not respecting their views on Brexit, Labour not being patriotic, and Labour not respecting. By the time of the 2019 election a key group of Labour's traditional working class supporters no longer felt the party represented them.

Voters were more willing to question Labour and look at the Conservatives as an alternative. This created an environment where voters who had previously concealed their growing preferences for the Tories due to social pressures, felt more comfortable revealing their true preferences. This was particularly the case after the publication of YouGov's first MRP poll revealed the scale of Conservative support. These events created a cascade effect: the more former Labour voters talked about voting Conservative, the more other former Labour voters felt able to reveal their preferences. A new narrative emerged that many labour voters were, for the first time, thinking of voting Conservative. A new and powerful challenger narrative emerged. A narrative that is essential in 'first past the post' electoral systems, namely that the challenging party can realistically win.

The future

The only silver lining for Labour in the disastrous loss of these former Red Wall seats was that many voters had no strong preference for the Conservatives. Indeed, many voters spoke of voting for the Tories with a heavy heart or of loaning them their votes. The general feeling was one of disillusionment with Labour. As Robert Langley notes "despite strong levels of support among the working class at the moment, blue-collar trust in the Conservative party remains fragile."[1]

The challenge for Labour is creating a new political narrative with an imagined future that connects with their former voters, their perceptions of reality and their aspirations. A narrative that appeals to both former Labour Red Wall voters and Labour's growing electoral base in the cities and amongst the young.

Part four of this book sets out the challenges facing Labour, and guidance for those crafting political narratives.

PART IV

THE FUTURE

15

LABOUR'S CHALLENGE

"I don't know what the Labour Party stands for anymore, they used to be the working person's go to party but now I don't really know what they stand for."

Focus group participant, Birmingham Northfield.[1]

This chapter looks at the challenges facing the Labour Party in creating a new political narrative following their fourth successive election defeat and the fourth consecutive increase in the Conservative vote share.

In April 2019, Keir Starmer was elected as the Labour Party's new Leader. The party is now going through an inevitable period of reflection and will develop a new political strategy. Whatever strategy the party adopts it will benefit from developing an overall narrative arc that will guide its strategic communications.

The new strategy will depend amongst many other things upon an assessment of the electoral geography and the importance of Red Wall seats and culturally conservative voters. Alex

Niven, writing in *The Guardian*, argues that Labour may need to forget traditional Red Wall voters and accept "some demographics in the North and Midlands may now be out of reach, for the time being at least."[2] However, in terms of the marginal swing needed to win parliamentary seats, it is these former Labour seats that dominate the party's target list for 2024.[3] Analysis by the Fabian Society shows that if the seats Labour needs to win are ordered simply by the swing required relative to the 2019 election result, then 63% of these seats are in the North, Midlands and Wales, and over 80% are in towns rather than cities. The Labour Together review of the election comments "there is no route back to power—even a minority government—without winning these seats."[4]

The number of culturally conservative voters in Red Wall seats may represent a small proportion of Labour's target electoral base nationally but they represent a very important group in terms of winning marginal seats.

Will former Labour voters return?

The potentially good news for Labour is that focus groups and interviews indicate that many former Labour voters in Red Wall seats switched to the Conservatives with feelings of sadness. As we previously noted many voters talked of lending their votes to the Conservatives. Simon Fell, the new Conservative MP for Barrow and Furness commented "I think the phrase lending your vote is absolutely spot on. The number of people who said to me my grandfather's voted Labour, my father voted Labour, I voted Labour all my life. This was a choice but it's one that they could very easily take back."[5]

Recent research by the Centre for Cities forecasts that the Red Wall seats won by the Conservatives are likely to be the hardest hit by the economic downturn from the coronavirus pandemic. The analysis reveals the highest levels of household debt are in towns and in cities in the North, Midlands and Wales. Households in these seats will have the smallest disposable incomes and are likely to suffer the most from job losses.[6]

Further research by the Institute for Employment Studies has already found that ex-industrial towns, including the central belt of Scotland, parts of Wales and the north of England are being disproportionately hit by job losses due to the pandemic.[7] In Redcar and Cleveland for example, the number of people vying for each job rose from 20 to 39 over the period of the lockdown. These findings will present challenges for the current Conservative government and it is possible that a narrative of 'buyer's remorse' could emerge.

Polling indicates that not all those who defected from Labour in 2019 would necessarily make the same decisions again. 14% said that 2019 was an unusual election and they would probably vote Labour again next time, 17% of switchers said they still identified with the party, and 24% said they could see themselves voting Labour again in future [8]

However, more than half of those who switched from Labour to the Conservatives in 2019 said they no longer think of the Labour Party as their party, and 27% said they could not see themselves voting Labour in future. Fully three quarters of Labour defectors in 2019 said the party will need to change very significantly before they would consider voting for them again.[9]

The importance of the former Red Wall seats won by the Conservatives to Boris Johnson's majority will ensure government policy is very cognisant of the needs of such constituencies. James Johnson has said that the Conservative Party is tracking these former Labour voters. He comments "previously assumed to be safe Labour voters, their new swing voter status means they will be at the heart of policymaking and political decisions over the coming years."[10] This is apparent in the Conservative's talk of 'levelling up' and introducing a 'new deal' for the regions. Labour party members in these Red Wall seats are already conscious that the Conservatives are seeking to develop a new narrative by creating and promoting stories of local change and success.[11]

Economic narrative

A major challenge for Labour is creating an economic narrative, which is an "absolutely central narrative" to any political narrative.[12] Equally importantly, the party has to create a narrative of economic competence. Robert Shrimsley, the UK chief political commentator for the *Financial Times*, claims that for Labour in 2020 "creating a cogent economic narrative is more important than new policies."[13]

For Blair and New Labour, the narrative was about embracing and leveraging the opportunities of a global economy. It was also about distancing the party from its previous commitment to nationalisation and actively supporting the privatisation of some industries. The narrative and discourse were about modernisation, the third way and the inevitability of globalisation. For Cameron, the economic narrative was austerity, which was required to save Britain from Labour's overspending and debt. For Trump it is economic nationalism and growth through cutting taxes and regulations.

The coronavirus pandemic may create an opportunity for a new economic narrative as the response has highlighted the role of the government in supporting the economy. Joseph Stiglitz has noted that it has also "been a powerful reminder that the basic political and economic unit is still the nation-state."[14] He argues governments must find a better balance between globalisation and economic self-reliance. This chimes with former Red Wall Labour MP Caroline Flint's call for a 'muscular economic nationalism'[15] and a greater focus on the manufacturing industry. The crisis might focus attention on greater national self-sufficiency and local purchasing policies.

Robert Schiller also argues that the pandemic might be a window of opportunity to look at new approaches, for example government emergency payments to individuals and furlough schemes might open the door to new ideas involving greater government intervention.

The good news for Labour is that their economic policies align with the views of Red Wall voters and are popular. According to the 2018 British Social Attitudes Survey, people want a new public settlement with greater investment in public services and less inequality.[16] Overall, there is less of a divide on economic policies, the left-right economic cleavage is not as marked. This can be seen in the analysis conducted by political sociologist Paula Surridge[17] and in the narrative emerging from the pandemic crisis. The Conservative Party has moved to the left on economic issues and supported large scale public borrowing and government investment. Robert Shrimsley notes that what is emerging is almost a 'new economic consensus'.[18] These developments mean that Labour may find it difficult to outflank the Conservatives on economic issues.

The Labour Party will also need to approach issues such as taxation with caution. Voters with traditional working class values of hard work and aspiration are comfortable with some people becoming much richer than others. They believe it is fair that if you work harder you become much wealthier. It is instructive to review Philip Gould's struggle with the issue of taxation when developing Labour's election strategies and taxation policies in the 1990s. Focus group after focus group raised concerns about increases in tax, even where the proposals were progressive. For example, a proposal to increase taxes for those earning over £100,000 a year met with much concern, people were "very uneasy as what they saw as a tax on the rich."[19] They felt it would penalise those who worked hard and would weaken the economy and jobs.

There clearly needs to be a narrative about regional

economies and a focus on the economic links between cities such as Manchester and Leeds and the surrounding towns. This will be an area of competing narratives. The Conservatives have already adopted the narrative of 'levelling up' and a New Deal approach, where they have packaged infrastructure projects, new house building, green projects, school building and apprenticeship investments as a programme for Red Wall areas.

The impact of the pandemic crisis and Brexit may create a long term economic crisis which will undermine the Conservative lead on perceptions of competence. People feel increasingly economically vulnerable and insecure, both economically and culturally. Secure, well-paid jobs have been replaced with poorly paid, precarious work and there is a desire to return to well paid jobs and greater job security. These trends are only likely to be reinforced by the current crisis. The Labour Together review recommends that "Labour focus on trying to build a coalition around the idea of transformational economic change rooted in voters' own lives and problems, and combine this with rebuilding "trust and credibility" in the party."[20] Matt Bishop has suggested that a Labour political economy narrative should be underpinned by the sense that "hard work is genuinely rewarded" and "everyone pays their fair share."[21] The development of discourses about work paying would fit the values of Red Wall voters and align with policies such as increases in the National Minimum Wage.

Regardless of the narrative the Labour Party develops around the economy, at its core has to be a strong story about economic competence. Labour's own internal review of the 2015 election found that the party failed "to shake off the myth that the last Labour government was responsible for crashing the economy."[22] Analysis by Thomas Prosser at Cardiff University shows that "millions of voters prioritise competence over values, including in Red Wall seats."[23] Yet in 2019, just 14 % of the public saw the Labour Party as economically competent, compared to 63 % who saw it as incompetent on economic issues.

Vision: an imagined future

A new Labour narrative has to connect the past and the present with an imagined future. To resonate with voters this imagined future must be desirable and perceived to be realistic. The future is by its very nature complex, there are so many economic, political, technological, social, and cultural strands. A vision has to act as a heuristic, something that is easily understandable, and which sets a clear direction and tone. Again, this may seem obvious but there are many examples of political campaigns which singularly failed to do this.

In the EU referendum the Remain campaign did not create a clear narrative about the future that resonated with voters in Red Wall seats. The future narrative that was created and promoted also did not align with people's perceptions of the past and the present. The campaign's slogan was 'stronger, safer, better off in Europe'. The slogan was created to support a historical narrative about the economic benefits of the EU and link these to the present and the future.

The phrase 'better off' is a good use of everyday language but it simply did not reflect the perceptions of many voters who did not feel safer or better off. In the ten years prior to the referendum, average wages had fallen in real terms. According to the Office for National Statistics average real weekly wages fell from £520 in 2008 to under £490 in 2016. After the 2008 financial crash, many employers began moving staff to zero hours contracts. By 2016, over 750,000 people had been moved to such contracts. Combined with the loss of secure, relatively well-paid manufacturing jobs many workers did not feel safer or better off. This growing insecurity coincided with a period of large-scale immigration from the EU following the Labour government's decision in 2004 not to impose restrictions on EU immigration. The failure of the Stronger in Europe campaign to create a narrative that resonated with Red Wall voters was reflected in the overwhelming vote in these seats to leave the EU.

Professor John Gaffney, in his book *Leadership and the Labour Party* argues that in the 2015 election the Labour Party "failed to develop a wider, more overarching narrative on politics, the economy and society" which countered the Conservative narrative.[24] Rather than developing an alternative coherent overarching counter narrative the party fought the election on a series of retail policy offers such as lowering energy prices.

By contrast, in 1997 the Labour party crafted a vision and overall narrative that did resonate with voters. The narrative was about renewal, that Britain deserved better and this could be achieved through its modernisation programme. It was supported through key policies that addressed concerns of voters, for example being tough on crime. The narrative also set a collective tone of social harmony. Blair himself was careful to use words such as 'we' and inclusive language in discourse.[25] This was in sharp contrast to the previous narrative of Thatcher which was one of enemies, of us versus them.

In developing a new narrative Labour has to be cognisant of a significant divide on cultural issues. Analysis by Datapraxis for the Labour Together review indicates this divergence on social and cultural issues is growing. This presents a major challenge for Labour in developing a narrative that reaffirms the audience's sense of identity and reflects a sense of shared values. In her book *The New Working Class*, Claire Ainsley, argues that to win working class hearts and minds political parties should root their policies in their collective values. Ainsley argues these working class values include family, fairness, hard work and decency.[26]

The appointment of Claire Ainsley as Head of Policy by Keir Starmer could signal that the party is serious about creating a narrative vision which connects with the identity and values of traditional working class voters. Ainsley has written about the positive aspects of Brexit and says "leaving the EU creates an opportunity to design a regional policy that responds to local priorities and opportunities, and increase the chance for local areas and city regions to determine their own futures."[27] Ainsley places a strong emphasis on family and communitarian values. Her views align with those of Stephen Kinnock who argued that Labour needs to move back towards the values and economic priorities of Communitarians. Importantly Ainsley says understanding and connecting with values is more important than specific policies.[28]

Traditional working class values also include patriotism and economic nationalism. The Labour party under Corbyn was seen by many as uncomfortable with national identity. Robert Shrimsley writing in the *Financial Times* observes that a major challenge for Labour "is to stop the party looking as though it hates its own country."[29] While Labour is unlikely to adopt more authoritarian policies around matters, such as immigration, there is a narrative to be developed around defending the national interest. Labour was perceived as too sympathetic to the Russian position in the case of the Skripal poisoning.

Effective political narratives include a basic patriotism and a story of promoting and defending the national interest. In the UK this can include support for reasonable expressions of British and English identity. Diane Kirkwood argues the Labour Party should create a narrative that includes "a generous dose of patriotism."[30] Keir Starmer appears to be taking some of these points on board and has said Labour must embrace patriotism, commenting: "In the Labour party we should be proud of being patriotic."[31]

It is easy to talk about coalition building but the cultural divides in Labour's electoral coalition are quite wide and cultural issues are becoming more salient as the gap on economic issues narrows. The majority of people that make up Labour's core voters have become increasingly socially liberal. However, Datapraxis note that while socially liberal voters make up the majority of Labour's core vote, they only comprise 21% of the electorate. Thus Labour has to build a wider alliance to win an election. Over recent years these socially liberal voters have also moved further away from traditional working class Red Wall voters. The extent of this gap is highlighted by recent research showing that many former Labour voters are to the right of Conservative Party members in supporting tougher policies on crime and tighter immigration restrictions.[32]

Creating a political narrative that will resonate with both socially liberal and culturally conservative voters is a major challenge. However, there are areas of common ground including greater government investment, reducing inequality, increasing affordable housing, improving elderly care, support for the NHS and localism, which is linked to the climate agenda. There is also scope for common ground on policies to redevelop towns, invest in regional infrastructure and to develop local communities. It is also possible to develop common ground on areas such as crime. New Labour successfully did this with its strong emphasis on issues such as crime and anti-social behaviour, issues which were mentioned extensively by voters in the 2019 election, but rarely referred to by Labour.

There is also scope to develop a future narrative that is about aspiration, hard work, dignity, pride, safety and community that will appeal to Labour's wider coalition. This narrative though has to resonate and align with what Labour does on the ground in constituencies. Local parties and Labour councils need to act and tell stories that align with the overall narrative.

Words also matter. David Goodhart has talked of how previously Labour celebrated change and globalisation too uncritically, and didn't give voice to the caution and anxiety of many voters.[33] This gave rise to a sense they were not being listened to.

An imagined future in relation to former Red Wall seats could include a new form of regionalism and localism. The narrative could take the form of a more populist regional and local discourse. This may give people a greater feeling of agency and control. Adopting a regional populist narrative may also mobilise passions, energise emotions, and increase the turnout of voters disillusioned with politics. There are obvious risks of adopting a populist narrative but research has found that such narratives can have a powerful mobilising effect and reach non-voters.[34] The Scottish National Party have used a populist narrative to mobilise voters and to be 'on their side' against a remote elite in Westminster. It is interesting to note that Andy Burnham, the Mayor of Manchester, who has been arguing strongly to protect the interests of the North, is also seen by voters as standing up for, and being in touch with, ordinary people.[35] This is in sharp contrast to voter's views of politicians in general.

Linking narrative to leadership

Leadership is a key cornerstone of an effective political narrative. It is therefore essential to align and associate Labour's new narrative with the Leader of the party. In the case of Blair, his youth and energy were associated with the party's vision of renewal and modernisation. Boris Johnson was strongly associated with the party's vision of breaking from the EU and greater economic nationalism. A leader's personal narrative needs to chime with and exemplify the overall political narrative. As Gaffney argues "the relationship between narrative and leadership, between rhetoric and performance, between doctrine and its voicing, are crucial to party politics, and are crucially underrated."[36]

A political leader's persona is a narrative construction that matters to voters. This narrative construction is constantly created, mediated, and challenged through the media and increasingly social media. The latter gives leaders and all public figures the opportunity to communicate directly and has created a new currency of authenticity. However, the reality is that we only see the projected persona of a political leader rather than the real person. This persona is constructed through a narrative.

One essential element of any Leader's persona must be a narrative around competence. The duality of party and Leader must work together as a coherent narrative. A party's narrative is likely to be undermined if the leader is not seen as competent and vice versa. The challenge for a party is to align the leader's narrative with their overall political narrative.

Listening and linking narrative to context and trends

Narratives are not static and cannot be conjured out of thin air. Former Labour MP for Leigh, Jo Platt, advised her colleagues to listen more to the people, saying, "Our party is viewed as entitled and elitist because key figures within the party are entitled, and have expressed their 'we know best' attitude for far too long."[37] Parties have to invest in understanding and responding to the public narratives in different regions and towns. This means listening to party members who are on the ground locally as well as conducting focus groups. In the run up to the 2019 election, a great many Labour members and MPs in Red Wall towns were not able to get the leadership in London to listen to their concerns.

Over the course of a parliament many things can change. If

a week is a long time in politics, things can change dramatically over just a few months. This has been exemplified by the coronavirus pandemic. Narratives therefore must be capable of adapting to circumstances and can gain momentum by leveraging contextual trends or events. Some events become salient political shocks that can cause major long-term political realignments. The nature of these shocks means that parties will compete around them and need to create narratives that place them into a political context. These narratives will influence public judgements about the parties including their competence and their image.

Summary

This chapter has outlined a number of major challenges for Labour in crafting a new narrative that will resonate with both its socially liberal membership and culturally conservative voters. There are specific challenges which Labour has to address regardless of the strategy it develops under its new leadership. These include developing a clear economic narrative and demonstrating Labour's economic competence; developing an imagined future that resonates, is easily understandable and is perceived as realistic; linking together the party's and the leader's narrative; and adopting a flexible approach based on continually listening to voters, tracking trends and crafting narratives around events that reinforce the overarching vision and narrative.

The next and final chapter, sets out some key principles to guide the development of a new political narrative.

16

CRAFTING AN EFFECTIVE POLITICAL NARRATIVE

"It is no surprise that so many of us held our noses and voted Conservative ... the reasons I voted for them is because of reasonable certainty over Brexit; rejection of unpatriotic far-left politics and rejection of antisemitism. I want Brexit completed and a recognition of the views of the working class; a reinvigoration of the economy outside the metropolitan areas and an improvement of our standing in the world."

Retired teacher and first-time Conservative voter in Bolsover[1]

I t is important to remember that narratives construct structures of meaning, making a sequence of complex events understandable. People comprehend the world through narrative, a grouping of events, ideas, and characters into a story.[2] Individuals draw on narrative to make sense of the world and their own life choices and decisions. Influential psychologist Ted Sarbin argues that "human beings think, perceive, imagine, and make moral choices according to narrative struc-

236

tures."[3] Given our identities guide our political decisions narratives can facilitate an identification process, whereby an individual links their identity to a political narrative. Powerful narratives conjure up stories that reaffirm an audience's sense of their collective and individual identity.

In political life, narratives are used to frame how events and issues are perceived, and to influence voting behaviour. While the media may direct public attention to certain issues the framing of these stories can be contested. Stories are not simply transmitted and received, they are decoded by an audience, based on their own experience and in the context of other stories. Stories are also shaped and reshaped in their retelling.

Stories that do not align with experiences or perceptions of reality will gain less traction than those that do. A story is also more likely to be shared if it can be retold simply in everyday language. It is therefore helpful to develop a concise narrative. This is not the same as a slogan. The fundamental feature of a political narrative is that it tells a story of the past, the present and of an imagined future. A concise narrative such as 'take back control' or 'make America great again' tell such stories and conjure up a worldview, along with multiple stories associated with the overall narrative. A concise narrative can become a slogan, however, a slogan that does not tell a story of the past, the present and the future can never be considered a narrative.

The purpose of a political narrative is to shape peoples' views of events and to influence their behaviour. This requires a coherent story, an overall narrative arc that resonates with voters, one that they use to make sense of the world. This may seem simple to the point of restating the obvious but there are many examples of political parties and campaigns that did not develop a clear overarching narrative. For example, following the global financial crash of 2008 the Conservatives created an overarching narrative that the previous Labour government had been profligate, overspent and built up debt, and that austerity was required to save the UK economy. This was not necessarily true but what mattered was the effectiveness of the story. It contrasted Conservative economic competence with the alleged incompetence of Labour. It was a powerful narrative which Labour has still not been able to overcome.

An effective political narrative must address three fundamental issues. First, the political economy and economic credibility. Second, a desirable and realistic vision for the future. Finally, it must demonstrate how the overarching political narrative aligns with the party leader's persona or personal narrative.

Some guiding principles

The coronavirus pandemic presents a major opportunity for Labour to create a new overarching political narrative. In developing this new narrative, Labour would be well advised to pay attention to and be guided by the following points.

There is no shortcut to creating a new political narrative even though there will be opportunities to leverage events such as the pandemic crisis. Developing a new narrative is a long-term project and needs to be viewed as such.

The aim of a political narrative is to influence and shape the public narrative, the stories that people share about themselves, their communities and what has to be done. It is therefore essential to be constantly listening to these public narratives, partly using focus groups but also by listening to feedback from members and councillors on the ground who are involved in public discourse. It is important to understand the stories that resonate, the language that is used and the way that stories are told. It is also important for a political party to demonstrate it is listening by reflecting the stories and language of communities.

The new political narrative must connect the past and the

present with a clear vision of Labour's imagined future. In the same way the Conservatives created a narrative of Labour's overspending and profligacy to explain the consequences of the 2008 financial crash, Labour needs to create a narrative of the recent past since 2010. Narratives have to be rooted in, and relate to, existing trends and events. The narrative created around the 2020 pandemic crisis will be critical, as this event will be subject to reports and inquiries that play out over the next four years and in the lead up to the next election.

Labour must craft a vision which is desirable and perceived to be realistic. Absolutely core to this is a clear narrative about the future political economy. The right has successfully developed a negative narrative about tax. It has become a deep story, calling up Benjamin Franklin's 1789 comment that there are only two things that are certain in life: death and taxes. Tax has been framed as something deeply negative, something that the monster of the state imposes to take your hard-earned money away from you. An alternative narrative is that tax is something that communities use to smooth the path through economically turbulent times. It is a shared selflessness that lets the community care for those who are ill or fall on hard times and to protect the community. The pandemic crisis has highlighted the critical role of government spending to support communities. This creates an opportunity to push an alternative narrative around taxation, highlighting the links to solidarity, community, public services and investment.

The new political narrative must reflect themes that voters are familiar with. This may include leveraging themes emerging from the pandemic economic crisis such as greater national self-sufficiency, the value of communities, localism and more active state intervention.

The narrative must also appeal to the voters' sense of collective and individual identity, where do they fit in this new world? The narrative will need to appeal to a British identity, and navigate the fraught issues of English, Welsh, Scottish and Irish identity.

The political narrative must be aligned with and exemplified by the leader's personal narrative.

The overall narrative architecture needs to bring many complex elements together into a single story and make sense of them as a coherent and meaningful whole. To do this the overall narrative arc must be supported by multiple stories that reinforce the overall message. It is not enough to identify the overall narrative arc, the multiple stories that support the arc must also be identified and shaped to support the whole.

Despite the dangers of heuristics and single stories, possibly even their lack of reality, the new political narrative must also be capable of being conveyed as a concise narrative that communicates the overall story, its symbolism, imagery and individual stories.

Finally, an effective political narrative must use vernacular language. The power of a political narrative is in the retelling. Hence, it must be capable of being understood, discussed, and retold in everyday language.

The fall of the Red Wall was one of the most important moments in British political history and its collapse will continue to reverberate for years to come. It demonstrates the importance of public narratives: *the stories that people share of themselves, their communities and their vision for the future.* But it is not the end of the story. It can be rebuilt. But only if Labour is prepared to acknowledge the real reasons that voters abandoned the party. The fall of these long-held Red Wall seats offers crucial lessons not only for Labour but for anyone that wants to understand and communicate with the voting public.

AFTERWORD

Dear Reader,

I hope you found this book interesting and thought provoking.

I would love to get your feedback and would particularly welcome a review on Amazon. It only takes a few minutes to post a couple of sentences that sum up your thoughts. I would really appreciate you taking the time. You can leave a review at the following link: https://amzn.to/2BZBSKA

Alternatively search for 'The Fall of the Red Wall' on Amazon.

Thank you.

NOTES

Introduction

1. Niven, A (2019) The north has changed. To win it back, Labour must recognise that. https://www.theguardian.com/commentisfree/2019/dec/22/north-changed-labour-grassroots-activism-devolving-power
2. Waugh, P (2017) Labour Voters Fear Family, Friends Will 'Disown' Them For Backing Tories https://www.huffingtonpost.co.uk/entry/labour-voters-fear-friends-and-family-will-disown-them-for-switching-to-tories-huffpost-edelman-focus-group_uk_59205461e4b03b485cb1e86b
3. Pickard, J (2020) Starmer blames Corbyn for Labour's election defeat, Financial Times. https://www.ft.com/content/031031ec-b9e6-4e06-ae7f-7ea8375a4760

1. Defining the Red Wall

1. Johnson, B (2019) Speech at Manchester Science and Industry Museum. https://www.gov.uk/government/speeches/pm-speech-at-manchester-science-and-industry-museum
2. Kanagasooriam, J (2019) Twitter thread. https://twitter.com/James-Kanag/status/1161639307536457730
3. Kanagasooriam, J (2019) How the Labour party's Red Wall turned blue, Financial Times. https://www.ft.com/content/3b80b2de-1dc2-11ea-81f0-0c253907d3e0
4. Kanagasooriam, J (2019) Twitter thread. https://twitter.com/James-Kanag/status/1190372058968068096
5. Payne, S (2019) Conservatives confident they can break through Labour's Red Wall, Financial Times. https://www.ft.com/content/9554b488-1b54-11ea-97df-cc63de1d73f4
6. Johnson, J (2019) Boris's New Swing Voters and Why They Are Here to Stay https://www.hanovercomms.com/blog/boriss-new-swing-voters-sceptical-of-business-and-here-to-stay/
7. Payne, S (2019) UK general election: Can Boris Johnson break Labour's 'red wall'? Financial Times. https://www.ft.com/content/fbd00ed6-ffd1-11e9-be59-e49b2a136b8d
8. Bastion, L (2019) The myth of the red wall, The Critic. https://thecritic.co.uk/the-myth-of-the-red-wall/
9. Cooper, C and Cooper, L (2020) The Devastating Defeat. https://www.europeforthemany.com/tdd-web.pdf

10. As an example see Mann, J (2019) Tweet https://twitter.com/LordJohnMann/status/1192107516072726529
11. BBC (2019) Sally Gimson: Bassetlaw Labour candidate deselected by NEC, BBC News. https://www.bbc.co.uk/news/uk-england-nottinghamshire-50322652
12. Centre for Towns (2017) Launch Briefing https://www.centrefortowns.org/reports/launch-briefing/viewdocument
13. YouGov (2019) How Britain voted in the 2019 general election https://yougov.co.uk/topics/politics/articles-reports/2019/12/17/how-britain-voted-2019-general-election
14. Fox, S (2019) Labour's Car Crash Result by Age Group, Brunel University. https://www.brunel.ac.uk/news-and-events/news/articles/Labours-car-crash-result-by-age-group
15. Gov UK (2018) Population of England and Wales. https://www.ethnicity-facts-figures.service.gov.uk/uk-population-by-ethnicity/national-and-regional-populations/population-of-england-and-wales/latest
16. Hanretty, C (2017). Areal interpolation and the UK's referendum on EU membership. *Journal of Elections, Public Opinion and Parties*, 27(4), 466-483.

2. The 2019 Earthquake

1. Jarvis, D (2019) Lessons from campaigning in the Labour heartland seat of Barnsley, Labour List. https://labourlist.org/2019/12/lessons-from-campaigning-in-the-labour-heartland-seat-of-barnsley/
2. Nandy, L (2019) What will the history books say about Brexit? Beyond Today, BBC podcast. https://www.bbc.co.uk/sounds/play/p07q0y14
3. Platt, J (2019) Labour forgot towns like mine, and that's why I lost my seat. It's time to start listening again, The Independent. https://www.independent.co.uk/voices/jo-platt-labour-election-result-lost-seats-leigh-northern-towns-a9252041.html
4. BBC (2019). General election 2019: "Leigh's voters on 'fantastic' seismic shift," BBC News. https://www.bbc.co.uk/news/election-2019-50781738
5. Surridge, P (2020) Twitter comment. https://twitter.com/p_surridge/status/1258069252495618051
6. Surridge, P (2020) How the Conservatives won the red wall. https://ukandeu.ac.uk/how-the-conservatives-won-the-red-wall/
   Datapraxis (2019) Tory Landslide, Progressives Split, Datapraxis. https://www.dataprax.is/tory-landslide-progressives-split
7. Resolution Foundation (2019) Election dissection. https://www.resolutionfoundation.org/comment/election-dissection/
8. Gibbon, G (2019) What Rory Did Next...| Politics: Where Next? Podcast. https://www.channel4.com/news/what-rory-did-next-politics-where-next-podcast

9. Datapraxis (2019) Tory Landslide, Progressives Split, Datapraxis. https://www.dataprax.is/tory-landslide-progressives-split

10. Langley, R (2019) My grandad hated Thatcher and the Tories. Here's why he voted for Boris, The Spectator. https://blogs.spectator.co.uk/2019/12/my-grandad-hated-thatcher-and-the-tories-heres-why-he-voted-for-boris/

11. British Election Study (2019) Wave 19 of 2014-2023 BES Internet Panel. https://www.britishelectionstudy.com/data-object/wave-19-of-the-2014-2023-british-election-study-internet-panel/

12. Surridge, P (2020) Twitter thread. Party identity and voting. https://twitter.com/p_surridge/status/1251480182814380033

13. Ibid

14. IGC, (2019) Northern Discomfort: Why Labour lost the General Election. https://institute.global/sites/default/files/articles/Northern-Discomfort-Why-Labour-lost-the-General-Election.pdf

15. Payne, S (2019) 'New dawn' as Conservatives turn Redcar into Bluecar, Financial Times. https://www.ft.com/content/0592a45a-1dab-11ea-97df-cc63de1d73f4

16. Mercouris (2019) Letter From Britain: Why Labour Lost. https://consortiumnews.com/2019/12/17/letter-from-britain-why-labour-lost/

17. Kellner, P (2020) Five crucially important but frequently ignored facts about the 2019, Prospect Magazine. election https://www.prospect-magazine.co.uk/politics/five-crucially-important-but-frequently-ignored-facts-about-the-2019-election-labour-conservatives-brexit-corbyn-johnson

18. Datapraxis (2019) Tory Landslide, Progressives Split. https://www.dataprax.is/tory-landslide-progressives-split

19. Tolhurst, A (2020) Leaked report by Labour into party's election failure blames Brexit and the media – not Jeremy Corbyn. Politics Home. https://www.politicshome.com/news/article/leaked-report-by-labour-into-partys-election-failure-blames-brexit-and-the-media--not-jeremy-corbyn

20. Pickard (2020) Starmer blames Corbyn for Labour's election defeat. Financial Times. https://www.ft.com/content/031031ec-b9e6-4e06-ae7f-7ea8375a4760?sharetype=blocked

21. Ashcroft (2020) Diagnosis Of Defeat Labour's turn to smell the coffee. https://lordashcroftpolls.com/wp-content/uploads/2020/02/DIAGNOSIS-OF-DEFEAT-LORD-ASHCROFT-POLLS-1.pdf

22. Ibid.

23. Ibid

24. Watson (2020) Lord Ashcroft: Tory pollster's analysis of Labour defeat sparks internal debate, BBC news. https://www.bbc.co.uk/news/uk-politics-51457739

25. Pickard (2020) Labour party report excuses Corbyn for election defeat,

Financial Times. https://www.ft.com/content/5dc2f7b0-41f5-11ea-a047-eae9bd51ceba

26. Labour Together (2020) Election Review 2019. https://electionreview.labourtogether.uk/

27. Rodgers, S (2020) Exclusive: Labour needs "major overhaul" to win again, says election review, Labour List. https://labourlist.org/2020/06/exclusive-labour-needs-major-overhaul-to-win-again-says-election-review/

28. Niven, A (2020) Forget the 'red wall', Labour can win by appealing to a new demographic, The Guardian. https://www.theguardian.com/uk-news/commentisfree/2020/mar/05/labour-red-wall-new-demographic

29. Lavery & Trickett (2020) Northern Discomfort, Tribune. https://tribunemag.co.uk/2020/03/northern-discomfort

30. Chakrabortty, A (2019) This Labour meltdown has been building for decades, The Guardian. https://www.theguardian.com/commentisfree/2019/dec/14/labour-meltdown-decades-govern-votes

31. Platt, J (2019) Labour forgot towns like mine, and that's why I lost my seat. It's time to start listening again, Independent. https://www.independent.co.uk/voices/jo-platt-labour-election-result-lost-seats-leigh-northern-towns-a9252041.html

32. Cutts, D., Goodwin, M., Heath, O., & Surridge, P. (2020). Brexit, the 2019 General Election and the Realignment of British Politics. *Political Quarterly, 91*(1), 7-23.

33. Surridge, P (2020) Beyond Brexit: Labour's Structural Problems. https://journals.sagepub.com/doi/pdf/10.1177/2041905820911741

34. Balls, K (2020) Toryism, but not as we know it: an interview with Ben Houchen, The Spectator. https://beta.spectator.co.uk/article/Toryism-but-not-as-we-know-it-an-interview-with-Ben-Houchen

35. Ibid.

36. Parveen, N (2019) Labour loses control of Bolsover for first time in 40 years, The Guardian. https://www.theguardian.com/politics/2019/may/03/labour-loses-control-of-bolsover-for-first-time-in-its-40-year-history

37. Halliday, J & Pidd, H (2019) Labour loses control of council strongholds of Bolton and Darlington, The Guardian. https://www.theguardian.com/politics/2019/may/10/labour-loses-control-bolton-darlington-councils-conservatives-local-elections

38. Rodgers, S (2019) How Labour Lost the Red Wall, Politics Home. https://www.politicshome.com/news/article/how-labour-lost-the-red-wall

39. Smeeth, R (2020) Podcast: Corbynism: The Post-Mortem. 9: The Red Wall Crumbles. https://podcasts.apple.com/za/podcast/9-the-red-wall-crumbles/id1494568978?i=1000468340080

40. Flint, C (2019) Sophy Ridge Podcast - Election Fallout. https://play-

er.fm/series/sophy-ridge-on-sunday/election-fallout-michael-gove-caro-
line-flint-richard-burgon-ian-blackford

41. Labour Together (2020) Election Review 2019. https://electionre-
view.labourtogether.uk/

42. Ibid.

43. Flint, C (2019) Sophy Ridge Podcast - Election Fallout. https://play-
er.fm/series/sophy-ridge-on-sunday/election-fallout-michael-gove-caro-
line-flint-richard-burgon-ian-blackford

3. Increasing Political Volatility in UK General Elections

1. Graham, M (2019) Mike Graham show on TalkRadio https://talkradio.co.
uk/radio/listen-again/1573552800 Clip at https://www.express.-
co.uk/news/uk/1203874/General-election-news-brexit-news-talkradio-
mike-graham-boris-johnson-labour-conservative

2. British Election Study (2019) Explaining Voter Volatility: A summary of
the British Election Study https://www.britishelectionstudy.com/wp-
content/uploads/2019/10/Explaining-Voter-Volatility.pdf

3. Fieldhouse, E. (2020). Electoral shocks : The volatile voter in a turbulent
world (First ed., Oxford scholarship online).

4. British Election Study (2019) Explaining Voter Volatility: A summary of
the British Election Study https://www.britishelectionstudy.com/wp-
content/uploads/2019/10/Explaining-Voter-Volatility.pdf

5. Dalton, R J (2016) Party Identification and Its Implications. Oxford
Research Encyclopedia of Politics. DOI:
10.1093/acrefore/9780190228637.013.72

6. Ibid

7. Campbell, A., & University of Michigan. Survey Research Center. (1960).
The American voter. New York, Wiley

8. Fieldhouse, E. (2020). Electoral shocks : The volatile voter in a turbulent
world (First ed., Oxford scholarship online).

9. Curtice, J (1989) The 1989 European Election" Protest or Green tide? Electoral Studies 8 (3):217-30

10. Hobolt, S., & Tilley, J. (2016). Fleeing the centre: The rise of challenger
parties in the aftermath of the euro crisis. West European Politics:
Europe's Union in Crisis: Tested and Contested, 39(5), 971-991.

11. Bølstad, J., Dinas, E., & Riera, P. (2013). Tactical Voting and Party Preferences:
A Test of Cognitive Dissonance Theory. Political Behavior, 35(3), 429-452.

12. Fieldhouse, E. (2020). Electoral shocks : The volatile voter in a turbulent
world (First ed., Oxford scholarship online).

13. Alex Salmond, quoted in Torrance, D (2011) Salmond: Against the Odds,
Berlin

14. Fieldhouse, E. (2020). Electoral shocks : The volatile voter in a turbulent world (First ed., Oxford scholarship online).
15. Eatwell, R., & Goodwin, Matthew J. (2018). National populism : The revolt against liberal democracy. London, Pelican.
16. Hansard Society. (2019). Audit of Political Engagement retrieved from https://assets.ctfassets.net/rdwvqctnt75b/7iQEHtrkIbLcrUkduG-mo9b/cb429a657e97cad61e61853c05c8c4d1/Hansard-Society_Audit-of-Political-Engagement-16_2019-report.pdf
17. UK Parliament (2018) Research Briefing: Political disengagement in the UK: who is disengaged? http://researchbriefings.files.parliament.uk/documents/CBP-7501/CBP-7501.pdf
18. Heath, O (2010) Policy Alienation, Social Alienation and Working-Class Abstention in Britain, 1964–2010 https://www.cambridge.org/core/journals/british-journal-of-political-science/article/policy-alienation-social-alienation-and-workingclass-abstention-in-britain-19642010/70E409B4E2274FAE7844449B95DA0EBB
19. Heath, O., & Goodwin, M. (2017). The 2017 General Election, Brexit and the Return to Two–Party Politics: An Aggregate–Level Analysis of the Result We're grateful to Chris Hanretty, Georgios Xezonakis and Elie Pelling for helpful comments and feedback on earlier drafts. Political Quarterly, 88(3), 345-358.
20. Heath, O., & Goodwin, M. (2017). The 2017 General Election, Brexit and the Return to Two–Party Politics
21. Labour Together (2020) Election Review 2019 https://electionreview.labourtogether.uk/
22. Ibid
23. British Election Study (2019) Explaining Voter Volatility: A summary of the British Election Study https://www.britishelectionstudy.com/wp-content/uploads/2019/10/Explaining-Voter-Volatility.pdf
24. Bruter, M & Harrison, S (2017) Understanding the emotional act of voting. Nature Human Behaviour, 1 (0024). pp. 1-3. ISSN 2397-3374campb
25. Ashcroft (2019) How Britain voted and why: My 2019 general election post-vote poll https://lordashcroftpolls.com/2019/12/how-britain-voted-and-why-my-2019-general-election-post-vote-poll/
26. Fieldhouse, E. (2020). Electoral shocks : The volatile voter in a turbulent world (First ed., Oxford scholarship online).

4. Deindustrialisation and Economic Decline in Towns

1. Beatty & Fothergill, (2016) Jobs, Welfare and Austerity. How the destruction of industrial Britain casts a shadow over present-day public finances. https://www4.shu.ac.uk/research/cresr/sites/shu.ac.uk/files/cresr30th-jobs-welfare-austerity.pdf

2. Comfort, N. (2013) The Slow Death of British Industry A Sixty-Year Suicide 1952-2012, BiteBack Publishing, London

3. Beatty & Fothergill, (2016) Jobs,Welfare and Austerity. How the destruction of industrial Britain casts a shadow over present-day public finances. https://www4.shu.ac.uk/research/cresr/sites/shu.ac.uk/files/cresr30th-jobs-welfare-austerity.pdf

4. GMB (2018) Almost 600,000 manufacturing jobs lost in decade. https://www.gmb.org.uk/news/almost-600000-manufacturing-jobs-lost-decade

5. Office for National Statistics (2018) Low and High Pay in the UK 2018. https://www.ons.gov.uk/employmentandlabourmarket/peopleinwork/earningsandworkinghours/bulletins/lowandhighpayuk/2018

6. EY (2020) Beyond Brexit: 'Levelling up' the UK. https://www.ey.com/en_uk/growth/ey-regional-economic-forecast-2020

7. Marmot, M (2010) Fair Society, Healthy Lives. The Marmot Review. http://www.instituteofhealthequity.org/resources-reports/fair-society-healthy-lives-the-marmot-review/fair-society-healthy-lives-full-report-pdf.pdf

8. Marmot, M (2020) Health Equity In England: The Marmot Review 10 Years On. https://www.health.org.uk/sites/default/files/2020-03/Health%20Equity%20in%20England_The%20Marmot%20Review%2010%20Years%20On_executive%20summary_web.pdf

9. Tomlinson, J (2017) Brexit: blame it on the loss of industrial jobs, not on globalisation, LSE. https://blogs.lse.ac.uk/businessreview/2017/04/28/brexit-blame-it-on-the-loss-of-industrial-jobs-not-on-globalisation/

10. Chakrabortty (2019) On the doorstep, Labour faces the question: who do you speak for? The Guardian. https://www.theguardian.com/politics/2019/nov/26/on-the-doorstep-labour-faces-the-question-who-do-you-speak-for

11. Goodhart, D. (2017). The road to somewhere : The populist revolt and the future of politics. Penguin, Hurst & Co

12. Centre for Towns (2017) Launch Briefing. https://www.centrefortowns.org/reports/launch-briefing/viewdocument

13. Chakrabortty, A (2019) This Labour meltdown has been building for decades, The Guardian. https://www.theguardian.com/commentisfree/2019/dec/14/labour-meltdown-decades-govern-votes

14. McKenzie, Lisa. (2017). 'It's not ideal': Reconsidering 'anger' and 'apathy' in the Brexit vote among an invisible working class. http://eprints.lse.ac.uk/83290/1/McKenzie_It's%20not%20ideal_2017.pdf

15. Tomlinson, J (2017) De-industrialisation rather than globalisation is the key part of the Brexit story https://blogs.lse.ac.uk/brexit/2017/04/28/de-industrialisation-rather-than-globalisation-is-the-key-part-of-the-brexit-story/

16. Ibid

17. Bank of England (2015) The impact of immigration on occupational wages: evidence from Britain. https://www.bankofengland.co.uk/-/media/boe/files/working-paper/2015/the-impact-of-immigration-on-occupational-wages-evidence-from-britain.pdf?la=en&hash=16F94BC8B55F06967E1F36249E90ECE9B597BA9C

18. Niven, A (2019) The Labour Party's Spectacular Defeat Had Been Coming for Decades, New York Times https://www.nytimes.com/2019/12/20/opinion/uk-election-labour.html?auth=login-google

19. Chakrabortty, A (2019) This Labour meltdown has been building for decades, The Guardian. https://www.theguardian.com/commentisfree/2019/dec/14/labour-meltdown-decades-govern-votes

20. Platt, J (2019) Labour forgot towns like mine, and that's why I lost my seat. It's time to start listening again, The Independent. https://www.independent.co.uk/voices/jo-platt-labour-election-result-lost-seats-leigh-northern-towns-a9252041.html

5. Labour's New Electoral Coalition and Declining Working Class Vote

1. Nivan, A (2019) The Labour Party's Spectacular Defeat Had Been Coming for Decades, New York Times. https://www.nytimes.com/2019/12/20/opinion/uk-election-labour.html

2. Evans & Tilley (2017) The New Politics of Class: The Political Exclusion of the British Working Class, Oxford University Press

3. Hunter, P (2015) Red alert: why Labour lost and what needs to change? http://www.smith-institute.org.uk/wp-content/uploads/2015/08/Red-alert-why-Labour-lost-and-what-needs-to-change.pdf

4. Kellner, P (2020) Five crucially important but frequently ignored facts about the 2019 election. https://www.prospectmagazine.co.uk/politics/five-crucially-important-but-frequently-ignored-facts-about-the-2019-election-labour-conservatives-brexit-corbyn-johnson

5. Payne, G (2013) Models of Contemporary Social Class: the Great British Class Survey https://journals.sagepub.com/doi/pdf/10.4256/mio.2013.001

6. Jennings and Stoker (2017) Tilting towards the cosmopolitan axis? Political change in England and the 2017 general election. https://eprints.soton.ac.uk/411956/1/Jennings_Stoker_PQ_FINAL.pdf and https://onlinelibrary.wiley.com/doi/abs/10.1111/1467-923X.12403

7. Cooper, C and Cooper, L (2020) The Devastating Defeat. https://www.europeforthemany.com/tdd-web.pdf

8. Jennings and Stoker (2017) Tilting towards the cosmopolitan axis? Political change in England and the 2017 general election. https://eprints.soton.ac.uk/411956/1/Jennings_Stoker_PQ_FINAL.pdf and https://onlinelibrary.wiley.com/doi/abs/10.1111/1467-923X.12403

9. Bickerton C (2019) Labour's lost working-class voters have gone for good, TheGuardian. https://www.theguardian.com/commentisfree/2019/dec/19/labour-working-class-voters-brexit

10. Ibid

11. See:
    1) Ludwigshafen, Piraeus & Valletta (2016) Rose thou art sick, Economist. https://www.economist.com/briefing/2016/04/02/rose-thou-art-sick
    2) Hanretty, C (2015) Electorally, West European social democrats are at their lowest point for forty years. https://medium.com/@chrishanretty/electorally-west-european-socialdemocrats-are-at-their-lowest-point-for-forty-years-ac7ae3d8ddb7

12. Mercouris (2019) LETTER FROM BRITAIN: Why Labour Lost. https://consortiumnews.com/2019/12/17/letter-from-britain-why-labour-lost/

13. Bale, T in Economist (2019) Who are the conservatives new voters in the north, The Economist. https://www.economist.com/britain/2019/12/18/who-are-the-conservatives-new-voters-in-the-north

14. Lavery & Trickett (2020) Northern Discomfort, Tribune. https://tribunemag.co.uk/2020/03/northern-discomfort

15. Kirkwood, D (2020) Why Britain's values divide should matter to Labour. https://ukandeu.ac.uk/why-britains-values-divide-should-matter-to-labour/

16. Flint, C (2019) Sophy Ridge Podcast - Election Fallout. https://player.fm/series/sophy-ridge-on-sunday/election-fallout-michael-gove-caroline-flint-richard-burgon-ian-blackford

17. Labour First (2020) Podcast: The Red Wall: How it was lost and how Labour wins it back https://www.facebook.com/watch/live/?v=1128965464107322&external_log_id=a021fc4ae3f03b29e4c869da961ffb90

18. Lavery & Trickett (2020) Northern Discomfort in Tribune https://tribunemag.co.uk/2020/03/northern-discomfort
    Smeeth, R (2020) Podcast: Corbynism: The Post-Mortem. 9: The Red Wall Crumbles https://podcasts.apple.com/za/podcast/9-the-red-wall-crumbles/id1494568978?i=1000468340080

19. Chakrabortty (2019) On the doorstep, Labour faces the question: who do you speak for? The Guardian. https://www.theguardian.com/politics/2019/nov/26/on-the-doorstep-labour-faces-the-question-who-do-you-speak-for

20. Surridge, P (2020) Beyond Brexit: Labour's Structural Problems. https://journals.sagepub.com/doi/pdf/10.1177/2041905820911741

21. Kellner, P (2020) Five crucially important but frequently ignored facts about the 2019 election. https://www.prospectmagazine.co.uk/politics/five-crucially-important-but-frequently-ignored-facts-about-the-2019-election-labour-conservatives-brexit-corbyn-johnson

22. Hunter, P (2011) Winning Back the Five Million. http://www.smith-institute.org.uk/wp-content/uploads/2015/10/Winning-back-the-5-million.pdf

23. Kellner, P (2012) Labour's Lost Votes, YouGov. https://yougov.co.uk/topics/politics/articles-reports/2012/10/22/labours-lost-votes

24. Skelton, D (2013) The working class vote is up for grabs - will it be Labour or the Tories that seizes it? New Statesman. https://www.newstatesman.com/politics/2013/02/working-class-vote-grabs-will-it-be-labour-or-tories-seizes-it

25. Cutts, D., Goodwin, M., Heath, O., & Surridge, P. (2020). Brexit, the 2019 General Election and the Realignment of British Politics. *Political Quarterly, 91*(1), 7-23.

26. Michell and Calvert Jump question the validity of the data from Cutts et al, as it is based on the 2011 census data. They also reproduce the 'falling ladder' analysis using the Standard Occupational Classification data for "elementary", "process", and "sales and customer service" occupations each year from the Annual Population Survey, which reveals a more stable Labour vote share. However, they also note that Labour's vote share has increased substantially in "areas with high blue-collar population shares, particularly in constituencies in cities such as Birmingham, Bradford, Liverpool and Manchester." By definition, if Labour's vote share in blue-collar constituencies has remained stable nationally, but increased substantially in major cities, it must have fallen elsewhere, such as in Red Wall seats.

    Michell, J and Calvert Jump, R (2020) Has Labour Really Lost The Working Class? https://politicalquarterly.blog/2020/03/31/has-labour-really-lost-the-working-class/

27. Burn-Murdoch et al, (2019) How class, turnout and the Brexit party shaped the general election result, Financial Times. https://www.ft.com/content/bc09b70a-1d7e-11ea-97df-cc63de1d73f4#

28. Joseph Rowntree Foundation (2019) Every voter counts: winning over low-income voters. https://www.jrf.org.uk/report/every-voter-counts-winning-over-low-income-voters

    Heath, O & Goodwin, M (2020) Low-income voters, the 2019 General Election and the future of British politics, Joseph Rowntree Foundation. https://www.jrf.org.uk/file/55326/download?token=fqm785hc&filetype=briefing

29. Ibid.

30. Ibid.

31. Ashcroft (2019) How Britain voted and why: My 2019 general election post-vote poll. https://lordashcroftpolls.com/2019/12/how-britain-voted-and-why-my-2019-general-election-post-vote-poll/

32. Surridge, P (2019) The long journey of Labour's voters into the Tory fold, Financial Times. https://www.ft.com/content/7990bd0e-1dc6-11ea-81f0-0c253907d3e0?shareType=nongift

33. Abrams, M (1960) Must Labour Lose? Penguin, London.

34. Trickett, J & Lavery, I (2020) Northern Discomfort, Jacobin. https://images.jacobinmag.com/wp-content/uploads/sites/4/2020/02/29233211/NORTHERN-DISCOMFORT-for-release.pdf

    Smeeth, R (2020) Podcast: Corbynism: The Post-Mortem. 9: The Red Wall Crumbles. https://podcasts.apple.com/za/podcast/9-the-red-wall-crumbles/id1494568978?i=1000468340080

35. Rentoul, J (2020) Gillian Duffy and how the Labour Party lost part of its working-class vote, The Independent. https://www.independent.co.uk/news/uk/politics/gillian-duffy-labour-party-brexit-gordon-brown-working-class-a9486306.html

36. Fabian Society (2018) For the Many?: Understanding and Uniting Labours core supporters. https://fabians.org.uk/publication/for-the-many/

37. Flint, C (2019) Sophy Ridge Podcast - Election Fallout. https://player.fm/series/sophy-ridge-on-sunday/election-fallout-michael-gove-caroline-flint-richard-burgon-ian-blackford

38. Kaonga, G (2020) Pollster exposes Labour Party's 'crumbling red wall' and shift to the north London elite, Daily Express. https://www.express.co.uk/news/uk/1240337/Labour-Party-red-wall-Deborah-Mattinson-London-elite-Politics-Live-news-latest

39. Mattinson, D (2019) The General Election Diaries. https://www.prweek.com/article/1668840/general-election-diaries-britain-normal-again

40. Labour Together (2020) Election Review 2019. https://electionreview.labourtogether.uk/

41. Economist (2019) Who are the conservatives new voters in the north. https://www.economist.com/britain/2019/12/18/who-are-the-conservatives-new-voters-in-the-north

42. Payne (2019) Conservatives plan to break Labour's Red Wall in north-east Wales https://www.ft.com/content/c6356734-ff00-11e9-b7bc-f3fa4e77dd47

43. Kanagasooriam, J (2019) How the Labour party's Red Wall turned blue, Financial Times. https://www.ft.com/content/3b80b2de-1dc2-11ea-81f0-0c253907d3e0

44. Waugh, P (2017) Labour Voters Fear Family, Friends Will 'Disown' Them For Backing Tories. Huffington Post. https://www.huffingtonpost.co.uk/entry/labour-voters-fear-friends-and-family-will-disown-them-for-switching-to-tories-huffpost-edelman-focus-group_uk_5920546e14b03b485cb1e86b

45. Ibid.

46. Surridge, P (2020) Twitter thread, 2005 Labour voters that switched to Conservatives in Red Wall seats. https://twitter.com/p_surridge/status/1262867405111525376

47. Evans and Mellon (2020) The Re-shaping Of Class Voting in the 2019 Election. https://www.britishelectionstudy.com/bes-findings/the-re-shaping-of-class-voting-in-the-2019-election-by-geoffrey-evans-and-jonathan-mellon/#.XmI39ZOTJBw

48. Burgin, R (2020) Copeland by-election ought to have been the canary in the coal mine, Labour List. https://labourlist.org/2020/01/copeland-by-election-ought-to-have-been-the-canary-in-the-coal-mine/
49. Datapraxis (2019) Tory Landslide, Progressives Split. https://www.dataprax.is/tory-landslide-progressives-split
50. Ray, J. (2019) Boris Johnson needs to deliver more than Brexit to keep Labour heartlands blue, ITV. https://www.itv.com/news/2019-12-19/boris-johnson-needs-to-deliver-more-than-brexit-to-keep-labour-heartlands-blue/
51. Hunter, P (2015) Red alert: why Labour lost and what needs to change? http://www.smith-institute.org.uk/wp-content/uploads/2015/08/Red-alert-why-Labour-lost-and-what-needs-to-change.pdf
52. Cadywould, C (2018) Labour in English towns, Policy Network. https://policynetwork.org/wp-content/uploads/2018/05/Labour-in-English-towns_FINAL.pdf
53. Balls, K (2020) Toryism, but not as we know it: an interview with Ben Houchen. The Spectator. https://beta.spectator.co.uk/article/Toryism-but-not-as-we-know-it-an-interview-with-Ben-Houchen
54. Demos (2018) Citizen's Voices. https://demos.co.uk/project/citizens-voices/
55. Ibid
56. Burn-Murdoch et al, (2019) How class, turnout and the Brexit party shaped the general election result, Financial Times. https://www.ft.com/content/bc09b70a-1d7e-11ea-97df-cc63de1d73f4#
57. Grylls, G (2019) Meet the Labour Leavers voting Tory: "I'm upset about what I've got to do," New Statesman. https://www.newstatesman.com/politics/uk/2019/11/meet-labour-leavers-voting-tory-i-m-upset-about-what-i-ve-got-do

6. Labour's Values Disconnect and Cross-Pressured Voters

1. Flint, C (2019) Sophy Ridge Podcast - Election Fallout. https://player.fm/series/sophy-ridge-on-sunday/election-fallout-michael-gove-caroline-flint-richard-burgon-ian-blackford
2. Knapp, A., Wright, Vincent, & ProQuest , issuing body. (2006). *The government and politics of France* (5th ed.). London: Routledge.
3. The UK in a Changing Europe (2020) Big differences on economic and social values between MPs and voters, new academic survey finds. https://ukandeu.ac.uk/big-differences-on-economic-and-social-values-between-mps-and-voters-new-academic-survey-finds/#
4. Ibid.
5. Lavery & Trickett (2020) Northern Discomfort, Tribune. https://tribunemag.co.uk/2020/03/northern-discomfort

6. O'Hara, G (2020) Labour has its post-mortem – but where is the plan for revival? https://capx.co/labour-has-its-post-mortem-but-where-is-the-plan-for-revival/

7. Burgin, R (2020) Copeland by-election ought to have been the canary in the coal mine, Labour List. https://labourlist.org/2020/01/copeland-by-election-ought-to-have-been-the-canary-in-the-coal-mine/

8. Swift, R (2019) Why did Labour lose in the north of England? https://theconversation.com/why-did-labour-lose-in-the-north-of-england-128940

9. Niven A (2019) Why Labour is losing the north, New Statesman. https://www.newstatesman.com/politics/uk/2019/08/why-labour-losing-north

10. Surridge, P (2019) The long journey of Labour's voters into the Tory fold, Financial Times. https://www.ft.com/content/7990bd0e-1dc6-11ea-81f0-0c253907d3e0?shareType=nongift

11. Datapraxis (2019) Tory Landslide, Progressives Split. https://www.dataprax.is/tory-landslide-progressives-split

12. The UK in a Changing Europe (2020) Big differences on economic and social values between MPs and voters, new academic survey finds. https://ukandeu.ac.uk/big-differences-on-economic-and-social-values-between-mps-and-voters-new-academic-survey-finds/#

13. Ibid.

14. Johnson, J (2019) Boris's New Swing Voters and Why They Are Here to Stay. https://www.hanovercomms.com/blog/boriss-new-swing-voters-sceptical-of-business-and-here-to-stay/

15. Labour Together (2020) Election Review 2019. https://electionreview.labourtogether.uk/

16. Chakrabortty, A (2019) On the doorstep, Labour faces the question: who do you speak for? The Guardian. https://www.theguardian.com/politics/2019/nov/26/on-the-doorstep-labour-faces-the-question-who-do-you-speak-for

17. Goodhart, D. (2017). The road to somewhere : The populist revolt and the future of politics. Penguin, Hurst & Co

18. Kinnock, S (2019) Labour's route to power lies in reflecting the communitarian values of its neglected heartlands. https://www.stephenkinnock.co.uk/labours-route-to-power-lies-in-reflecting-the-communitarian-values-of-its-neglected-heartlands/

19. Ibid

20. Koopmans, R., & Zürn, M. (2019). Cosmopolitanism and Communitarianism – How Globalization Is Reshaping Politics in the Twenty-First Century. In P. De Wilde, R. Koopmans, W. Merkel, O. Strijbis, & M. Zürn (Eds.), The Struggle Over Borders: Cosmopolitanism and Communitarianism (pp. 1-34). Cambridge: Cambridge University Press.

21. Goodwin, M (2019) Nine lessons from the election: Boris was lucky - but he also played his hand right. https://www.spectator.co.uk/article/nine-

lessons-from-the-election-boris-was-lucky---but-he-also-played-his-hand-right

22. Ford, R & Goodwin, M (2014). Revolt on the right: Explaining support for the radical right in Britain (Routledge studies in extremism and democracy).

23. Bickerton (2019) Labour's lost working-class voters have gone for good, The Guardian. https://www.theguardian.com/commentis-free/2019/dec/19/labour-working-class-voters-brexit

24. Cutts, D., Goodwin, M., Heath, O., & Surridge, P. (2020). Brexit, the 2019 General Election and the Realignment of British Politics. *Political Quarterly, 91*(1), 7-23.

25. Ibid

26. Ipsos MORI (2019) How Britain voted in the 2019 election. https://www.ipsos.com/ipsos-mori/en-uk/how-britain-voted-2019-election

27. Farrage, N (2019) Tweet. https://twitter.com/nigel_farage/status/1205880267220668416?lang=en

28. Evans and Mellon (2020) The Re-shaping Of Class Voting in the 2019 Election https://www.britishelectionstudy.com/bes-findings/the-re-shaping-of-class-voting-in-the-2019-election-by-geoffrey-evans-and-jonathan-mellon/#.XmI39ZOTJBw

29. Curtis (2017) How Britain voted at the 2017 general election, YouGov. https://yougov.co.uk/topics/politics/articles-reports/2017/06/13/how-britain-voted-2017-general-election

30. Evans and Mellon (2020) The Re-shaping Of Class Voting in the 2019 Election https://www.britishelectionstudy.com/bes-findings/the-re-shaping-of-class-voting-in-the-2019-election-by-geoffrey-evans-and-jonathan-mellon/#.XmI39ZOTJBw

31. Cutts, D., Goodwin, M., Heath, O., & Surridge, P. (2020). Brexit, the 2019 General Election and the Realignment of British Politics. *Political Quarterly, 91*(1), 7-23.

32. Nat Cen (2018) The emotional legacy of Brexit. https://whatuk-thinks.org/eu/wp-content/uploads/2018/10/WUKT-EU-Briefing-Paper-15-Oct-18-Emotional-legacy-paper-final.pdf

33. Datapraxis (2019) Tory Landslide, Progressives Split. https://www.dataprax.is/tory-landslide-progressives-split

34. Skelton, D (2019) Labour's complacency lost it northern seats — the Tories must change to keep them, New Statesman. https://www.new-statesman.com/politics/uk/2019/12/labour-s-complacency-lost-it-north-ern-seats-tories-must-change-keep-them

35. Labour First (2020) Podcast: The Red Wall: How it was lost and how Labour wins it back. https://www.facebook.com/watch/live/?v=1128965464107322&external_log_id=a021fc4ae3f03b29e4c869da961ffb90

36. British Election Study (2019) Explaining Voter Volatility: A summary of the British Election Study. https://www.britishelectionstudy.com/wp-content/uploads/2019/10/Explaining-Voter-Volatility.pdf

37. Hunter, P (2015) Red alert: why Labour lost and what needs to change? http://www.smith-institute.org.uk/wp-content/uploads/2015/08/Red-alert-why-Labour-lost-and-what-needs-to-change.pdf

38. Curtice, J (2018) The Emotional Legacy of Brexit. https://whatuk-thinks.org/eu/wp-content/uploads/2018/10/WUKT-EU-Briefing-Paper-15-Oct-18-Emotional-legacy-paper-final.pdf

39. YouGov (2019) How Britain voted in the 2019 general election. https://yougov.co.uk/topics/politics/articles-reports/2019/12/17/how-britain-voted-2019-general-election

40. Surridge, P (2020) How the Conservatives won the red wall. https://ukan-deu.ac.uk/how-the-conservatives-won-the-red-wall/

41. British Social Attitudes Survey, (2013) https://www.britsocat.com

7. The Importance of Narrative

1. Polkinghorne, D. (1988) *Narrative knowing and the human sciences* (SUNY series in philosophy of the social sciences).

2. Seargeant, P (2020) *The art of political storytelling*, Bloomsbury, London

3. Polletta, F; Callahan, J (2017). "Deep stories, nostalgia narratives, and fake news: Storytelling in the Trump era." *American Journal of Cultural Sociology.* 5 (3): 392–408. doi:10.1057/s41290-017-0037-7.

4. Ganz, M (2015) Public Narrative Worksheet. http://marshallganz.usm-blogs.com/files/2012/08/Public-Narrative-Worksheet-Fall-2013-.pdf

5. Polletta, F (2008) Storytelling in Politics, University of California. http://faculty.sites.uci.edu/polletta/files/2011/03/Contexts-Storytelling-in-Politics.pdf

6. Obama, B (2012) My Biggest Failure Was Not Telling A Story. https://www.youtube.com/watch?v=QXI-rIXoUsk

7. Westen, D (2011) What Happened to Obama? New York Times. https://www.nytimes.com/2011/08/07/opinion/sunday/what-happened-to-obamas-passion.html

8. Prince, G. (1982). Narrative Analysis and Narratology. *New Literary History*, 13(2), 179-188.

9. Maines, D. (1993). Narrative's Moment and Sociology's Phenomena: Toward a Narrative Sociology. *The Sociological Quarterly, 34*(1), 17-38.

10. Davis, J.E. (2002). *Stories of Change: Narrative and Social Movements.* Albany: State University of New York Press. muse.jhu.edu/book/4482.

11. Griffin, L. (1993). Narrative, Event-Structure Analysis, and Causal Interpretation in Historical Sociology. *American Journal of Sociology, 98*(5), 1094-1133.

12. Polkinghorne, D. (1988). Narrative knowing and the human sciences (SUNY series in philosophy of the social sciences).

13. Graef, J., da Silva, R., & Lemay-Hebert, N. (2018): *Narrative, Political*

Violence, and Social Change, Studies in Conflict & Terrorism, DOI:10.1080/1057610X.2018.1452701

14. Briggs, M (2018) Storytelling and politics: How history myths and narratives drive our decisions. https://www.psa.ac.uk/psa/news/storytelling-and-politics-how-history-myths-and-narratives-drive-our-decisions

15. Shenhav, S R (2015) *Analyzing Social Narratives*, New York: Routledge.

16. Hall, S (1973) Encoding and Decoding in the Television Discourse. https://www.birmingham.ac.uk/Documents/college-artslaw/history/cccs/stencilled-occasional-papers/1to8and11to24and38to48/SOP07.pdf

17. Iser, W (1972). The Reading Process: A Phenomenological Approach. *New Literary History*, 3(2), 279-299.

18. Mary Louise Pratt, Toward a speech act theory of literary discourse. Bloomington: Indiana University Press, 1977. Pp. xix 236. *Journal of Linguistics*, 16(1), 110-113.

19. Davis, J (2002) *Stories of Change: Narrative and Social Movements*. State University of New York Press.

20. Mayer, F (2014) Why Stories are Powerful Spurs to Political Action. https://scholars.org/sites/scholars/files/ssn_key_findings_mayer_on_narrative_politics.pdf

21. Rathje, S (2017) The power of framing: It's not what you say, it's how you say it. The Guardian. https://www.theguardian.com/science/head-quarters/2017/jul/20/the-power-of-framing-its-not-what-you-say-its-how-you-say-it

22. Johnson, Fleming, Chazan (2020) Coronavirus: Is Europe losing Italy? Financial Times. https://www.ft.com/content/f21cf708-759e-11ea-ad98-044200cb277f

23. Morrison, P (2018) Column: Linguist George Lakoff on what Democrats don't understand — and Republicans do — about how voters think. LA Times. https://www.latimes.com/opinion/op-ed/la-ol-patt-morrison-george-lakoff-20181128-htmlstory.html

24. Morrison, P (2018) Linguist George Lakoff on what Democrats don't understand — and Republicans do — about how voters think. LA Times. https://www.latimes.com/opinion/op-ed/la-ol-patt-morrison-george-lakoff-20181128-htmlstory.html

25. Anderson, B. (2016). *Imagined communities : Reflections on the origin and spread of nationalism* (Revised ed.).

26. Ibid

27. McAdams, D (1997) *The Stories We Live By: Personal Myths and the Making of the Self*. Guildford Press, London.

28. Potter, M. (2017). Critical junctures: place-based storytelling in the Big Stories, Small Towns participatory documentary project. Media International Australia, 164(1), 117–127. https://doi.org/10.1177/1329878X17694754

29. Mckenzie, L. (2015). *Getting By : Estates, class and culture in austerity Britain*. Bristol: Policy Press.

30. Graef, J., da Silva, R., & Lemay-Hebert, N. (2018): Narrative, Political Violence, and Social Change, *Studies in Conflict & Terrorism*, DOI: 10.1080/1057610X.2018.1452701

31. Waugh (2017) Labour Voters Fear Family, Friends Will 'Disown' Them For Backing Tories. Huffington Post. https://www.huffingtonpost.co.uk/entry/labour-voters-fear-friends-and-family-will-disown-them-for-switching-to-tories-huffpost-edelman-focus-group_uk_59205461e4b03b485cb1e86b

32. Mueller, B (2019) How Labour's Working-Class Vote Crumbled and Its Nemesis Won the North. New York Times. https://www.nytimes.com/2019/12/13/world/europe/uk-election-labour-redwall.html

33. Waugh (2017) Labour Voters Fear Family, Friends Will 'Disown' Them For Backing Tories https://www.huffingtonpost.co.uk/entry/labour-voters-fear-friends-and-family-will-disown-them-for-switching-to-tories-huffpost-edelman-focus-group_uk_59205461e4b03b485cb1e86b

34. Graef, J., Da Silva, R., & Lemay-Hebert, N. (2020). Narrative, Political Violence, and Social Change. *Studies in Conflict & Terrorism: Special Issue: Narrative, Political Violence and Social Change. Guest Editors: Raquel Da Silva, Josefin Graef and Nicolas Lemay-Hébert, 43*(6), 431-443.

35. Hammack, P. L. (2015). Mind, story, and society: The political psychology of narrative. In M. Hanne, W. D. Crano, & J. S. Mio (Eds.), Claremont symposium on applied social psychology series. *Warring with words: Narrative and metaphor in politics* (p. 51–77). Psychology Press.

36. Shiller, R (2019) *Narrative Economics*, Princeton University Press

37. Cialdini, R.B., Rhoads, K.V.L.: Human behavior and the marketplace. *Marketing Research.* 13, 8–13 (2001).

38. Hammack, P (2014) in Hanne, M et al, *Warring with Words: Narrative and Metaphor in Politics* (Claremont Symposium on Applied Social Psychology Series) Psychology Press

39. Mayer , F(2014) Why Stories are Powerful Spurs to Political Action. https://scholars.org/sites/scholars/files/ssn_key_findings_mayer_on_narrative_politics.pdf

40. Ibid

41. Klandermans, B (199). The Social Psychology of Protest. Oxford: Blackwell

8. Political and Public Narratives

1. Seargeant, P (2020) *The art of Political Storytelling*. Bloomsbury, London.

2. Graef, J., da Silva, R., & Lemay-Hebert, N. (2018): Narrative, Political Violence, and Social Change, *Studies in Conflict & Terrorism*, DOI: 10.1080/1057610X.2018.1452701

3. Ganz, M (2011) Public Narrative, Collective Action, and Power. 2011.

http://marshallganz.usmblogs.com/files/2012/08/Public-Narrative-Collective-Action-and-Power.pdf
4. Peston, R (2017) *WTF?* Hodder & Stoughton
5. Baquet, D (2018) The Axe Files [Audio Podcast] Dean Baquet & Marty Baron retrieved from https://player.fm/series/the-axe-files-with-david-axelrod-2046673/ep-264-dean-baquet-marty-baron
6. The North Pole (2019) Podcast. https://browse.entale.co/show/5cd4df34-debc-4560-ac09-3c679d77682c
7. Easton, M (2019) Why vox pops are important, BBC. https://www.bbc.co.uk/news/uk-46946442
8. Daschmann, G. (2000). Vox Pop Polls: The Impact Of Poll Results And Voter Statements In The Media On The Perception Of A Climate Of Opinion. International Journal of Public Opinion Research, 12(2), 160-181.
9. Beckers, K. (2019). What Vox Pops Say and How That Matters: Effects of Vox Pops in Television News on Perceived Public Opinion and Personal Opinion. Journalism & Mass Communication Quarterly, 96(4), 980-1003.
10. Ibid
11. James, Moynihan, Olsen & van Ryzin (2020) Behavioral public performance: Making effective use of metrics about government activity. https://blogs.lse.ac.uk/politicsandpolicy/behavioral-public-performance/
12. Harris, J & Dokomos, J (2019) We spent 10 years talking to people. Here's what it taught us about Britain, The Guardian. https://www.theguardian.com/news/2019/dec/03/anywhere-but-westminster-vox-pops-understanding-uk-political-landscape
13. Johansson, B and Mörtenberg, E,W (2013) Local or Not? The Impact of Political System Factors on Media Election Coverage https://www.hilarispublisher.com/open-access/local-or-not-the-impact-of-political-system-factors-on-media-election-coverage-2165-7912.1000164.pdf
14. Graef, J., da Silva, R., & Lemay-Hebert, N. (2018): Narrative, Political Violence, and Social Change, Studies in Conflict & Terrorism
15. Shenhav, S R (2015) Analyzing Social Narratives, New York: Routledge.
16. Polletta, F; Callahan, J (2017). "Deep stories, nostalgia narratives, and fake news: Storytelling in the Trump era." American Journal of Cultural Sociology. 5 (3): 392–408.
17. Shenhav, Shaul R. (2006). "Political Narratives and Political Reality." International Political Science Review. 27 (3): 245–262.
18. Polletta, F; Callahan, J (2017). "Deep stories, nostalgia narratives, and fake news: Storytelling in the Trump era." American Journal of Cultural Sociology. 5 (3): 392–408.
19. Vonnegut, K (2005) A man without a country, Seven Stories Press
20. Brooker, C (2004) The seven basic plots, Bloomsbury, London
21. Shrimsley, R (2020) The Art of Political Storytelling — how leaders win hearts, Financial Times. https://www.ft.com/content/d0d0f4ec-a4d2-11ea-92e2-cbd9b7e28ee6
22. McKinnon, M (2016) in Klein and Wilson, How to win an election, New

York   Times.   https://www.nytimes.com/video/opin-
ion/100000004216589/how-to-win-an-election.html

23. Ngozi Adichie, C (2009) The danger of a single story, TED. https://www.t-
    ed.com/talks/chimamanda_adichie_the_danger_of_a_single_story/tran-
    script?language=en#t-145080
24. Klein,   E   (2020)   Why   we're   polarized,   Vox.   https://www.vox.-
    com/2020/1/28/21077888/why-were-polarized-media-book-ezra-news
25. Mance, H. (2017) Former Obama adviser Jim Messina under scrutiny
    after   UK   election,   Financial   Times.   https://www.ft.com/con-
    tent/479aeddo-4f5e-11e7-a1f2-db19572361bb
26. Bai, M (2012) Still Waiting for the Narrator in Chief, New York Times.
    https://www.nytimes.com/2012/11/04/magazine/still-waiting-for-the-
    narrator-in-chief.html
27. Hasher, L., Goldstein, D., & Toppino, T. (1977). Frequency and the confer-
    ence of referential validity. Journal of Verbal Learning and Verbal Behav-
    ior, 16(1), 107-112.
28. Polletta, F; Callahan, J (2017). "Deep stories, nostalgia narratives, and fake
    news: Storytelling in the Trump era." American Journal of Cultural Soci-
    ology. 5 (3): 392–408.
29. Bai, M (2012) Still Waiting for the Narrator in Chief, New York Times.
    https://www.nytimes.com/2012/11/04/magazine/still-waiting-for-the-
    narrator-in-chief.html

9. Understanding Social and Political Change

1. Sims, P (2019) How the North was won, The Sun. https://www.thesun.co.
   uk/news/10550284/tory-working-revolution-smashed-red-walls-corbyn-
   heartlands/
2. Hegel, G W. (1874). The Logic. Encyclopaedia of the Philosophical
   Sciences. 2nd Edition. London: Oxford University Pres
3. Sunstein, C (2019) How Change Happens, MIT Press, Boston
4. Elster, J. (1989). Social Norms and Economic Theory. Journal of
   Economic Perspectives, 3(4), 99-117.
5. Sunstein, C (2020) How change happens, LSE lecture. https://www.
   youtube.com/watch?v=_WNQEN8m534&feature=youtu.be
6. Margetts, H., John, P., Hale, S., & Yasseri, T. (2016) Political turbulence :
   how social media shape collective action. New Jersey: Princeton University Press.
7. Sunstein, C (2019) How Change Happens, MIT Press, Boston
8. Sunstein, C (2020) How change happens, LSE lecture https://www.y-
   outube.com/watch?v=_WNQEN8m534&feature=youtu.be
9. Braha, D,. de Aguiar, M (2017) Voting Contagion: Modeling and Analysis
   of a Century of U.S. Presidential Elections, PLoS ONE 12(5): e0177970.
   doi/10.1371/journal.pone.0177970.

10. Thompson, D (2018) Hit Makers: How Things Become Popular. Amazon media, US.

11. Cialdini, R. (2007). Influence : The psychology of persuasion (Rev. ed. ; 1st Collins business essentials ed.). New York: Collins.

12. Cialdini, R. B. (2016). *Pre-Suasion: A Revolutionary Way to Influence and Persuade.* New York: Simon & Schuster.

13. Cialdini, R (2017) Robert Cialdini on how persuasion works in business and politics. https://ftalphaville.ft.com/2017/04/03/2186724/podcast-robert-cialdini-on-how-persuasion-works-in-business-and-politics/

14. Lau in Suhay, E., Grofman, Bernard, & Trechsel, Alexandre H. (2019). The Oxford Handbook of Electoral Persuasion.

15. Cotter in Suhay, E., Grofman, Bernard, & Trechsel, Alexandre H. (2019). The Oxford Handbook of Electoral Persuasion.

16. Ibid.

17. Kunda, Z. (1990). The Case for Motivated Reasoning. Psychological Bulletin, 108(3), 480-498.

18. Buffet, W (2002) Warren Buffet and Charlie Munger: Become a Better Investor by Using Feedback Mechanisms https://finance.yahoo.com/news/warren-buffet-charlie-munger-become-013827950.html

19. Curtice, J (2018) The Emotional Legacy of Brexit. https://whatukthinks.org/eu/wp-content/uploads/2018/10/WUKT-EU-Briefing-Paper-15-Oct-18-Emotional-legacy-paper-final.pdf

20. Cotter in Suhay, E., Grofman, Bernard, & Trechsel, Alexandre H. (2019). The Oxford Handbook of Electoral Persuasion.

21. Child, D (2019) Labour's Red Wall creaks as loyal voters consider other parties, Aljazeera. https://www.aljazeera.com/news/2019/12/labour-red-wall-creaks-loyal-voters-parties-191207144943188.html

22. Mason, P (2019) In Leigh, my hometown, far right propaganda and hostility to Jeremy Corbyn could unseat Labour. https://inews.co.uk/opinion/polling-general-election-2019-paul-mason-leigh-369891

23. Waugh, P (2017) Labour Voters Fear Family, Friends Will 'Disown' Them For Backing Tories. Huffington Post. https://www.huffingtonpost.co.uk/entry/labour-voters-fear-friends-and-family-will-disown-them-for-switching-to-tories-huffpost-edelman-focus-group_uk_59205461e4b03b485cb1e86b

24. Kellner, P (2015) We got it wrong. Why? YouGov. https://yougov.co.uk/topics/politics/articles-reports/2015/05/11/we-got-it-wrong-why

25. While the Market Research Society has previously found that 'shy Tories' explain part of the error in opinion polls nationally, the British Polling Council found that this factor was marginal in 2015 and the polling errors were due mainly to unrepresentative polling samples.

26. Larson et al, (2020) Free Expression and Constructuve Dialogue at the University of North Carolinia Chapel Hill. https://fecdsurveyreport.web.unc.edu/files/2020/02/UNC-Free-Expression-Report.pdf

27. Balls, K (2020) Toryism, but not as we know it: an interview with Ben

Houchen, The Spectator. https://beta.spectator.co.uk/article/Toryism-but-not-as-we-know-it-an-interview-with-Ben-Houchen

10. Developing an Effective Election Campaign Narrative

1. McKinnon, M (2017) It's Storytelling, Stupid: What Made Donald Trump Smarter Than Hillary Clinton. https://www.thedailybeast.com/its-storytelling-stupid-what-made-donald-trump-smarter-than-hillary-clinton

2. Cruddas, Pecorelli & Rutherford (2016) Report of the independent inquiry into why Labour lost in 2015. http://www.cultdyn.co.uk/ART067736u/313245238-Labour-s-Future-19-05-16.pdf

3. Cummings (2018) On the referendum 24I: new research on Facebook & 'psychographic' microtargeting. https://dominiccummings.com/tag/polls/

4. Shaw, E (2019) How Labour failed to connect with the British working class. https://theconversation.com/how-labour-failed-to-connect-with-the-british-working-class-128082

5. Gould, P. (2011). The unfinished revolution : How New Labour changed British politics for ever. London: Abacus.

6. Butler, D & Kavanagh, D (1988) The British General Election of 1987. Palgrave.

7. Dalton, R J (2016) Party Identification and Its Implications. Oxford Research Encyclopedia of Politics. DOI: 10.1093/acrefore/9780190228637.013.72
    Dassonneville, R., & Hooghe, M. (2017). Economic indicators and electoral volatility: Economic effects on electoral volatility in Western Europe, 1950–2013. Comp Eur Polit,15(6), 919-943.

8. Qvortrup (2016) Farewell to focus groups. https://ukandeu.ac.uk/farewell-to-focus-groups/

9. Gould, P. (2011). The unfinished revolution : How New Labour changed British politics for ever. London: Abacus.

10. Ibid

11. Qvortrup (2016) Farewell to focus groups. https://ukandeu.ac.uk/farewell-to-focus-groups/

12. Howell, S (2018) Game Changer - Eight Weeks That Transformed British Politics, Headline Accent

13. Issenberg, S. (2013). The victory lab : The secret science of winning campaigns (First Paperback ed.).

14. Gould, P. (2011). The unfinished revolution : How New Labour changed British politics for ever. London: Abacus.

15. Downs, A. (1957). An Economic Theory of Political Action in a Democracy. Journal of Political Economy, 65(2), 135-150.

16. Mullen, T (2019). General election 2019: "Leigh's voters on 'fantastic'

seismic shift," BBC News. https://www.bbc.co.uk/news/election-2019-50781738

17. Cialdini, R. (2007). *Influence : The psychology of persuasion* (Rev. ed. ; 1st Collins business essentials ed.). New York: Collins.

18. Goodhart, D. (2017). *The road to somewhere : The populist revolt and the future of politics*. Penguin, Hurst & Co

19. Hooghe and Marks (2017) Cleavage theory meets Europe's crises: Lipset, Rokkan, and the transnational cleavage. https://www.eui.eu/Documents/RSCAS/JMF-25-Presentation/Hooghe-Marks-Cleavage-theory-meets-Europes-crises-Lipset-Rokkan-and-the-transnational-cleavage.pdf

20. Marks, G. and Wilson, C. (2000) 'The past in the present: a cleavage theory of party response to European Integration', *British Journal of Political Science* 30(3): 433–59.

21. Hooghe and Marks (2017) Cleavage theory meets Europe's crises: Lipset, Rokkan, and the transnational cleavage. https://www.eui.eu/Documents/RSCAS/JMF-25-Presentation/Hooghe-Marks-Cleavage-theory-meets-Europes-crises-Lipset-Rokkan-and-the-transnational-cleavage.pdf

22. Kalla, J., & Broockman, D. (2018). The Minimal Persuasive Effects of Campaign Contact in General Elections: Evidence from 49 Field Experiments. *American Political Science Review*, 112(1), 148-166.

23. Jacobson, G. (2015). How Do Campaigns Matter? *Annual Review of Political Science*, 18(1), 31-47.

24. Campbell, A., Converse, P.E., Miller, W.E., & Stokes, D.E. (1980) *The American Voter* University of Chicago Press.

25. Kalla, J., & Broockman, D. (2018). The Minimal Persuasive Effects of Campaign Contact in General Elections: Evidence from 49 Field Experiments. *American Political Science Review*, 112(1), 148-166.

26. Shaw D. (2008) Swing voting and U.S. presidential elections. In Mayer (2008) *The making of presidential candidates 2008* pp. 75–101, Lanham, Md.: Rowman & Littlefield.

    Gerber, A., & Green, D. (2000). The Effects of Canvassing, Telephone Calls, and Direct Mail on Voter Turnout: A Field Experiment. *The American Political Science Review, 94*(3), 653-663.

27. Jacobson, G. (2015). How Do Campaigns Matter? *Annual Review of Political Science, 18*(1), 31-47.

28. Hansen, K., M., Slothuus, R., & Stubager, R. (2012). Late Deciders: Changing Patterns in Which Voters Make Up Their Mind during Campaigns? In J. Blom-Hansen, C. Green-Pedersen, & S-E. Skaaning (Eds.), *Democracy, Elections and Political Parties* (pp. 130-137). Aarhus: Politica.

29. Dalton, R J (2016) Party Identification and Its Implications. *Oxford Research Encyclopedia of Politics*. DOI: 10.1093/acrefore/9780190228637.013.72

    Dassonneville, R., & Hooghe, M. (2017). Economic indicators and electoral volatility: Economic effects on electoral volatility in Western Europe, 1950–2013. *Comp Eur Polit*,15(6), 919-943.

Issenberg, S. (2013). *The victory lab : The secret science of winning campaigns* (First Paperback ed.).

30. Gould, P. (2011). *The unfinished revolution : How New Labour changed British politics for ever.* London: Abacus.

31. Johann, D,. Kleinen-von Königslöw, K,. Kritzinger, S. & Thomas K (2018) Intra-Campaign Changes in Voting Preferences: The Impact of Media and Party Communication, *Political Communication*, 35:2, 261-286.

32. Fournier, P., Nadeau, R., Blais, A., Gidengil, E., & Nevitte, N. (2004). Time-of-voting decision and susceptibility to campaign effects. *Electoral Studies*, 23(4), 661–681.

33. Dalton, R J (2016) Party Identification and Its Implications. *Oxford Research Encyclopedia of Politics.* DOI: 10.1093/acrefore/9780190228637.013.72

34. British Election Study (2017) The 2017 General Election: Volatile Voting, Random Results retrieved from https://www.electoral-reform.org.uk/latest-news-and-research/publications/the-2017-general-election-report/

35. New Statesman (2018) Why did so many voters switch parties between 2015 and 2017? https://www.newstatesman.com/politics/uk/2017/09/why-did-so-many-voters-switch-parties-between-2015-and-2017

36. Dalton, R J (2016) Party Identification and Its Implications. *Oxford Research Encyclopedia of Politics.* DOI: 10.1093/acrefore/9780190228637.013.72

37. European Consortium for Political Research (2018) New Parties in Europe. https://ecpr.eu/Events/SectionDetails.aspx?SectionID=778&EventID=115

38. Jacobson, G. (2015). How Do Campaigns Matter? *Annual Review of Political Science*, 18(1), 31-47.

39. Gerber, A., & Green, D. (2000). The Effects of Canvassing, Telephone Calls, and Direct Mail on Voter Turnout: A Field Experiment. *The American Political Science Review*, 94(3), 653-663.

40. Bond RM, Fariss CJ, Jones JJ, et al. (2012) A 61-million-person experiment in social influence and political mobilization. *Nature.* 2012;489(7415):295–298. doi:10.1038/nature11421

41. Scammell, M(2014) *Consumer Democracy: The Marketing Of Politics.* New York, NY USA: Cambridge University Press.

11. The 2019 Election: An Overview of the Major Party Campaigns

1. Staunton, D, (2019) The inside story of how Boris Johnson won the UK election, Irish Times. https://www.irishtimes.com/news/world/uk/the-inside-story-of-how-boris-johnson-won-the-uk-election-1.4114943?mode=amp

2. Cummings, D (2017) How the Brexit campaign was won, The Spectator.

https://blogs.spectator.co.uk/2017/01/dominic-cummings-brexit-referendum-won/

3. Payne, S (2019) UK general election: Can Boris Johnson break Labour's 'red wall'? Financial Times. https://www.ft.com/content/fbd00ed6-ffd1-11e9-be59-e49b2a136b8d

4. McElvoy (2020) The inside story of election 2019, BBC. https://www.bbc.co.uk/programmes/m000f5rr

5. Cummings, D (2017) How the Brexit campaign was won, The Spectator. https://blogs.spectator.co.uk/2017/01/dominic-cummings-brexit-referendum-won/

6. Staunton, D, (2019) The inside story of how Boris Johnson won the UK election, Irish Times. https://www.irishtimes.com/news/world/uk/the-inside-story-of-how-boris-johnson-won-the-uk-election-1.4114943?mode=amp

7. Thomson, A. (2019) From manifestos to mantras: only one political message is cutting through, The Times. https://www.thetimes.co.uk/article/from-manifestos-to-mantras-only-one-political-message-is-cutting-through-wqpwtrvdn

8. Swinford, S (2019) Election 2019: Isaac Levido secured Tory triumph with skill and sharp slogan, The Times. https://www.thetimes.co.uk/edition/news/election-2019-isaac-levido-secured-tory-triumph-with-skill-and-sharp-slogan-ddg2hot5g

9. Labour Together (2020) Election Review 2019. https://electionreview.labourtogether.uk/

10. Cowley & Ford (2019) Sex, Lies and Politics: The Secret Influences That Drive our Political Choices. Biteback Publishing

11. Crampton, R (2019) Labour's Red Wall collapsed along faultline of broken towns, The Times. https://www.thetimes.co.uk/article/labour-s-red-wall-collapsed-along-faultline-of-broken-towns-npzhvjnkb

12. Green, M (2019) 'Workington man' is just the latest depressing political caricature, Financial Times. https://www.ft.com/content/9f8e831e-fafe-11e9-98fd-4d6c20050229

13. Cooney, C (2019) '1970S CLICHE' Workington Man hits back at 'patronising stereotype' after election experts say Northern voters hold keys to No10, The Sun. https://www.thesun.co.uk/news/10246693/workington-man-patronising-stereotype-election-northern-voters/

14. Burrows, T (2019) So farewell then, Workington man ... we hardly knew you, The Guardian. https://www.theguardian.com/commentisfree/2019/nov/22/workington-man-voter-caricature-essex-man

15. Payne, S (2019) 'New dawn' as Conservatives turn Redcar into Bluecar, Financial Times. https://www.ft.com/content/0592a45a-1dab-11ea-97df-cc63de1d73f4

16. Goodwin, M (2020) Presentation to Labour MPs January 15, 2020 http://www.matthewjgoodwin.org/uploads/6/4/0/2/64026337/presentation_to_labour_-_jan_15.pdf

17. IGC (2019) Northern Discomfort: Why Labour lost the General Election https://institute.global/tony-blair/northern-discomfort-why-labour-lost-general-election

18. Bale et al (2016) Middle-class university graduates will decide the future of the Labour Party. https://esrcpartymembersproject.org/2016/07/18/middle-class-university-graduates-will-decide-the-future-of-the-labour-party/

19. Goodwin, M (2020) Presentation to Labour MPs January 15, 2020 http://www.matthewjgoodwin.org/uploads/6/4/0/2/64026337/presentation_to_labour__-_jan_15.pdf

20. Perraudin, F (2019) Jeremy Corbyn reveals dossier 'proving NHS up for sale', The Guardian. https://www.theguardian.com/society/2019/nov/27/jeremy-corbyn-reveals-dossier-proving-nhs-up-for-sale

21. Pogrund, G (2019) Tweet, first draft of Labour's grid for a Brexit election. https://twitter.com/Gabriel_Pogrund/status/1188178898598748161

22. Labour Together (2020) Election Review 2019. https://electionreview.labourtogether.uk/

23. Williams, P (2020) Listening to Voters. https://www.twitlonger.com/show/n_1sr4lc2

24. Ashcroft (2020) Diagnosis Of Defeat Labour's turn to smell the coffee https://lordashcroftpolls.com/wp-content/uploads/2020/02/DIAGNOSIS-OF-DEFEAT-LORD-ASHCROFT-POLLS-1.pdf

25. Swinford, S (2019) Election 2019: Isaac Levido secured Tory triumph with skill and sharp slogan, The Times. https://www.thetimes.co.uk/edition/news/election-2019-isaac-levido-secured-tory-triumph-with-skill-and-sharp-slogan-ddg2h0t5g

26. Rodgers, S (2019) "I don't think our narrative was good enough," says McDonnell, Labour List. https://labourlist.org/2019/12/i-dont-think-our-narrative-was-good-enough-says-mcdonnell/

27. Gould, P. (2011). The unfinished revolution : How New Labour changed British politics for ever. London: Abacus.

28. Shaw, E (2019) How Labour failed to connect with the British working class. https://theconversation.com/how-labour-failed-to-connect-with-the-british-working-class-128082

29. Institute for Fiscal Studies (2019) Labour's nationalisation policy. https://www.ifs.org.uk/publications/14622

30. Brand, P (2019) Breaking news Tweet. https://twitter.com/PaulBrandITV/status/1184772053636964352

31. New Statesman (2019) Leader: The Labour Party's Brexit confusion https://www.newstatesman.com/politics/uk/2019/09/leader-labour-party-s-brexit-confusion

32. BBC (2019) Thornberry on Brexit: 'I'd negotiate a deal... but campaign against it.' https://www.bbc.co.uk/news/av/uk-politics-49605019/thornberry-on-brexit-i-d-negotiate-a-deal-but-campaign-against-it

33. Drury, C (2019) 'I feel dirty – but Labour took us for granted': Why Work-

ington Man has no regrets about voting Tory. https://www.independent.-co.uk/news/uk/politics/general-election-results-boris-johnson-conservatives-workington-man-a9245496.html

34. Sims, P (2019) How the North was won, The Sun. https://www.thesun.co.uk/news/10550284/tory-working-revolution-smashed-red-walls-corbyn-heartlands/

35. Malnick, E (2019) How strategy borrowed from Dominic Cummings's Vote Leave wooed voters to Tories https://www.telegraph.co.uk/politics/2019/12/14/strategy-borrowed-vote-leave-wooed-voters-tories/

36. Stiff, J., & Mongeau, Paul A. (2002). Persuasive communication. (2nd ed. / James B. Stiff and Paul A. Mongeau. ed.). New York, London: Guilford.

37. Smith, M (2019) Labour economic policies are popular, so why aren't Labour? YouGov. https://yougov.co.uk/topics/politics/articles-reports/2019/11/12/labour-economic-policies-are-popular-so-why-arent-

38. Rayner, T (2018) Salisbury attack: 'Sheer fury' at Corbyn's response to spy poisoning, Sky News. https://news.sky.com/story/salisbury-attack-jeremy-corbyn-accused-of-appeasement-towards-russia-11289753

39. Ibid.

40. Skelton, D (2013) The working class vote is up for grabs - will it be Labour or the Tories that seizes it? New Statesman. https://www.newstatesman.com/politics/2013/02/working-class-vote-grabs-will-it-be-labour-or-tories-seizes-it

41. Loughborough (2019) UK wide television and print media reporting of the 2019 UK General Election. https://www.lboro.ac.uk/news-events/general-election/report-1/

42. Smith, M (2019) Labour economic policies are popular, so why aren't Labour? YouGov. https://yougov.co.uk/topics/politics/articles-reports/2019/11/12/labour-economic-policies-are-popular-so-why-arent-

43. IGC, (2019) Northern Discomfort: Why Labour lost the General Election. https://institute.global/tony-blair/northern-discomfort-why-labour-lost-general-election

44. Labour Together (2020) Election Review 2019. https://electionreview.labourtogether.uk/

45. IGC, (2019) Northern Discomfort: Why Labour lost the General Election. https://institute.global/tony-blair/northern-discomfort-why-labour-lost-general-election

46. Ashcroft (2020) DIAGNOSIS OF DEFEAT Labour's turn to smell the coffee. https://lordashcroftpolls.com/wp-content/uploads/2020/02/DIAGNOSIS-OF-DEFEAT-LORD-ASHCROFT-POLLS-1.pdf

47. Williams, J (2019) 'Don't vote Labour' warn former Labour MPs in extraordinary eleventh hour election ad, Manchester Evening News. https://www.manchestereveningnews.co.uk/news/greater-manchester-news/dont-vote-labour-warn-former-17397217

48. Ashcroft (2020) DIAGNOSIS OF DEFEAT Labour's turn to smell the

coffee. https://lordashcroftpolls.com/wp-content/uploads/2020/02/
DIAGNOSIS-OF-DEFEAT-LORD-ASHCROFT-POLLS-1.pdf

49. Ashcroft (2020) DIAGNOSIS OF DEFEAT Labour's turn to smell the
coffee. https://lordashcroftpolls.com/wp-content/uploads/2020/02/
DIAGNOSIS-OF-DEFEAT-LORD-ASHCROFT-POLLS-1.pdf

50. Ibid.

51. Howell, S (2019) Tweet.
https://twitter.com/FromSteveHowell/status/1208750678195232769

52. Shipman, Pogrund and Wheeler (2019) General election 2019: Labour
and Lib Dems jettison old strategies — and Tories fear their lead could
go pop. Sunday Times. https://www.thetimes.co.uk/article/general-elec-
tion-2019-labour-and-lib-dems-jettison-old-strategies-and-tories-fear-
their-lead-could-go-pop-dr96ppwbq

53. Payne & Pickard (2019) The campaign teams behind Jeremy Corbyn and
Boris Johnson, Financial Times. https://www.ft.com/content/8610dc48-
0148-11ea-b7bc-f3fa4e77dd47

54. Pogrund, G (2019) Tweet of Murphy speech to Labour campaign. https://
twitter.com/Gabriel_Pogrund/status/1205301163786199041

55. Pogrund, G (2019) Twitter.
https://twitter.com/Gabriel_Pogrund/status/1208503645584666626

56. Brickell, P (2019) Twitter.
https://twitter.com/Phil_Brickell/status/1208821887326990336

57. Shipman, Pogrund and Wheeler (2019) General election 2019: Labour
and Lib Dems jettison old strategies — and Tories fear their lead could
go pop. Sunday Times. https://www.thetimes.co.uk/article/general-elec-
tion-2019-labour-and-lib-dems-jettison-old-strategies-and-tories-fear-
their-lead-could-go-pop-dr96ppwbq

58. Rodgers, S (2019) How Labour Lost the Red Wall, Politics Home.
https://www.politicshome.com/news/article/how-labour-lost-
the-red-wall

59. Labour Together (2020) Election Review 2019. https://electionre-
view.labourtogether.uk/

60. McElvoy (2020) The inside story of election 2019, BBC. https://www.bbc.-
co.uk/programmes/m000f5rr

61. Watson, I (2020) General election 2019: Labour to change strategy with
two weeks to go, BBC News. https://www.bbc.co.uk/news/election-2019-
50580699

62. Thornhill, D (2020) 2019 Election Review, Liberal Democrats. https://
www.libdems.org.uk/2019-election-review

63. Cutts, D., Goodwin, M., Heath, O., & Surridge, P. (2020). Brexit, the 2019
General Election and the Realignment of British Politics. *Political Quarterly, 91*(1), 7-23.

64. Burn-Murdoch et al, (2019) How class, turnout and the Brexit party
shaped the general election result, Financial Times. https://www.ft.-
com/content/bc09b70a-1d7e-11ea-97df-cc63de1d73f4#

65. Ibid.
66. Fisher, S D, (2004) Definition and measurement of tactical voting: the role of rational choice.' British Journal of Political Science 34 152-166
67. Fisher, S. D. (2000) Intuition versus formal theory: tactical voting in England 1987–1997, Paper prepared for APSA Annual Meeting, Washington, DC, 31 August–September.
68. Johnston, R., & Pattie, C. (2011). Tactical Voting at the 2010 British General Election: Rational Behaviour in Local Contexts? Environment and Planning A, 43(6), 1323-1340.
69. Hanretty, C (2019) The effects of tactical voting sites. https://medium.com/@chrishanretty/the-effects-of-tactical-voting-sites-4d264d8ef89e

12. Red Wall Public Narratives and the Labour Party In 2019

1. Kirby, D (2019) General election 2019: Meet the ex-miners who are planning to vote Tory in Bolsover. https://inews.co.uk/news/general-election-2019-miners-vote-tory-bolsover-derbyshire-shirebrook-brexit-1262531
2. Daschmann, G. (2000). Vox Pop Polls: The Impact Of Poll Results And Voter Statements In The Media On The Perception Of A Climate Of Opinion. International Journal of Public Opinion Research, 12(2), 160-181.
3. Mckenzie, L. (2015). Getting By : Estates, class and culture in austerity Britain. Bristol: Policy Press.
    Mckenzie, L. (2017). The class politics of prejudice: Brexit and the land of no–hope and glory. British Journal of Sociology, 68(S1), S265-S280.
4. Gibbon, (2020) Focus group: Can Tories win over Labour supporters who back Leave? https://www.youtube.com/watch?v=Ry9SMUurM_k
5. Sims, P (2019) How the North was won, The Sun. https://www.thesun.co.uk/news/10550284/tory-working-revolution-smashed-red-walls-corbyn-heartlands/
6. Kirby, D (2019) 'I voted Labour until Jeremy Corbyn became leader': Meet voters in former mining community of Blyth Valley who chose Boris Johnson. https://inews.co.uk/news/long-reads/general-election-result-blyth-valley-voters-mining-community-boris-johnson-1341193
7. Ashcroft (2020) DIAGNOSIS OF DEFEAT Labour's turn to smell the coffee https://lordashcroftpolls.com/wp-content/uploads/2020/02/DIAGNOSIS-OF-DEFEAT-LORD-ASHCROFT-POLLS-1.pdf
8. Ibid.
9. Bates, L (2019) Lisa Nandy: "There are huge swathes of the country that are now up for grabs" Politics Home https://www.politicshome.com/the-house/article/lisa-nandy-there-are-huge-swathes-of-the-country-that-are-now-up-for-grabs
10. Crampton, R (2019) Labour's Red Wall collapsed along faultline of

broken towns https://www.thetimes.co.uk/article/labour-s-red-wall-collapsed-along-faultline-of-broken-towns-npzhvjnkb

11. Glaze, B (2020) How did Jeremy Corbyn's Labour lose Tony Blair's old seat of Sedgefield? Daily Mirror. https://www.mirror.co.uk/news/politics/how-jeremy-corbyns-labour-lose-21423488

12. Waller, J (2019) Corbyn's lack of pride and support for armed forces cost him votes in Grimsby says Melanie Onn. Grimsby Telegraph. https://www.grimsbytelegraph.co.uk/news/grimsby-news/corbyns-lack-pride-support-armed-3672312

13. Ibid.

14. Flint, C (2019) Sophy Ridge Podcast - Election Fallout. https://player.fm/series/sophy-ridge-on-sunday/election-fallout-michael-gove-caroline-flint-richard-burgon-ian-blackford

15. English Labour Network (2020) General Election 2019: How Labour lost England. https://englishlabournetwork.files.wordpress.com/2020/02/ge2019-how-labour-lost-england-pdf.pdf

16. Ibid

17. Ibid

18. Goodhart, D. (2017). The road to somewhere : The populist revolt and the future of politics. Hurst & Co

19. English Labour Network (2020) General Election 2019: How Labour lost England https://englishlabournetwork.files.wordpress.com/2020/02/ge2019-how-labour-lost-england-pdf.pdf

20. Ashcroft (2020) DIAGNOSIS OF DEFEAT Labour's turn to smell the coffee https://lordashcroftpolls.com/wp-content/uploads/2020/02/DIAGNOSIS-OF-DEFEAT-LORD-ASHCROFT-POLLS-1.pdf

21. Nanan-Sen, S (2019) Lifelong Labour voters reveal why they 'switched from red to blue' this election, Daily Express. https://www.express.co.uk/news/uk/1216904/Labour-Party-Conservative-Party-General-Election-Boris-Johnson

22. Mullen, T (2019)General election 2019: Leigh's voters on 'fantastic' seismic shift, BBC News. https://www.bbc.co.uk/news/election-2019-50781738

23. Ashcroft (2020) DIAGNOSIS OF DEFEAT Labour's turn to smell the coffee https://lordashcroftpolls.com/wp-content/uploads/2020/02/DIAGNOSIS-OF-DEFEAT-LORD-ASHCROFT-POLLS-1.pdf

24. Curtis, C (2020) New Tory voters think Labour left them, not the other way around, The Times. https://www.thetimes.co.uk/article/new-tory-voters-think-labour-left-them-not-the-other-way-around-f0j5r7w6p

25. Hardman, I (2019) The Tory MPs who broke down the 'red wall'. Podcast. https://podcasts.apple.com/ec/podcast/the-tory-mps-who-broke-down-the-red-wall/id1101754136?i=1000460402739

26. Ainsley, C & Menon, A (2019) We asked people from deprived areas what matters to them after Brexit - this is what they told us. https://inews.co.uk/opinion/comment/we-asked-people-from-deprived-areas-what-matters-to-them-after-brexit-this-is-what-they-told-us-497470

27. Jennings, W (2017) Understanding public attitudes, Centre for Towns. https://www.centrefortowns.org/blog/17-understanding-public-attitudes

28. Green E (2019) Defeated Grimsby MP Melanie Onn talks voters and Labour Party. https://www.shoutoutuk.org/2019/12/20/defeated-grimsby-mp-melanie-onn-talks-voters-and-labour-party/

29. Ibid

30. Platt, J (2019) Labour forgot towns like mine, and that's why I lost my seat. It's time to start listening again. https://www.independent.co.uk/voices/jo-platt-labour-election-result-lost-seats-leigh-northern-towns-a9252041.html

31. Burgin, R (2020) Copeland by-election ought to have been the canary in the coal mine. https://labourlist.org/2020/01/copeland-by-election-ought-to-have-been-the-canary-in-the-coal-mine/

32. Smith, A (2019) U.K. election: How Boris Johnson's Conservatives won Labour's Red Wall heartlands, NBC. https://www.nbcnews.com/news/world/u-k-election-how-conservatives-won-labour-s-red-wall-n1101771

33. Child, D (2019) Labour's Red Wall creaks as loyal voters consider other parties, Aljazeera. https://www.aljazeera.com/news/2019/12/labour-red-wall-creaks-loyal-voters-parties-191207144943188.html

34. Mullen, T (2019). General election 2019: "Leigh's voters on 'fantastic' seismic shift," BBC News. https://www.bbc.co.uk/news/election-2019-50781738

35. Kirby, D (2019) General election 2019: Meet the ex-miners who are planning to vote Tory in Bolsover. https://inews.co.uk/news/general-election-2019-miners-vote-tory-bolsover-derbyshire-shirebrook-brexit-1262531

36. Ibid

37. Glaze, B (2020) How did Jeremy Corbyn's Labour lose Tony Blair's old seat of Sedgefield? Daily Mirror. https://www.mirror.co.uk/news/politics/how-jeremy-corbyns-labour-lose-21423488

38. Hall, D & Kellaway, B (2019) Furious residents of Grimsby swing seat on why they're shunning Labour after town left to sink into decay. https://www.thesun.co.uk/news/10400145/brexit-party-campaign-grimsby-labour-christopher-barker/

39. Johnson, B (2019) Speech in Downing Street calling the 2019 Election. YouTube https://www.youtube.com/watch?v=kSNQcZcK1hM

40. Rodgers, S (2019) How Labour Lost the Red Wall. https://www.politicshome.com/news/article/how-labour-lost-the-red-wall

41. Halliday et al (2019) 'They're getting their just deserts': how traditional voters ditched Labour, The Guardian. https://www.theguardian.com/politics/2019/dec/13/theyre-getting-their-just-desserts-how-traditional-voters-ditched-labour

42. Drury, C (2019) 'I feel dirty – but Labour took us for granted': Why Workington Man has no regrets about voting Tory. https://www.independent.

co.uk/news/uk/politics/general-election-results-boris-johnson-conservatives-workington-man-a9245496.html

43. Ibid.

44. Ashcroft (2020) DIAGNOSIS OF DEFEAT Labour's turn to smell the coffee https://lordashcroftpolls.com/wp-content/uploads/2020/02/DIAGNOSIS-OF-DEFEAT-LORD-ASHCROFT-POLLS-1.pdf

45. Ibid.

46. Sims, P (2019) How the North was won, The Sun. https://www.thesun.co.uk/news/10550284/tory-working-revolution-smashed-red-walls-corbyn-heartlands/

47. Clyne (2019) Reflections on our defeat and the challenge ahead. https://eyalclyne.wordpress.com/2019/12/13/reflections-on-our-defeat-and-the-challenge-ahead/

48. Gibbon, (2020) Focus group: Can Tories win over Labour supporters who back Leave? https://www.youtube.com/watch?v=Ry9SMUurM_k

49. Langley, R (2019) My grandad hated Thatcher and the Tories. Here's why he voted for Boris. The Spectator. https://blogs.spectator.co.uk/2019/12/my-grandad-hated-thatcher-and-the-tories-heres-why-he-voted-for-boris/

50. Ainsley, C. (2018). The new working class : How to win hearts, minds and votes. Policy Press. Bristol.

51. Jones, O (2011) Chavs: The demonisation of the working class. London, Verso.

52. Mason, P (2019) Twitter https://twitter.com/paulmasonnews/status/1205247632135872516

53. IGC, (2019) Northern Discomfort: Why Labour lost the General Election. https://institute.global/tony-blair/northern-discomfort-why-labour-lost-general-election

54. Glaze, B (2020) How did Jeremy Corbyn's Labour lose Tony Blair's old seat of Sedgefield? Daily Mirror. https://www.mirror.co.uk/news/politics/how-jeremy-corbyns-labour-lose-21423488

55. Grylls (2019) Meet the Labour Leavers voting Tory: "I'm upset about what I've got to do," New Statesman. https://www.newstatesman.com/politics/uk/2019/11/meet-labour-leavers-voting-tory-i-m-upset-about-what-i-ve-got-do

56. Kirkby, D (2019) 'I voted Labour until Jeremy Corbyn became leader': Meet voters in former mining community of Blyth Valley who chose Boris Johnson. https://inews.co.uk/news/long-reads/general-election-result-blyth-valley-voters-mining-community-boris-johnson-1341193

57. Gibbon, (2020) Focus group: Can Tories win over Labour supporters who back Leave? https://www.youtube.com/watch?v=Ry9SMUurM_k

58. Ipsos Mori (2019) Ipsos MORI's new Political Monitor poll reveals Jeremy Corbyn now has the lowest net satisfaction ratings of any opposition leader since the survey began in 1977. https://www.ipsos.com/ipsos-

mori/en-uk/jeremy-corbyn-has-lowest-leadership-satisfaction-rating-any-opposition-leader-1977

59. Bale quoted in Child, D (2019) Labour's Red Wall creaks as loyal voters consider other parties, Aljazeera. https://www.aljazeera.com/news/2019/12/labour-red-wall-creaks-loyal-voters-parties-191207144943188.html

60. Ibid.

61. Coastes, S (2018) John Woodcock abandons Labour calling Jeremy Corbyn a 'clear risk to national security', The Times. https://www.thetimes.co.uk/article/mp-john-woodcock-abandons-labour-calling-jeremy-corbyn-a-clear-risk-to-national-security-as-pm-mqz38rdvd

62. Leatherhead, D (2019) Cafe politics in coal country, BBC. https://www.bbc.co.uk/news/extra/ALSU1CqK3U/election-2019-battleground-bishop-auckland

63. Glaze, B (2020) How did Jeremy Corbyn's Labour lose Tony Blair's old seat of Sedgefield? Daily Mirror. https://www.mirror.co.uk/news/politics/how-jeremy-corbyns-labour-lose-21423488

64. Langley, R (2019) My grandad hated Thatcher and the Tories. Here's why he voted for Boris, The Spectator. https://blogs.spectator.co.uk/2019/12/my-grandad-hated-thatcher-and-the-tories-heres-why-he-voted-for-boris/

65. Labour First (2020) Podcast: The Red Wall: How it was lost and how Labour wins it back. https://www.facebook.com/watch/live/?v=1128965464107322&external_log_id=a021fc4ae3f03b29e4c869da961ffb90

66. Demos (2018) Citizen's Voices. https://demos.co.uk/project/citizens-voices/

67. Drury, C (2019) 'I feel dirty – but Labour took us for granted': Why Workington Man has no regrets about voting Tory. https://www.independent.co.uk/news/uk/politics/general-election-results-boris-johnson-conservatives-workington-man-a9245496.html

68. Smith, S (2019) General election 2019: Why Labour is lost in the middle in Scotland, BBC. https://www.bbc.co.uk/news/uk-scotland-scotland-politics-50405399

69. Blakely, A (2019) Wigan General Election 2019 results in full, Manchester Evening News. https://www.manchestereveningnews.co.uk/news/uk-news/lisa-nandy-wigan-labour-17389814

70. IGC, (2019) Northern Discomfort: Why Labour lost the General Election. https://institute.global/tony-blair/northern-discomfort-why-labour-lost-general-election

71. Barker, C (2019) Twitter video. https://twitter.com/Barker4Grimsby/status/1182911797898174465

72. Leatherdale, D (2019) Cafe politics in coal country, BBC News. https://www.bbc.co.uk/news/extra/ALSU1CqK3U/election-2019-battleground-bishop-auckland

73. Fabian Society (2018) For the Many?: Understanding and Uniting

Labours core supporters. https://fabians.org.uk/publication/for-the-many/

74. Ibid.

75. Ibid

76. Curtis, C (2020) New Tory voters think Labour left them, not the other way around, The Times. https://www.thetimes.co.uk/article/new-tory-voters-think-labour-left-them-not-the-other-way-around-foj5r7w6p

77. Chaos with podcast (2020) The Panel (Winning Back The Red Wall). https://soundcloud.com/chaoswith/red-wall-panel-discussion

78. Labour First (2020) Podcast: The Red Wall: How it was lost and how Labour wins it back. https://www.facebook.com/watch/live/?v=1128965464107322&external_log_id=a021fc4ae3f03b29e4c869da961ffb90
    Glaze, B (2020) How did Jeremy Corbyn's Labour lose Tony Blair's old seat of Sedgefield? Daily Mirror. https://www.mirror.co.uk/news/politics/how-jeremy-corbyns-labour-lose-21423488

79. Harris, J (2019) Anywhere but Westminster: how Labour lost, and the hope that endures, The Guardian. https://www.theguardian.com/commentisfree/video/2019/dec/13/anywhere-but-westminster-how-labour-lost-and-the-hope-that-endures-video

80. English Labour Network (2020) General Election 2019: How Labour Lost England. https://englishlabournetwork.files.wordpress.com/2020/03/ge2019-how-labour-lost-england-pdf.pdf

81. Mckenzie, L. (2017). The class politics of prejudice: Brexit and the land of no–hope and glory. *British Journal of Sociology, 68*(S1), S265-S280.

82. Lord Ashcroft, 'How Britain voted and why: My 2019 general election post-vote poll', Lord Ashcroft Polls, 13 December 2019: https://lordashcroftpolls.com/2019/12/how-britain-voted-and-why-my-2019-general-election-post-vote-poll/

83. Mattinson, D (2019) The General Election Diaries. https://www.prweek.com/article/1668840/general-election-diaries-britain-normal-again

84. Payne, S (2019) Conservatives confident they can break through Labour's Red Wall, Financial Times. https://www.ft.com/content/9554b488-1b54-11ea-97df-cc63de1d73f4

85. Glaze, B (2020) How did Jeremy Corbyn's Labour lose Tony Blair's old seat of Sedgefield? Daily Mirror. https://www.mirror.co.uk/news/politics/how-jeremy-corbyns-labour-lose-21423488

86. Ashcroft (2019) My latest focus groups from three Leave-voting, Labour-held Tory targets in Wales, Conservative Home. https://www.conservativehome.com/platform/2019/11/lord-ashcroft-my-latest-focus-groups-from-three-leave-voting-labour-held-tory-targets-in-wales.html

87. IGC, (2019) Northern Discomfort: Why Labour lost the General Election. https://institute.global/tony-blair/northern-discomfort-why-labour-lost-general-election

13. A New Challenger Narrative in Red Wall Seats

1. Williams, J (2019) Leigh and Bury South could both go Tory in a fortnight's time, says a shock new poll' Manchester Evening News. https://www.manchestereveningnews.co.uk/news/greater-manchester-news/leigh-bury-south-could-both-17328300

2. Johnston, R., Rossiter, Hartman, Pattie, Manley, & Jones. (2018). Exploring constituency-level estimates for the 2017 British general election. International Journal of Market Research, 60(5), 463-483.

3. Cutts, D., Goodwin, M., Heath, O., & Surridge, P. (2020). Brexit, the 2019 General Election and the Realignment of British Politics. *Political Quarterly, 91*(1), 7-23.

4. Johnston, Pattie and Hartman (2020) Testing the 'wisdom of the crowds' argument: local opinion in the 43 Red Wall constituencies that Labour lost, LSE. https://blogs.lse.ac.uk/politicsandpolicy/red-wall-local-opinion/

5. Langley, R (2019) My grandad hated Thatcher and the Tories. Here's why he voted for Boris. https://blogs.spectator.co.uk/2019/12/my-grandad-hated-thatcher-and-the-tories-heres-why-he-voted-for-boris/

6. Johnston, Pattie and Hartman (2020) Testing the 'wisdom of the crowds' argument: local opinion in the 43 Red Wall constituencies that Labour lost, LSE. https://blogs.lse.ac.uk/politicsandpolicy/red-wall-local-opinion/

7. Mullen, T (2019)General election 2019: Leigh's voters on 'fantastic' seismic shift, BBC News. https://www.bbc.co.uk/news/election-2019-50781738

8. Mason, P (2019) In Leigh, my hometown, far right propaganda and hostility to Jeremy Corbyn could unseat Labour. https://inews.co.uk/opinion/polling-general-election-2019-paul-mason-leigh-369891

9. Grundy, J (2019) Facebook post 28th November 2019 https://www.facebook.com/pg/james4leigh/posts/

10. Williams, J (2019) Leigh and Bury South could both go Tory in a fortnight's time, says a shock new poll, Manchester Evening News. https://www.manchestereveningnews.co.uk/news/greater-manchester-news/leigh-bury-south-could-both-17328300

11. Mulligan, S (2019) Leigh could vote in Tory MP, says YouGov MRP poll, Leigh Journal. https://www.leighjournal.co.uk/news/18066143.leigh-vote-tory-mp-first-time-says-poll/

12. Griffiths, N (2019) 'I'm voting Tory for the first time': Things appear to be changing in Leigh, Manchester Evening News. https://www.manchestereveningnews.co.uk/news/greater-manchester-news/im-voting-tory-first-time-17334596

13. Griffiths, N (2019) Leigh constituency election portrait. https://www.leighjournal.co.uk/news/18070162.wigan-leigh-constituency-election-portrait/

14. Ibid.

15. Kirby, D (2019) General election 2019: Meet the ex-miners who are planning to vote Tory in Bolsover. https://inews.co.uk/news/general-election-2019-miners-vote-tory-bolsover-derbyshire-shirebrook-brexit-1262531

16. Gibbon, (2020) Focus group: Can Tories win over Labour supporters who back Leave? https://www.youtube.com/watch?v=Ry9SMUurM_k

17. Ibid

18. Chao-Fong, L (2019) Labour CRUMBLES in North 'First time I'm voting Tory!' Heartland voters ABANDON Corbyn, Daily Express. https://www.express.co.uk/news/politics/1210915/general-election-news-labour-party-jeremy-corbyn-leigh-red-wall-crumbling

19. Ibid

20. Daschmann, G. (2000). Vox Pop Polls: The Impact Of Poll Results And Voter Statements In The Media On The Perception Of A Climate Of Opinion. International Journal of Public Opinion Research, 12(2), 160-181.

21. Mullen, T (2019) General election 2019: Leigh's voters on 'fantastic' seismic shift, BBC News. https://www.bbc.co.uk/news/election-2019-50781738

14. Summary: The Perfect Storm Which Brought Down the Red Wall

1. Langley, R (2019) My grandad hated Thatcher and the Tories. Here's why he voted for Boris. https://blogs.spectator.co.uk/2019/12/my-grandad-hated-thatcher-and-the-tories-heres-why-he-voted-for-boris/

15. Labour's Challenge

1. Gibbon, G (2020) Participant comment from 'Focus group: Can Tories win over Labour supporters who back Leave?' Channel 4. https://www.youtube.com/watch?v=Ry9SMUurM_k

2. Niven, A (2020) Forget the 'red wall', Labour can win by appealing to a new demographic, The Guardian. https://www.theguardian.com/uk-news/commentisfree/2020/mar/05/labour-red-wall-new-demographic

3. Election Polling (2020) Labour's target seats 2024. http://www.election-polling.co.uk/battleground/targets/labour

4. Labour Together (2020) Election Review 2019. https://electionreview.labourtogether.uk/

5. Hardman, I (2019) The Tory MPs who broke down the 'red wall'. Podcast. https://podcasts.apple.com/ec/podcast/the-tory-mps-who-broke-down-the-red-wall/id1101754136?i=1000460402739

6. Centre for Cities (2020) Household debt and problem debt in British

cities   https://www.centreforcities.org/publication/household-debt-british-cities/

7. Narwan, G (2020) Red-wall towns worst hit by lockdown job losses, The Times.   https://www.thetimes.co.uk/article/red-wall-towns-worst-hit-by-lockdown-job-losses-ht5qwwk73

8. Ashcroft (2020) DIAGNOSIS OF DEFEAT Labour's turn to smell the coffee   https://lordashcroftpolls.com/wp-content/uploads/2020/02/DIAGNOSIS-OF-DEFEAT-LORD-ASHCROFT-POLLS-1.pdf

9. Ibid.

10. Johnson, J (2019) Boris's New Swing Voters and Why They Are Here to Stay.   https://www.hanovercomms.com/blog/boriss-new-swing-voters-sceptical-of-business-and-here-to-stay/

11. Smeeth, R (2020) Podcast: Corbynism: The Post-Mortem. 9: The Red Wall Crumbles   https://podcasts.apple.com/za/podcast/9-the-red-wall-crumbles/id1494568978?i=1000468340080

12. Gaffney, J. (2017). Leadership and the Labour Party : Narrative and performance (Palgrave studies in political leadership series).

13. Shrimsley, R (2020) Labour needs a Tony Blair for the Twenties, Financial Times.   https://www.ft.com/content/51b08e5e-3072-11ea-a329-0bcf87a328f2

14. Stiglitz, J (2020) We Need a Better Balance Between Globalization and Self-Reliance.   https://foreignpolicy.com/2020/04/15/how-the-economy-will-look-after-the-coronavirus-pandemic/

15. Flint, C (2020) in Institute for Prosperity report Manufacturing a recovery from Coronavirus.   https://instituteforprosperity.org.uk/admin/resources/reports/manufacturing-a-recovery-from-coronovirus.pdf

16. Nathan (2018) British Social Attitudes.   https://www.bsa.natcen.ac.uk/media/39284/bsa35_full-report.pdf

17. Surridge, P (2019) The long journey of Labour's voters into the Tory fold, Financial Times.   https://www.ft.com/content/7990bd0e-1dc6-11ea-81f0-0c253907d3e0?shareType=nongift

18. Shrimsley, R (2020) New Deal Tories show the scale of Labour's challenge   https://www.ft.com/content/ac6ad3ae-13b3-4727-bf14-614353563528

19. Gould, P. (2011). The unfinished revolution : How New Labour changed British politics for ever. London: Abacus.

20. Labour Together (2020) Election Review 2019.   https://electionreview.labourtogether.uk/

21. Bishop, M (2014) What is Labour's narrative?   http://speri.dept.shef.ac.uk/2014/08/06/labours-narrative/

22. Mason, R (2016) Beckett report: Labour lost election over economy, immigration and benefits.   https://www.theguardian.com/politics/2016/jan/14/beckett-report-labour-lost-2015-election-economy-immigrants-benefits

23. Prosser, T (2020) What do Red Wall voters want from Labour?

https://thomasjprosser.wordpress.com/2020/05/29/what-do-red-wall-voters-want-from-labour/

24. Gaffney, J. (2017). Leadership and the Labour Party : Narrative and performance (Palgrave studies in political leadership series).

25. Fairclough, N. (2000). New Labour, new language? New York : Routledge

26. Ainsley, C. (2018). The new working class : How to win hearts, minds and votes. Policy Press. Bristol.

27. Ainsley, C (2016) Brexit presents us with the opportunity to transform the prospects of many who voted Leave and politicians must not squander it. https://brexitcentral.com/claire-ainsley-brexit-opportunities/

28. Ainsley, C. (2018). The new working class : How to win hearts, minds and votes. Policy Press. Bristol.

29. Shrimsley, R (2020) Labour needs a Tony Blair for the Twenties. https://www.ft.com/content/51b08e5e-3072-11ea-a329-0bcf87a328f2

30. Kirkwood, D (2020) Why Britain's values divide should matter to Labour. https://ukandeu.ac.uk/why-britains-values-divide-should-matter-to-labour/

31. Proctor, K (2020) Labour should not shy away from patriotism, says Starmer, The Guardian. https://www.theguardian.com/politics/2020/apr/30/labour-should-not-shy-away-from-patriotism-says-starmer

32. The UK in a Changing Europe (2020) Big differences on economic and social values between MPs and voters, new academic survey finds. https://ukandeu.ac.uk/big-differences-on-economic-and-social-values-between-mps-and-voters-new-academic-survey-finds/#

33. Goodhart, D. (2017). The road to somewhere : The populist revolt and the future of politics. Penguin, Hurst & Co

34. Hameleers, M., Bos, L., Fawzi, N., Reinemann, C., Andreadis, I., Corbu, N., . . . Weiss-Yaniv, N. (2018). Start Spreading the News: A Comparative Experiment on the Effects of Populist Communication on Political Engagement in Sixteen European Countries. The International Journal of Press/Politics, 23(4), 517-538.

35. YouGov (2020) Andy Burnham public popularity ratings. https://yougov.co.uk/topics/politics/explore/public_figure/Andy_Burnham

36. Gaffney, J. (2017). Leadership and the Labour Party : Narrative and performance (Palgrave studies in political leadership series).

37. Platt, J (2019) Labour forgot towns like mine, and that's why I lost my seat. It's time to start listening again. https://www.independent.co.uk/voices/jo-platt-labour-election-result-lost-seats-leigh-northern-towns-a9252041.html

16. Crafting an Effective Political Narrative

1. Guardian Readers (2019) 'I feel betrayed': readers in the 'red wall' react to Labour's collapse, The Guardian. https://www.theguardian.com/commentisfree/2019/dec/13/readers-red-wall-labour-collapse

2. Hammack, P. L. (2015). Mind, story, and society: The political psychology of narrative. In M. Hanne, W. D. Crano, & J. S. Mio (Eds.), Claremont symposium on applied social psychology series. Warring with words: Narrative and metaphor in politics (p. 51–77). Psychology Press.

3. Sarbin, T. R. (Ed.) (1986). Narrative psychology: The storied nature of human conduct. Praeger Publishers/Greenwood Publishing Group.

ABOUT THE AUTHOR

Steve Rayson is a researcher and author. He completed his MSc on Political Communication at the London School of Economics and won the best dissertation prize for his work on political podcasts.

He was previously the co-founder of three successful companies: BuzzSumo, Kineo and Totara. He was also a public sector consultant at KPMG and the Director of Resources at Brighton & Hove Council.

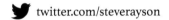 twitter.com/steverayson

Printed in Great Britain
by Amazon

44365333R00169